MW01286047

A COMBAT ENGINEER WITH PATTON'S ARMY

The Fight Across Europe with
the 80th "Blue Ridge" Division in World War II

Lois Lembo and Leon Reed

Savas Beatie
California

©2020 Leon Lembo and Lois Reed

All rights reserved. No part of this publication may be reproduced, stored in a retrieval system, or transmitted, in any form or by any means, electronic, mechanical, photocopying, recording, or otherwise, without the prior written permission of the publisher.

Library of Congress Cataloging-in-Publication Data

Names: Lembo, Lois, author. | Reed, Leon, authors.
Title: A Combat Engineer with Patton's Army: The Fight Across Europe with the 80th "Blue Ridge" Division in World War II / by Lois Lembo and Leon Reed.
Description: El Dorado Hills, California : Savas Beatie, [2020] | Includes bibliographical references.
Identifiers: LCCN 2018058534 | ISBN 9781611214031 (hardcover: alk. paper) | ISBN 9781611214048 (ebk)
Subjects: LCSH: Lembo, Frank T., 1930-2006. | United States. Army. Engineer Combat Battalion, 305th—Biography. | Military engineers—United States—Biography. | United States. Army. Infantry Division, 80th (1942-1946)—Biography. | World War, 1939-1945—Campaigns—Western Front. | World War, 1939-1945—Regimental histories—United States. | World War, 1939-1945—Personal narratives, American. Classification: LCC D769.335 305th .L46 2020 | DDC 940.54/1273092 [B] --dc23
LC record available at https://lccn.loc.gov/2018058534

First Edition, First Printing

SB
Savas Beatie
989 Governor Drive, Suite 102
El Dorado Hills, CA 95762
916-941-6896 / sales@savasbeatie.com / www.savasbeatie.com

All of our titles are available at special discount rates for bulk purchases in the United States. Contact us for information.

Proudly published, printed, and warehoused in the United States of America.

Dedicated to Frank and Betty and the boys of B Company, 305th Engineers

I was just thinking about that last day together that we had, and how perfect it was, and how long a way I've come since then. I can remember that boat ride to England, our trip across the Channel, going into action and suffering a thousand deaths when we heard our first artillery shell. The mad dash across France—a ride with its wine, flowers, ripe tomatoes and eggs—the storming of our first river and the fighting beyond, Christmas in Belgium, New Year in Luxembourg. . . . Yes we've come a long way. We're a little tired, a little older, and a little bitter. We fight hoping each battle is the last one, with thoughts of going home and enjoying a peaceful life—our thoughts run to our sweethearts who we long for, each letter being a five minute furlough with the one you love.

Frank T. Lembo
January 2, 1945

Frank and Betty, high school sweethearts. *Michelina Lembo*

Table of Contents

Table of Contents (continued)

Maps and photos have been distributed through the book
for the convenience of the reader.

DAD AND WORLD WAR II

My father, Frank T. Lembo, was like other young men of his generation whose lives were interrupted by the call to serve in the U.S. Army during World War II. He was a man of his time: intelligent, resourceful, ambitious, and committed to doing his part to win the war. I'm not just saying this because he's my father. I know it because he wrote hundreds of letters to my mother, Betty (née) Craig, and she kept every one. Articulate and perceptive, the letters relate his wartime thoughts and experiences with real-time immediacy.

The letters—86 of them from Europe alone—comprise a window into the life of a GI. He wrote about the horrors of war and weather but also with humor about small pleasures and the camaraderie among the soldiers. He didn't let a letter go by without reflecting on his yearning for his sweetheart, which only deepened during his months away.

Lembo was an engineer in Lt. Gen. George S. Patton Jr.'s Third Army. He was assigned to the 305th Engineer Combat Battalion, 80th Infantry Division, and fought in many of the major battles of World War II. After one and a half years in training, Lembo got his orders to deploy across the Atlantic to aid the American servicemen who were breaking out from Normandy. The 80th raced across the Atlantic without an escort in less than a week on the RMS *Queen Mary*.

Even more than in previous wars, the highly mechanized armies of World War II depended on engineers to keep on the move. Patton's Third Army, which reflected its commander's slashing offensive style of war, may have needed engineering support on an even more urgent basis than other Allied forces.

The engineers performed a wide variety of tasks, but the most common jobs for Frank Lembo's unit were clearing mines, booby traps, and other obstacles;

building, maintaining, and repairing roads; performing reconnaissance of riverbanks, roads, and bridges, often behind enemy lines; building or repairing bridges; and fighting as infantry.

Within two weeks of its arrival in France, the 80th went into its first major battle at the Argentan-Falaise Gap and then chased the escaping Germans across France, traveling 684 miles in little over a week. The engineers then took the lead in a series of hazardous river crossings, including the Moselle, Seille, and Nied, amid drenching rain and record floods. It was during this time, patrolling behind enemy lines in preparation for the Seille River crossing, that Lembo earned a Silver Star, saving his men from a German ambush.

The GIs were about to celebrate Christmas and their thoughts were turning toward home and holiday packages (and the impending assault across the Saar River into Germany) when the Wehrmacht launched a surprise counteroffensive in what became known as the Battle of the Bulge. As part of Patton's historic rush from the Saar to Luxembourg, the 80th Division went into action around Ettelbruck. After several days of savage fighting and heavy losses, Lembo's 1st Platoon of B Company, 305th Engineers, acted as complement to a segment of the 80th that rushed forward to relieve the surrounded 101st Airborne in Bastogne. While on this mission, Lembo and his platoon earned the Presidential Unit Citation as an "attached unit" to the 2nd Battalion of the 318th Infantry Regiment.

FRANK'S LETTERS TO BETTY

All the while, Lembo wrote letters to his then-fiancé Betty whenever he could. They told of other ETO adventures as well: impromptu rodeos, R&R in Paris, celebrating the liberation of French villages, movies and dances, and the occasional beer party. And always clearing mines. Coupled with the few memories he shared after the war—like being responsible for the 80th Division's July 4th fireworks show in 1945, his frustration when an injury prevented him from the honor of demonstrating bridge-building techniques for Patton, accidentally setting off a German 75 mm howitzer and destroying a company truck—his letters provide a remarkably vivid portrait of a GI engineer's experiences in Europe.

Although his letters came to an end before the war was over—the last batch was never found—the story of Lembo and B Company continued. Lembo and his fellow GIs were present for the liberation of concentration camps, the final battles of the European war, the signing of the German surrender, and the lazy days of occupation. Before he came back to the States, Lembo received his long-coveted promotion to first lieutenant.

Dad and me, 1951. *Betty Lembo*

FRANK COMES HOME

Frank Lembo was a young man whiling away his time in a blue-collar job before he was drafted, but he emerged from the army a mature man ready to establish a family and meet the world.

Like other veterans, my father returned from Europe with souvenirs and reminders of his days in the field. He treasured a captured German Luger, a Nazi flag "appropriated" from the wall of a newly liberated Nazi meeting hall, and his company's battle flag. My mother added to this stockpile, documenting the highlights of Frank's military career in "His Service Record"—a type of ready-made scrapbook with that title on its cover, designed for spouses or families to keep track of their GIs—plus keeping a scrapbook of her own with photographs and other items that Frank sent home for safekeeping.

I loved looking through these souvenirs when I was growing up. The item I enjoyed the most was the diary kept by my father's unit, "B Company of the 305th Engineer Combat Battalion, 80th Infantry" neatly typewritten on onionskin. The diary followed the movements and actions of the company as it paved the way for the Third Army across Europe. After my father gave me his collection, I became committed to filling in the blanks and fleshing out the story of his war. The diary was the basis for this chronicle, which I started writing before my father died and continued working on for many years. At some point, it became a family project as my husband, Leon Reed, joined me in the adventure.

THE PROJECT

The story of Frank Lembo and his unit took shape when supplemented by other contemporary accounts from the 305th Engineers and the 80th Division's three infantry regiments, primarily morning reports and monthly after-action reports. Firsthand accounts, especially the army interviews of 80th Division commanders and junior officers, were essential to filling in the "why" associated with the "where" and "when" from the company diary.

A second tier of sources includes manuscripts, memoirs, theses, and reports written by 80th Division veterans, descendants, and military analysts. These are listed in the bibliography.

The book approaches the story from four different levels. First, we give Frank's perspective, based on his letters, the souvenirs he sent home to Betty Craig, and his postwar recollections. Second, primarily based on the Company diary and 305th Battalion after-action reports and interviews, we describe what the engineers were doing day by day. These engineering tasks were performed in support of the war effort, and we report what the infantry regiments were doing based on their after-action reports, interviews, and memoirs from the 80th Division's infantry and field artillery units. Finally, we give some insight into the division, corps, Third Army, and SHAEF personalities and their decisions that set the direction for the actions of the men at the point of the spear.

Frank with army buddies Scotty (left) and Whitey (right). *A GI using Frank's camera*

ORGANIZATION

After a brief introduction about Frank and his family and a quick summary of 80th Division training, the book describes the division's deployment, its brief stopover in England, and its early August 1944 arrival in France. From there, chapters 3 and 4 proceed chronologically through the Normandy Campaign to Argentan and the chase across France. Chapters 5 through 9 describe the frustrating campaigns in the province of Lorraine and the German borderlands, starting with the division's first hotly contested river crossing at the Moselle and including the fighting in the hills beyond the river.

Then came the frustrating October pause, the crossing of the Seille River, the fight for Delme Ridge, and the brutal November slog to the German border. Chapters 10 and 11 recount the story of the Ardennes Campaign, including the race from the Saar to Luxembourg, the 80th's fighting around Ettelbruck, the relief of Bastogne, and the bitter fighting in January 1945 to close the bulge.

Drawing of Frank during his visit to Paris.

Copy photo by Leon Reed

Chapters 12 through 17 describe the 1945 campaigns to cross the Sauer River and cut through Germany to the war's end in Austria. The book closes with a chapter on occupation duty and a postscript describing Frank Lembo's return home and the life he made with Betty Craig (Lembo) after the war.

Lois Lembo
January 2020

CHAPTER 1

JOINING THE U.S. ARMY

FRANK Lembo's wartime odyssey began when he received his induction notice on November 21, 1942.

On the day the notice arrived in the mail, Frank was working at Wright Aeronautical Corporation, the aircraft engine division of Curtiss-Wright Corp., in Paterson, New Jersey. He had started working at the factory soon after finishing Hawthorne High School in June 1939. War was declared on December 8, 1941, the day after the Japanese attack on Pearl Harbor. Frank's employment in an essential defense industry had given him an exemption from the draft for several months, but as mobilization continued, his number finally came up.

Frank would be leaving behind his parents, Joseph and Michelina (Mary), his older sister Genevieve, and his beloved younger sisters, Josephine and Mary. The elder Lembos had both lived in Southern Italy before immigrating to the United States in the early part of the century. As the only male child in the family, Frank had been a central fixture in the Lembo household and the apple of his father's eye.

Besides Frank's job at Wright, he worked at his father's business—Joseph Lembo, General Contractor—gaining experience in roadwork that would serve him well as an army combat engineer. He had started helping at his father's business when he was still young, and the word "engineer" had become so ingrained in his personality that it was used under his high school yearbook picture. Frank lived with his family at 144 Parker Avenue in Hawthorne, New Jersey. The Lembo family was close, and Frank would be sorely missed. His parents were devastated when he was finally called up to the war.

Above: Frank Lembo holds up his draft notice. *Mary Lembo (Randall)*; Right: Frank Lembo and his mother, Michelina (Mary) Aliegro Lembo. *Betty Craig (Lembo)*; Below: Frank Lembo and his father, Joseph Lembo. *Mary Lembo (Randall)*

Frank Lembo's fiancé, Betty Craig (Lembo).

Frank Lembo

Frank would also be saying goodbye to his girlfriend, Beatrice (Betty) Craig. Frank (or Lem) and Betty had had an on-again, off-again romance since high school. Betty also had a job at Wright. She worked as a secretary to one of the bosses after graduating from Hawthorne High School and Berkeley Secretarial School. It was sometimes slow in the office, and Betty would have plenty of time to write Frank long letters every day.

Betty was the beloved daughter of Alexander and Nellie Craig, who also lived in Hawthorne. Betty's only brother, Leslie, was considerably older, so Betty grew up as basically an only child. Betty's parents didn't think much of Frank Lembo at first and didn't believe the couple had a future together. Their attitude changed as the war went on and it became apparent that Betty and Frank would be a couple for good.

Frank and Betty were a study in contrasts. Betty was timid and Frank had an easy self-confidence and independent spirit. She was reserved and he was outgoing; she was refined while he was a little rough around the edges. At times Betty thought Frank made fun of her, and she may have been right. Nevertheless, she was attracted to Frank's good looks. Their attraction was obvious and their romance grew deeper as the years wore on.

On November 22, 1942, Frank Lembo reported to the Newark Armed Forces Induction Center for his Selective Service examination, and less than a week later, on November 28, he boarded a bus headed for the reception center at Fort Dix, New Jersey.[1] The Hawthorne newspaper reported, "Borough organizations,

---

1 Frank was forced to make a minor change to his identity when he filled out his U.S. Government paperwork for the draft. He didn't have a middle name and the army wouldn't

Frank Lembo and Betty Craig. *Mary Lembo (Randall)*

relatives and friends will unite tomorrow morning in giving a sendoff to the 40 men who will leave from the headquarters of Draft Board No. 3 at Lafayette School." The Hawthorne Veterans of Foreign Wars and American Legion post "request their respective members and color guards to be present at the school at 9 o'clock to take part in the sendoff." After a "quiet, simple ceremony," the departing men were presented with "metal mirrors and cases from the Citizens Committee and cigarettes from the Red Cross." Frank and other men from St. Anthony's Parish

induct him without one. He pulled "Thomas" out of the air and would be "Frank T. Lembo" for life.

were given Miraculous Medals and Serviceman's Prayer Books by the Holy Name Society. A group photograph from the local newspaper shows the 40 men smiling and giving a thumbs-up to the camera.

The Lembo family and Betty went to see Frank board the bus with the other local boys. It was an emotional farewell and the only time Sister Jo would see her father cry. Betty immediately set to work on "His Service Record," which she would keep assiduously for the entire war.[2]

After arriving at the Fort Dix reception center, Frank was sworn in, inoculated, processed, and issued a uniform. He was sent home for a week to say goodbye to his family before training began. On his first night at Fort Dix, Frank wrote the first of hundreds of letters to Betty, chronicling his observations and experiences in training and eventually in wartime Europe.[3] His November 29, 1942, letter began simply enough: "Well honey I am a soldier boy."

On December 4, 1942, Pvt. Frank T. Lembo left for basic and specialized training at Camp Forrest in Tullahoma, Tennessee.[4] Frank would be joining the 80th "Blue Ridge" Infantry Division, which had been reactivated at Camp Forrest on July 15, 1942. Through the early stages of training, it was under the command of Maj. Gen. Joseph Patch, a longtime army officer who had served as a junior officer during World War I. The 80th was made up almost entirely of draftees like Frank from the mid-Atlantic region.

Army specialists interviewed Frank about his background, experience, and aptitude to determine his army occupational specialty. Often these designations were made according to what the army needed rather than what the recruit was

2 In "His Service Record" Betty kept close track of Frank's progression through training and across Europe. She noted such things as times he visited home, bases where he served, friends he made in service, letters and gifts, and the record of his promotions. The record also included treasured items such as an 80th Division patch and the induction notice as well as photographs Frank sent home to her for safekeeping. Betty also separately kept a scrapbook consisting mainly of newspaper articles about the progress of the Third Army in Europe.

3 In total, Frank wrote more than 500 letters to Betty, 86 of them during his time in Europe. (Unfortunately, at present, the final letters are missing, and the collection only extends to the end of February 1945.) The letters sometimes refer to events of the war to the extent that the censors allowed, but they were mainly filled with rich detail about the GIs' lives in the field as well as Frank's feelings about the home front, his surroundings, and his dreams for the future. He was occasionally downbeat, but his positive attitude and his pleasure in small things made the war bearable.

4 A companion manuscript (in process) is based on letters that detail Frank's thoughts and experiences during his many months of training at Camp Forrest, Tennessee; Camp Phillips, Kansas; and the army's desert proving ground in Yuma, Arizona (between December 1942 and March 1944).

suited for; however, in this case the army assigned a specialty that was as close to Frank's civilian occupation as possible. In its wisdom, the army did not assign Frank to the infantry, as Frank had feared; rather, he was to be part of the 305th Engineer Combat Battalion, "the organic" engineering element of the 80th Division. For the duration of the war, the 305th would operate with other 80th Division units, most notably the 317th, 318th, and 319th Infantry Regiments.

80th Infantry Division—Table of Organization

317th Infantry Regiment

318th Infantry Regiment

319th Infantry Regiment

80th Reconnaissance Troop (Mechanized)

305th Engineer Combat Battalion

305th Medical Battalion

80th Division Artillery

313th Field Artillery Battalion (105mm Howitzer)

314th Field Artillery Battalion (105mm Howitzer)

315th Field Artillery Battalion (155mm Howitzer)

905th Field Artillery Battalion (105mm Howitzer)

Special Troops

780th Ordnance Light Maintenance Company

80th Quartermaster Company

80th Signal Company

Military Police Platoon

Headquarters Company

Band

The 305th Engineer Combat Battalion was divided into a headquarters and three letter-named companies, each of which was divided into three numbered platoons. Captain Robert C. Marshall was in command of B Company, and Frank Lembo was assigned to B Company's 1st Platoon, which in turn was commanded by Lt. Arthur Henke. Unofficially, but in practice, each platoon was divided into three squads, and Lembo became the leader of one of these toward the end of training.[5]

---

5 Frank unsuccessfully applied to Officer Candidate School (OCS) when he entered the army. His failure to be accepted was one of his greatest disappointments in his military career, and it

Soldiers in Sgt. Lembo's squad would have thought themselves lucky to be part of Lembo's outfit. Frank was a born leader and possessed unfailing self-confidence. He was decisive and seldom questioned his own judgment. As the 80th would later come into regular contact with the Germans, Lembo found himself with the responsibility of keeping the men in his squad safe and effective. As willing as he may have been to enjoy GI humor—and at times instigate it—his primary concern was the welfare of his men. Lembo's squad would be assigned particularly challenging missions, regularly entering hostile territory on reconnaissance patrols.[6]

The U.S. Army's *Engineer Soldier's Handbook* summarizes what the army expected of its combat engineers:

> You are an engineer. You are going to build bridges and blow them up. You are going to stop tanks and destroy them. You are going to build roads, airfields, and buildings. You are going to construct fortifications. You are going to fight with many kinds of weapons. You are going to make sure that our own troops move ahead against all opposition, and you are going to see to it that enemy obstacles do not interfere with our advance. You are an engineer.[7]

As Frank's recounting of the agonies of physical conditioning and weapons training in his letters attest, basic training at Camp Forrest was grueling, leaving Frank and the other recruits exhausted but stronger after their accelerated six-week program. It was a welcome relief when he moved across the camp to begin his specialized engineer training with the 305th. With that, Frank entered a new world that suited him well.

Frank and the men in the 305th had to be highly trained to perform a wide-ranging set of complex missions before they would be ready to enter the war

---

was no doubt disappointing to Betty as well. Frank would say later in life that the sticking point was his inability to stay afloat in water, notwithstanding the countless hours he would spend working in swollen rivers. He ultimately reached the rank of second lieutenant in March 1945 (and was promoted to first lieutenant after the war) by moving up through the ranks.

6 The army promoted Frank while stateside from private to PFC in April 1943, to corporal on December 26, 1943, and to sergeant on January 10, 1944, at which point he was given command of a squad. He was promoted to staff sergeant and temporary command of a B Company platoon in February 1945; the assignment would become permanent with his battlefield promotion to second lieutenant on March 8, 1945, and then first lieutenant before his stay in Europe ended on September 15, 1945.

7 U.S. War Department, *Basic Field Manual: Engineer Soldier's Handbook* (FM 21-105) (Washington, DC: Government Printing Office, 1943), 1.

Frank stands on a bridge recently built by 305th engineers. *Battalion photographer*

zone. One combat engineer website noted, "The U.S. military mission in WWII depended on, more than any other time in history, the efforts of combat engineers. Tanks, artillery, and infantry were only as mobile as the roads they traveled on, the bridges they crossed, and the obstacles they overcame." By the time they were done with training, Frank and the men in his battalion would be some of the most highly trained men in the army.

Combat engineers are traditionally known as bridge builders, and Frank and the other 700 enlisted men in the battalion learned how to build Bailey bridges, trestle bridges, pontoon[8] bridges and a host of other kinds, both fixed and floating. They were also trained in the conduct of assault crossings. To fulfill another important engineering function, the recruits practiced roadwork over Camp Forrest's rugged terrain. This not only entailed building and maintaining roads, culverts, and bypasses but also clearing roads of wrecked enemy tanks, vehicles, and mines, as well as snow and ice, which would be critical in the frigid winter in Europe. They laid and removed abatis and other obstacles and became adept in the use of explosives. The army's *Basic Field Manual* stated, "Demolitions are usually ordered at critical times; and the failure of a single demolition could cost the lives of hundreds of men. YOU MUST NOT FAIL."[9]

The 80th Division's new combat engineers were also cross-trained, and on January 9, 1943, Frank T. Lembo qualified as expert with a rifle. The engineers were

8 During WWII, the army's preferred spelling for a floating bridge resting on shallow-draft boats or floats was "ponton," but in this book we have used the more common spelling "pontoon."

9 U.S. War Department, *Basic Field Manual*, 77.

often called on to act as infantry when numbers were short, despite the light weapons load they carried.

In March 1943, Maj. Gen. Horace McBride, who had served as a battery commander during World War I, was appointed commander of the 80th Division, and he remained in command until the last months of the war.

Frank came home for furlough between March 15 and March 22, 1943. Betty commented that Frank "looks wonderful. Gained 18 lbs. Applied for OCS. Has a great deal of confidence in himself."[10] Frank was promoted to PFC the following month.

The trainees enjoyed a special occasion on April 17, 1943, when the 80th Division was reviewed by President Franklin Delano Roosevelt during a tour of inspection at Camp Forrest. From all accounts, the parade was exhilarating for the men. Presidential secretary Grace Tully's papers included a short description of the tour. FDR was met by an honor band of the 318th and 319th infantry regiments, and then he reviewed the division's troops and bivouac area. "Their armament and equipment, which was prominently displayed for the President, was most ominous looking—and they had everything out, from socks to jeeps and long-barreled rifles. These boys presented the appearance of well seasoned, and completely equipped, troops—ready for combat duty anywhere."[11]

It apparently wasn't all work at Camp Forrest, though. On May 5, Frank wrote Betty, "Still sitting in the woods and having a lazy time. We had another beer party last night and we all enjoyed ourselves."

One of the major features of training at Camp Forrest was the "Tennessee Maneuvers," a large-scale training exercise held on the old Civil War stomping grounds between Nashville and Chattanooga. From July to August 1943, the 80th Division tested its mettle against the 83rd Infantry Division under simulated combat conditions. As the 80th's engineering complement, the 305th tested the full range of its offensive engineering functions, including guarding vital bridges, constructing fords, simulating bridge repairs, assembling footbridges, and making assault crossings.

Together with other units from the division, the 305th additionally exercised such defensive operations as laying hasty minefields, setting up roadblocks and obstacles, and preparing bridges for demolition. One of the engineers' highlights

---

10 "His Service Record," 7.

11 "Log of the President's Trips: Inspection Tour, April 13-29 1943," Grace Tully Papers, Grace Tully Archive, Box 7, Franklin D. Roosevelt Library and Museum, accessed January 16, 2017, www.fdrlibrary.marist.edu/_resources/images/tully/7_08a.pdf.

GI postcard from 80th division maneuvers.

Pvt. Ralph Owen, 80th Division special service

during the Tennessee Maneuvers was building a 540-foot assault bridge across the Cumberland River.

Lembo and others from the 80th left Camp Forrest for Camp Phillips, situated near Salina, Kansas, in late August 1943. Just before the transfer, Frank came home again for a visit from August 29 to September 9. Army food seemed to be agreeing with Frank, Betty noted in his Service Record; he "put on more weight and looks good."

Frank came home again for an unexpected Thanksgiving furlough and at long last gave Betty the engagement ring he had picked out for her. Betty mentioned the ring in "His Service Record" and said Frank was "Just as handsome as ever!" But she didn't formally accept right away, and Frank's mother put the ring in her bedroom drawer. Betty would go to the Lembo's for friendly conversation, coffee, and sneak peeks at the ring during the long, hard months Frank was away.

On November 17, 1943, the 80th Division again pulled up stakes. This time it went to the California-Arizona Maneuver Area (CAMA) in the Mojave Desert, where the GIs prepared for the harsh conditions they might encounter at the front in either the Mediterranean, the Pacific, or Northern Europe—they didn't yet know where they would be sent. Arizona would be their home for the next five months.

It was here the draftees were turned into soldiers prepared, to the extent possible, for the rigors of wartime. A soldier from the 317th Infantry Regiment said, "I found out later that part of the training included purposefully cutting back on rations, something we would experience time and time again during the Battle of the Bulge. Training under these conditions not only built us physically but demonstrated how we would fight as teams: squads, platoons, companies, battalions, regiments, and divisions."[12] This phase of their training culminated in a three-week corps-level maneuver in which they exercised against the 104th Infantry Division in a highly competitive, stressful environment.

On December 26, 1943, Frank Lembo was promoted to corporal. He was promoted to sergeant a short time later, on January 10, 1944. He was to take charge of his own 13-man squad in the 1st Platoon of Company B, 305th Combat Engineers.[13] As a squad leader, Sergeant Lembo would be responsible for the training, discipline, counseling, morale, health, and welfare of his men. Later, in combat, Lembo would lead his men in hundreds of missions.

After completing their training in the desert, Frank's battalion spent several days on a crowded troop train from Arizona back to Fort Dix, New Jersey, their final staging area before deploying overseas. They reached Fort Dix on April 5, 1944. Over the course of the next three months the men did their final training prior to deployment. They were outfitted with weapons, equipment, and clothing and given their inoculations. They didn't know their destination, but according to the grapevine, there was going to be a major operation in Europe and they were going be part of it.

The 305th Engineer Combat Battalion moved to the division staging area at Camp Kilmer, New Jersey. After a short break, their next destination was England.

---

12 Andrew Z. Adkins Jr. and Andrew Z. Adkins III, *You Can't Get Much Closer than This: Combat with Company H, 317th Infantry Regiment, 80th Division* (Havertown, PA: Casemate, 2005), 9-10.

13 Toward the end of training, Frank wrote of his growing pride in his squad. "My job as a sergeant is to handle thirteen men. I have one heavy machine gun under me and one truck. . . . The squad I've got was more or less a joke when I got them, but now are considered the best in the platoon."

CHAPTER 2

THE TRIP TO ENGLAND AND FRANCE: JULY 1-AUG. 6, 1944

ON July 1, 1944, some 15,000 U.S. troops, primarily from the 80th Infantry Division, crowded aboard the RMS *Queen Mary*, a former luxury liner reborn as an enormous army troopship, and set sail on a transatlantic journey to Europe. Stripped of its luxury fittings, the *Queen Mary* sailed the Atlantic alone, painted in gray-tinted camouflage. Dubbed the "Grey Ghost," the *Queen* relied on speed to evade prowling enemy ships and submarines.

RMS *Queen Mary* in New York harbor. *US Navy*

From all reports, the voyage across the Atlantic was uneventful. During their five days aboard ship, the men of the 80th were indoctrinated and inculcated in the mission that lay ahead. As Frank recalled in his July 8, 1944, letter to Betty—his first letter from Europe—the trip was tedious, as rattled as the men's nerves must have been. "I'm glad the boat ride is over with and be damned if I didn't get sick one day, but almost everyone else did so it wasn't Mr. Lembo alone." He continued, "All in all it was a rather nice trip. Most of the time you were bored waiting. The food was lousy, two meals a day, and the smell alone was enough to kill you."

Amid the humdrum aboard ship, the army distributed a kit that contained "razor blades, cards, stationery, soap, a book, and a carton of cigarettes." At least the playing cards helped break the monotony. Frank let Betty know that "Scotty, Eddy and Whitey and I spent most of our time playing cards and Whitey and I made four dollars off of them playing pinochle."[1]

The book Frank got in his onboard "kit" may have been a pocket guide to France prepared by the Information Branch of the Army Service Forces.[2] The book warned against prostitutes, spies, and secret agents and introduced the servicemen to many aspects of French life, including language, geography, food and drink, national characteristics (the French are "big talkers" and "good cooks"), and acceptable modes of address (especially toward women). It also advised servicemen on such matters as billeting with French families, advising them that "the man of the house may be a prisoner of the Nazis, along with a million and one half others like him" or "The allied invasion will bring extra problems and lots of talk. Stay out of these local discussions, even if you have had French II in high school."

But as they closed on the British coast, some of the indoctrination became more serious. Division commander Maj. Gen. Horace McBride issued an order during the crossing, informing his soldiers, "The members of the Division can enter into battle with confidence in themselves, their comrades, and their units." The order was brutally clear about the GIs' mission in Europe:

---

1 Paul "Scotty" Scott, "Eddy," and George "Whitey" White were Frank's best buddies in B Company from the earliest days of training. While he was friendly with all the members of the company, the four of them were particularly close. Frank constantly referred to them in his letters home.

2 U.S. Army Information and Education Branch, Army Service Forces, *Instructions for American Servicemen in France During World War II* https://www.youtube.com/watch?v=etM2jk4Jb0c (1944, reprint, Chicago: University of Chicago Press, 2008).

Kill Germans. Only by killing Germans can we break and destroy their will to fight. Every member of this Division must keep foremost in mind that his job in combat is to kill, kill Germans." McBride further warned the men they faced "a dangerous, dirty, bloody job. It will require the best that is in everyone. You cannot fail your comrades; you must not be a shirker; every man must do his part. I know you can and will earn the respect, admiration, and gratitude of your comrades, your families, and your nation during the days ahead when you will be making history.[3]

The *Queen Mary* docked at Gourock (Greenoch), Firth of Clyde, Scotland, on July 7, 1944. A group of bagpipers was on the dock to greet the ship. A group of WACS took turns on the bagpipes, and local residents tossed food to the GIs.

The men quickly boarded trains and headed 225 miles south to Northwich, Cheshire, England, where final preparations for duty in the European theater were made. The 305th was billeted in the village of Newton-le-Willows, along with the 313th Field Artillery.

The 305th Engineer Combat Battalion would spend only about a month in England, training and preparing for their arrival in France. Frank had enough free time to write often about his new environment as well as the personal issues with Betty that tended to dominate their correspondence. Soon enough, his mind would be on combat.

Once he settled into camp, Frank's eyes were opened to the cultural differences in the new world he'd entered, as would be the case on the Continent as new countries went by one after another. He reported to Betty, "We have daylight here from six in the morning until eleven thirty at night and I must say it's just as well because we don't have any electricity here." He also commented he enjoyed watching the townsfolk make their way around town on their bicycles—a national pastime and the only mode of transportation available to them—joking to Betty that he'd like to see her ride her bicycle to work at Wright's.

He mentioned the men had made friends with some of the English locals around camp, which was refreshing after so much time spent with other males in training and aboard ship. He wrote, "The boys have got one of the little kids that live around in our tent, and they are stuffing him with chocolate and gum. You would also be surprised at the amount of kids about ten years old who plead for cigarettes."

---

3 Berry Craig, *80th "Blue Ridge" Infantry Division* (Paducah, KY: Turner, 1991), 15. References in this chapter to locations, movements, and training activities are from this book and are not footnoted.

Frank wrote again on July 10, complaining about the nonstop English rain. But before a week had passed, he let her know, "I can say that I'm used to the weather now. That is, I don't curse it as much as I did when we first came here." The rain apparently made him think about the upcoming winter, because he suggested, "By the way you better get to work on a heavy sweater for me."

On July 13, the boys went on their first trip to a local pub to spend their English money—they'd finally been able to exchange their American currency, but with some difficulty. "I can't say much for the beer here but we did have a lot of fun. There isn't a bar we go to that we don't end up with Scotty singing and he made a hit with the town folks. The pubs here seem to be the neighborhood gathering place and the people quite friendly." When he got to town on a Sunday, "the church bells were ringing out a tune on the chimes and it sounds strange so close to a combat area and yet everything is so peaceful."

It wasn't long before the novelty wore off and Frank wrote, "I'm hoping we get a crack at someone pretty soon. This camp life doesn't agree with me and as long as we are sitting around the war will go on that much longer." The routine, however, was broken when Frank was sent away from his unit to a specialized training program. An 80th Division history says the officers and noncommissioned officers (noncoms) were sent to school in St. George to learn about waterproofing equipment for the Channel crossing, so this may have been the training he attended.[4] On July 19, he wrote, "This morning I had a chance to listen to one of the best lectures that I ever had. We are at an English school and up to today it's been rather boring. But so far today it's been enjoyable. We have class from 9-12 and 2-4:30 so it's more or less a vacation. Plenty of sunshine and the countryside is beautiful." He planned to go into town where there was "plenty of beer and women." He later clarified, "I'll have to watch out for these English girls, they are all looking for a trip to America." It's doubtful this would have made Betty feel much better.

After his return to camp, he wrote, "I finally got back to the outfit and I had about sixteen letters. I'm glad to get back, because here I know everyone and although the past week was a picnic, I'm not used to an easy life." He celebrated his return by going to town with Eddy, Whitey, and Scotty and getting "high. I guess it's the first time I felt like that."

Back at home, Betty was embroiled in a conflict over access to Frank's prized 1942 Chevy. Frank had left the keys with his sister, Gen, with the understanding

4 Ibid.

Frank and Betty beside Frank's car.

Mary Lembo (Randall)

that Betty could use it whenever she pleased. But Gen was keeping a tight rein on it, to Betty's chagrin. Frank wrote, "I hope you are using the car as much as you want," and Betty replied, obviously miffed, that she wasn't able to touch it. This was still a sore subject with Betty 60 years later. Faced with the need to resolve a clash between his girlfriend and his sister from 4,000 miles away, Frank tried to mollify Betty: "I'm sorry about the car, I had no idea that was going to happen. If I had known I'd have turned it completely over to you. I think, though, after reading your letter I've been hurt more than you, in fact I'm shocked and I'm going to blow my top."

Frank was always mulling over the amount of money he was able to send home and how much Betty would save. He wanted to be sure they could settle down comfortably once they got married after the war. But Frank couldn't help but be cynical about Betty's willingness to meet his savings targets. He wrote on July 23, "I'm glad to hear that you're intending to save after your trip but I bet it's about 6 months before you start. When you don't work for a month it runs into money, but you deserve a vacation so have a good time."[5]

Frank might have been charmed by the English girls, but he was not enthusiastic about the boys he feared Betty would meet on the vacation she was

---

5 Several patterns that would continue throughout Frank's correspondence with Betty were already clear by the time he left England. The first category was his preoccupation with (1) local conditions, such as weather, food, and lodging; (2) money, regrets they hadn't already gotten married, and postwar plans; (3) mail from home; and (4) the hijinks and pranks of "the boys." Second, although none of Betty's letters to Frank survived, echoes of her letters survive in Frank's. It was clear from Frank's correspondence that they both enjoyed "poking" at each other: Betty complained that Frank wasn't loving enough and she worried about other women, while Frank enjoyed nagging Betty about money and egging on her jealousy with stories about English, French, and German women, followed quickly by "oh, but we were just joking around" or "I only think of you."

planning. Not for the first time, Frank took the opportunity to raise the issues of Betty's vacations and the fun he thought she would have while he was sacrificing himself for his country. "Soon you'll be going on your trip to California and I hope you and [best friend] 'Ish' have a good time. It should be quite an experience." Betty may have been innocently planning a bus trip to see her cousin Maizie, a navy brat, in San Diego, but Frank's next words revealed his true feelings: "I guess by the time this letter reaches you you'll be ready to go out to the coast and I'm a little afraid. I know what happened last time you took off for a vacation, but we aren't married yet so maybe I shouldn't talk. How long are you planning on staying?"

Frank couldn't get his mind off the trip, and he soon wrote, "What are you doing on your trip about mail? Do you want me to stop writing until you get back home or what? It's useless for me to write if you won't get my letters for a month." Shortly thereafter, he reminded Betty, "I'm awaiting a letter in answer to the question." Whether Betty replied in the negative or Frank decided to put his communications on hold while Betty was away, there would not be another letter from Frank in Betty's collection until August 12. Meanwhile, the 80th was getting closer to deploying to the Continent.

By the third week of July, Dwight D. Eisenhower, supreme commander of the Allied Expeditionary Forces, had determined his men were ready to break through and destroy the enemy in France. The 80th Division would be part of George Patton's Third Army, which was due to be activated. On July 26, the 80th finally got the word to move to a marshaling area near the port of Southampton, England, to ready for its Channel crossing to Normandy. It soon boarded cargo ships, left Southampton, and crossed the choppy English Channel to France.

CHAPTER 3

NORMANDY AND THE FALAISE POCKET: AUG. 6-26, 1944

THE 80th "Blue Ridge" Division landed on Utah Beach on August 6, 1944, two months after D day. The scene when the 305th Engineer Combat Battalion came ashore was still chaotic, and B Company faced logistical nightmares. Disembarkation was frustratingly slow because the company had crossed the Channel in an ordinary Liberty (cargo) ship rather than the specialized LSTs (landing ship tanks) that transported other 80th units.[1] The engineers and their equipment were squeezed onto the crowded shore only by increments.

Once disembarkation was complete, the men of the 305th Engineer Combat Battalion loaded onto their trucks for the first time in Europe and drove to an assembly area in St. Jores, about six miles from the beachhead. They had finally reached the battle zone. One chronicler of the 80th Division observed, "The Blue Ridgers were close to combat, but not in battle. They had slept on the ground before, but never in a war zone. Some prayed quietly while others joked. Still others preferred thought to talk."[2]

Most of the troops arriving with the 80th that day never forgot the sights and smells of their first few days in France. One soldier remembered, "The second day we were in France I was told there was a dead German soldier in the field next to us. . . . Someone had already set fire to the body according to the instructions we

1 LSTs permitted unloading directly onto the beach or in shallow water because a ramp dropped off the front end; troops arriving in regular ships had to transfer to a landing boat and make their way ashore.

2 Robert T. Murrell, *317th Infantry Regiment History WWII* (Luxembourg: CreateSpace, 2015), 2.

received in England. . . . It was a stench the likes I had never smelled before. It was a long time before I finally got that smell of burning flesh out of my nose."[3] A veteran of the 80th's 317th Infantry Regiment recalled, "I can still see the long line of single-file troops going up to the hill to Saint Mére-Eglise. . . . The sight of unburied decomposing German soldiers is a reoccurring vision in my memory."[4] The time at the assembly area was consumed by a dizzying array of organizational and logistics tasks. Combat aside, activities taken on in St. Jores, listed in the 305th after-action report, included establishing procedures for mail distribution, graves registration, storing clothing and equipment, carrying gasoline, transporting water, obtaining supplies, and setting up ordnance points.[5] A staff sergeant at the 305th Battalion's headquarters prepared monthly after-action reports for the duration of the war. A sergeant from B Company also prepared handwritten morning reports and typed diary entries for the company every day, even when the company was in intense combat.

On August 7, the 80th Division received an order to move. The American breakthrough at Avranches was occurring even as the 305th Engineers crossed the Channel. After Omar Bradley's First Army had hammered an opening into the German front, the newly activated Third Army of Lt. Gen. George S. Patton Jr. was ordered to exploit the breakthrough. The 80th's first combat mission would be to block a massive Panzer counterattack that threatened to cut off the American spearheads. If the Germans could retake Avranches on the coast, through Mortain, they would cut off Patton's supply line and make his lead divisions easy prey.[6] On the night of August 6-7, the Germans launched Operation Lüttich to cut through the narrow coastal corridor and strangle Patton's forward divisions.

This campaign against the Germans in Normandy had been months in the making. Through the spring of 1944 the Germans knew an Anglo-American

3   Frank Lankford, "Adjusting to the Combat Zone," in John Beard, *Tales from Henpeck: Folklore of the 314th FA BN* (Ann Arbor, n.d.), 3, https://www.80thdivision.com/OralHistories/314FABn_Folklore_2.pdf, see also https://www.80thdivision.com/OralHistories/314FABn_Folklore_Intro.pdf.

4   Lester Kuhnert, quoted in Dean James Dominique and James Hayes, *One Hell of a War: Patton's 317th Infantry Regiment in WWII* (Gainesville: Wounded Warrior Publications, 2014), 23.

5   "Personnel and Allied Administration for the Month of August," After-Action Report, 305th Engineer Combat Battalion, August 1944.

6   Orientation Section, Information and Education Division, "80th Division Ever Forward," 4.

invasion was in the offing, but they didn't know where or when it would hit. In anticipation of an Allied landing on the Continent, over 50 German divisions were stationed in France, comprising almost a million men. Field Marshal Erwin Rommel, the famed "Desert Fox," was responsible for defending the coast directly opposite England and constructed an extensive defense network. Thanks largely to an elaborate Allied deception plan, Operation Fortitude, the Germans believed the invasion was focused on Calais, the closest point of France to Britain, and their entire Fifteenth Army was kept in that area.[7]

The Allies caught the Germans off guard on June 6, 1944, when they sidestepped Calais and instead came across the Channel onto five beaches in Normandy, on what became known as D day. The initial landings were conducted in two phases: an airborne assault followed by the largest amphibious landing of soldiers and equipment in history. The American First Army, under the command of Lt. Gen. Omar Bradley, made slow progress breaking out from its beachhead into the interior of Normandy. British and Canadian troops farther east were also stymied. The Americans struggled during the remainder of June and into July to expand the Omaha and Utah beachheads, fighting against fierce opposition. The French hedgerows were formidable obstacles, consisting of mounds of stone and dirt covered with old-growth bushes and small trees. The Americans had never seen anything like this claustrophobic terrain and were ill-prepared to fight in it. Sunken roads and deep drainage ditches between the hedgerows provided the Germans superb defensive positions.[8]

First Army struggled through the Normandy hedgerows until July 25, when the Americans launched Operation Cobra and quickly broke through the German defenses near St. Lo.[9] After Bradley's First Army successfully broke through, the newly arrived U.S. Third Army, made operational on August 1, 1944, under the command of Patton, exploited and widened the breakthrough by fanning out from Normandy, sweeping through Avranches, and then turning west to occupy much

---

7 The D-day Campaign, the fighting in Normandy's hedgerow country, and Operation Cobra are discussed in John Keegan, *Six Armies in Normandy: From D-Day to the Liberation of Paris, June 6th-August 25th, 1944* (New York: Viking, 1982), 115-251; Dwight D. Eisenhower, *Crusade in Europe* (Garden City, NY: Doubleday, 1948); Martin Blumenson, ed., *The Patton Papers, Volume 2: 1940-1945* (Boston: Houghton Mifflin, 1974), 464-511; and Michael Green and James D. Brown, *Patton's Third Army in WWII: An Illustrated Guide* (Minneapolis: MBI and Zenith, 2010), 5-62, among many other sources.

8 Craig, *The 80th Infantry Division*, 18.

9 Eisenhower, *Crusade in Europe*, 253-65; Blumenson, *Patton Papers*, 483-89.

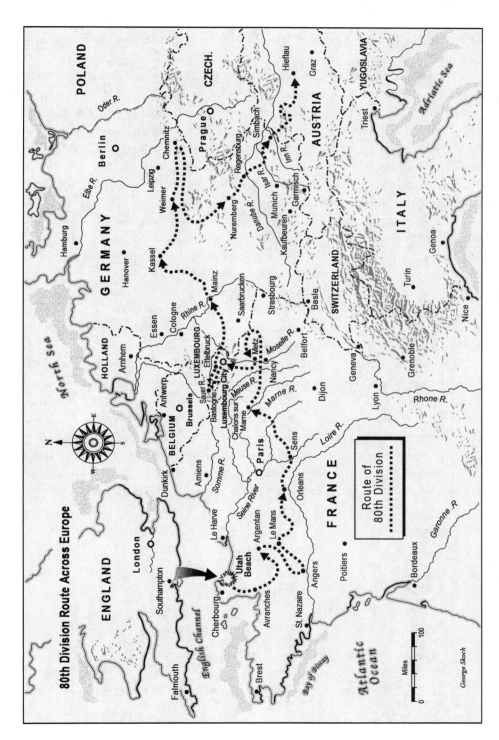

of Brittany, including the ports of Brest, St. Malo, and the notorious U-boat pens of Lorient.[10]

The sudden breakthrough from the hedgerow country by Third Army left the Germans in disarray. The German generals on the spot favored an organized withdrawal from lower Normandy, where they faced likely defeat and possible losses of significant infantry, armor, and artillery. But Hitler, increasingly out of touch with conditions on the ground, demanded the Wehrmacht hold the line. His forces regrouped, and on August 7, six understrength panzer divisions launched a counterattack toward Avranches to cut off the advance divisions of Third Army and restore the Normandy front.[11]

This was the situation on August 8, when the newly arrived 80th Division and the 305th Engineers B Company trucks left their assembly area at St. Jores and drove toward Avranches. On its first night out, the company bivouacked in Montinmy, 11 miles southeast of Avranches.[12]

The German counterattack was stopped around the town of Mortain, primarily by the U.S. 30th Division, and the panzers suffered heavy losses to Allied airpower and artillery. Once this threat was resolved, the 80th Division advanced farther south while the Luftwaffe bombed the column en route.

On August 8, the 80th was ordered to attack and seize Le Mans, site of the headquarters of the German Seventh Army, in order to protect the left and rear flanks of Patton's XV Corps as it moved rapidly across Normandy.[13] The high command concluded the Germans were reinforcing the area around Le Mans and possibly preparing for a counterattack against the extended Allied supply lines. But the threat never materialized, and the attack on Le Mans was suspended before the division reached the city. The 80th was instead ordered to attack any German forces it encountered on its route toward Le Mans. The 317th and 318th Infantry

---

10 Green and Brown, *Patton's Third Army*, 38-53.

11 Blumenson, *Patton Papers*, 503.

12 In general, references to movements of the 305th Engineers, mileage traveled, locations left and arrived at, and routine engineering functions (clearing mines, ferrying troops, scouting) are from the company diary unless referenced to another source. Most references to the diary are not footnoted.

13 80th Infantry Division Summary of Operations, August 3-31, 1944, 1; Company A, 317th Infantry Regiment Morning Report, August 10, 1944.

Regiments met pockets of resistance and engaged in firefights in villages and towns along the Germans' escape route.[14]

B Company's motor convoy left its bivouac in the vicinity of Avranches on August 9 and drove a long 75 miles to Bazouge-sur-le-Loir, a village 27 miles from Le Mans. For the moment, the strategic situation was uncertain, and the company stayed in Bazouge for two days while plans for employment of the 80th Division were still being formulated by the Allied command.

The 80th, however, soon found itself in its first real engagement of the war. On August 10, the 317th Infantry attacked and took Evron in only two hours while the 318th followed in support. That night, the 1st Battalion of the 317th attacked the enemy in the strategically situated town of Conlie, which lay astride a main highway into Le Mans.[15] The infantry took the town, and that night B Company bivouacked seven miles away. The 305th stayed with the infantry, sweeping the roads of mines and clearing away obstacles, abatis, and other roadblocks.[16]

On August 11, a 318th combat team[17] overran a German communications center at Sille-le-Guillaume (dubbed "Silly William" by the GIs) after three platoons of the 80th's Reconnaissance Cavalry, bolstered by tanks, infantry, and engineers, probed the enemy's defenses.[18] One of the platoons hit a minefield that the 305th Engineer Combat Battalion had cleared the previous day. The Germans had remined the field and claimed two jeeps, a tank, and several American casualties. The 80th seized Pré-en-Pail shortly afterward, but the 317th walked into an artillery barrage and had to fight house-to-house before the day ended.

After a week in the combat zone, Frank Lembo broke his self-imposed silence and wrote his first letter to Betty Craig on August 12 from France. He grudgingly asked, "I'd like to hear what kind of vacation you had. I hope this thing ends sometime so I can take a vacation too."

---

14 Craig, *The 80th Infantry Division*, 16.

15 After-Action Report, S-3, 317th Infantry Regiment, August 1944, 1; Craig, *The 80th Infantry Division*, 16.

16 Dominique and Hayes, *One Hell of a War*, 29.

17 A combat team was an ad hoc, task-oriented unit consisting of all or a portion of an infantry regiment, along with attached units, such as tanks, field artillery, and engineers. Like an armored combat command, it was designed to be self-supporting in combat. The German term for such improvised units was *Kampfgruppe* (battle group).

18 Craig, *The 80th Infantry Division*, 17; "Baptism of Fire," in Summary of Actions of Company F, 2nd Battalion, 318th Infantry Regiment, August 44 to May 45, 1.

American soldiers celebrate with recently liberated French citizens. *Frank Lembo*

The violence that engulfed the GIs during the first weeks of the war left them without words to describe their experiences to the folks back home. France stood in stark contrast to the relative security and serenity of the homes the American soldiers recalled. Throughout the war and afterward, Frank, like many other soldiers, did not discuss the horrors of the war in any depth.[19]

As Frank told Betty, "The weather is perfect here now and just like our summers back home. In a way I feel sorry for the French, their towns take a beating, but then I guess they would rather be free again. The Germans take the best they have, and it must be a relief to them not to be haunted by fear all the time." Nevertheless, it was hard for him to avoid, even during these early days, the magnitude of the destruction in France. Some of it had been at the hands of the

19 Several books written by the children of veterans note the reticence of many World War II combat veterans to discuss their experiences, even years after the war. See James Bradley and Ron Powers, *Flags of Our Fathers* (New York: Bantam, 2000); Jan Elvin, *The Box from Braunau: In Search of My Father's War* (New York: AMACOM/American Management Association, 2009); Lelia Levinson, *Gated Grief: The Daughter of a GI Concentration Camp Liberator Discovers a Legacy of Trauma* (Brule, WI: Cable Publishing, 2011); Carol Schultz Vento, *The Hidden Legacy of World War II: A Daughter's Journey of Discovery* (Mechanicsburg, PA: Sunbury Press, 2011); and Thomas Childers, *Soldier from the War Returning: The Greatest Generation's Troubled Homecoming from World War II* (Boston: Houghton Mifflin Harcourt, 2009).

Allies. A short time later he wrote, "It seems as if the French are going to have to rebuild most of their towns where we have been fighting. They are usually nothing more than shambles. The people move out when we move in to take a town, then when it's all over they head back with their few belongings."

Most of the GIs had never been outside the continental United States before their deployment to Europe, and their only familiarity with the French people was the little they had learned from propaganda materials disseminated on the way over. B Company's engineers appreciated the obvious gratitude of the French citizens they met along the way. Frank wrote to Betty, "You should see the towns as they are liberated and the last Germans gone. People are on the streets with flowers and our jeeps look like flower gardens. They are rather liberal with their wine, but we lay off the stuff. The bells start ringing, and singing goes on far into the night, then the war moves on to the next town or village."

The camaraderie within his platoon also kept up Frank's spirits. He wrote, "I'm feeling fine and as healthy as ever, and I'm glad to say that Scotty and the rest of the gang are in the same condition. I had a good night's sleep last night and I must say I needed it because I was dead tired. It's just the same dirty war again, but I don't mind."

On August 13, B Company motored 30 miles from Conlie and bivouacked at St. Aubin De Desert.

Boys from Frank Lembo's squad pose with "Lem's Junk" in the background. *Frank Lembo*

Scotty, his wife Tess, and Betty pose at Easter 1944 get-together. *Frank Lembo*

Sergeant Lembo cared about the men in his squad, and they were apparently affectionate toward their sergeant in return. He proudly told Betty, "The boys were in a painting mood yesterday and painted all our names on the trucks, and also since it's about to fall apart they named it 'Lem's Junk.' I imagine I'll catch hell for it all, but I don't care because I like to see and keep them in a good mood."

In the same vein, on August 13, he reported,

> The boys are threatening to blackmail me. We stopped in a town and the people were all out as usual, so the boys posed for pictures with the girls and they coaxed me into one with a girl. If we ever get it developed I'll send it along. These liberated towns are all alike, wine, people and flowers. We came in one and the people had just put up a sign in screwy English 'Hurrah for the U.S.—Long life to Americans.' Well, I'm glad this fighting is making some people happy, soon maybe everyone will be happy and the world peaceful again.

Frank ended his August 13 letter on a more somber note. Combat had clearly gotten him thinking philosophically. "Honey, I wish as much as you that we had got married, but if anything happens to me, I want you when you do get married to someone (it's the way I want it) and have children to give our ring to your first girl. I've wanted to tell you a long time ago, but there wasn't any danger then. It would make me happy wherever I am."

B Company's motor convoy moved to St. Pierre-des-Nids on August 14. On August 15, the company traveled another 13 miles to Evron, liberated a few days earlier by the 317th.

The two nights in Evron gave the engineers a chance to wash and clean up for the first time since their arrival in France. Frank was no different from the others in finding personal hygiene important, regardless of the circumstances. He found the filth of the battlefield to be abhorrent, but as combat persisted, he frequently found himself with no alternative for weeks on end. The word "dirty" came up frequently in his correspondence, whether he was referring to his body, a creek, his laundry, life in the field, or, as was most often the case, the war itself.

Frank found time to compose a letter on August 16, his last night in Evron. He confessed, "I shaved almost a week's growth of whiskers off a few minutes ago and it was a great relief. We also had our first bath in seventeen days yesterday and it sure felt swell, even if the creek was rather dirty. Now I'm going to put my head in the hands of fate and let Scotty give me a haircut. Thank god you can't see me." Betty met Scotty and his wife, Tess, when he and Frank were in training together, and by now Scotty was Betty's friend too.

GI hijinks did indeed keep the boys in a "painting mood" once they were able to enjoy a short breather in Evron. Lembo relished recounting the platoon's exploits in his letters. Even being transported into a war zone didn't diminish the boisterousness of a "gang" of American boys far away from home. Frank told Betty the story of how

> last night we sort of had a rodeo here in the cow pasture. The boys were lassoing the cattle and trying to ride them, war and army were completely forgotten and everyone had a good time. I hope the good laughs and humor are never taken out of this bunch, come what may.

A few days later he wrote to Betty, "Scotty, Joe and Eddy are still as good as ever and I guess there's a lot less kidding now."

Vacations would be a continual source of friction between Betty and Frank and would dominate their correspondence, even after Betty got home from the West Coast. Frank was well aware that, as he was withstanding grueling combat conditions, life went on back home much the same as it always had, at least as far as Betty was concerned. At times, Betty seemed like she was untouched by events in Europe. It rankled Frank, but he wanted his sweetheart to maintain her innocence without having to face the "dirty truths" about war.

Frank was undoubtedly irate about Betty's apparent shenanigans with the navy boys in California during her vacation, and Betty rubbed it in. When she suggested she might join the WAVES (the navy branch of women's service),[20] Frank indignantly told her, "No that idea of your joining the WAVES doesn't appeal to me and if I hear anymore I'll blow my top. Enough said." But it clearly wasn't

---

20 The WAVES (Women Accepted for Voluntary Emergency Service) were the women's branch of the naval reserve. Members of the WAVES did a variety of noncombat tasks. They wore naval uniforms and carried military rank.

enough said, because a week or so later he dropped a bombshell on her plans: "I thought I told you my opinion about the WAVES. All I can say is forget all about it, or forget me."

As always, Frank loved Betty and couldn't help but soften his angry words as he closed his letter, reassuring her that "I've got your double picture sitting in front of me on the hood and the radio is playing something romantic, so you know where my heart is and I just wish you were here to appreciate the loving mood, or better thought, I'd rather be with you in the States."

On August 17, the company traveled 38 miles to a bivouac near Montree, where the engineers took their first two prisoners of war. Montree was the last stop before they would reach the chaotic and bloody battlefield at Argentan on August 18.

Argentan lay astride the main highway and rail line from Caen to Le Mans and a main road that linked it with Paris. This road and rail network gave the town considerable strategic importance, especially since the tide of Germans now retreating toward the Seine and across France to the German border had to flow through a narrow corridor between the towns of Argentan and Falaise. This corridor became known as the Argentan-Falaise Gap.

An Allied plan devised by Bernard Montgomery, Bradley, and Patton sought to entrap the Germans as they moved through the gap, using a pincer maneuver. American troops would close off the escape route from the south while a multinational force, led by Canadians, would push the Germans into the pocket from the north. The 80th would be on the southwestern flank of the maneuver.

On August 17, the 80th Division was ordered to advance on Argentan to eliminate the German strongpoints and to close the gap.[21]

The Germans were intent on preventing the Allies from cutting their escape route. They held strong positions around the corridor and had several defensive advantages. They held the high ground and controlled the approaches to Argentan from all directions. Their positions on the hill were protected by tanks, artillery, machine guns, and antiaircraft guns as well as the natural obstacles presented by hedgerows and deep woods.

Patton's Third Army steered north to seal the German escape route. The 80th Division (minus the 319th Infantry, which was temporarily assigned elsewhere) approached the enemy at Argentan, 13 miles south of Falaise, at the southern end of the pocket. The 305th Engineers accompanied the 317th and 318th Regiments.

---

21 Orientation Section, "80th Division Ever Forward," 5-6.

Patton originally planned to bypass Argentan and proceed toward Falaise, where his forces would rendezvous with Canadians approaching from the north. On August 13, a few Third Army patrols proceeded beyond the agreed-upon boundary, only six miles from Falaise. According to his autobiography, Bradley was furious. Concerned about overextended positions, confusion, and friendly fire, Bradley ordered Patton to halt his advance and withdraw any Third Army forces from the vicinity of Falaise and anywhere north of Argentan.[22]

The fighting at Argentan had begun on August 8, shortly after the 80th's arrival in France. By the time the 80th Division reached Argentan on August 17, the Nazis were dug in and had blocked the roads and prepared minefields and booby traps.

The 80th was ordered to lead an assault on Argentan on August 18, and the 318th moved in at 8:00 a.m. The order was to seize the high ground to the northeast and then swing southwest to take the city. The road at the edge of the town quickly became crowded with men and equipment. Troops from the 318th were exposed and vulnerable, and they suffered many casualties when the Germans ripped into them with artillery, machine guns, tanks, and 88s.[23] American light tanks moved in to support the 318th, but the shelling destroyed them all; the medium tanks that the 318th required were unavailable. The 318th slowly withdrew while the 305th Medical Battalion pushed through to attend to the casualties and bring the wounded to safety.[24]

That day, B Company, assigned responsibility for mine clearing, bivouacked four miles from the town.

Division commander Horace McBride developed a second attack plan, which again relied on the 318th Infantry. This time a massive artillery barrage preceded the assault to soften German defenses. The attack jumped off on the morning of August 19. Again there were significant casualties among the 318th's ranks, and

---

22 Green and Brown, *Patton's Third Army*, 102; Omar N. Bradley and Clay Blair, *A General's Life: An Autobiography* (New York: Simon and Schuster, 1983), 298-99. Bradley confessed worry that the new U.S. infantry divisions would not be able to hold before the concentrated thrust of an entire battle-hardened German Army trying to reach safety. He preferred "a hard shoulder at Argentan," as he put it, "to a broken neck at Falaise." In fact, he also expected the Canadians and British to advance more quickly from the north without having to plug the gap with U.S. troops.

23 The German 88mm gun was the most feared antitank weapon of the war. Also present in the German arsenal were *Neblewerfers* (multibarreled heavy mortars). The soldiers called their rounds "screaming meemies" because of the deafening sound the shells made as they approached.

24 American Battle Monuments Commission, *80th Infantry Division, Summary of Operations in the World War* (Washington DC: Government Printing Office, 1944), August 3-31, 1944.

317th Infantry soldiers in the ruins of Argentan. *US Army photo*

several key officers were killed. When the 318th's combat team was not able to break through the German defenses by late afternoon, McBride ordered the 317th Infantry to move forward.[25]

Casualties among the 317th mounted as the regiment fought into the city under the enemy artillery and automatic weapons fire. American artillery and tank destroyers, however, found their mark, and the GIs were able to get partway up the objective hill before digging in for the night.[26]

The next day the GIs resumed the attack on Argentan and the surrounding woods, which were strongly held by the Germans. The 318th Combat Team took up the attack from the southern end of the city. The Germans were caught between the two 80th Division infantry regiments. By fighting house to house, and supported by the 610th Tank Destroyer Battalion, the infantry began to push the

25 HQ Company, Company E, and Company F, 317th Infantry Regiment Morning Reports, August 19, 1944.

26 Craig, *The 80th Infantry Division*, 20.

Germans back. Enemy artillery continued to fire on the American forces, but by nightfall the Americans controlled the city.[27]

Just before midnight, seven U.S. artillery battalions concentrated their fire over the town and set it ablaze.[28] Elements of the 317th infantry were subsequently able to fight their way to the objective, Hill 244, which overlooked Argentan. The 317th and 318th Infantry liberated Argentan on August 20.[29] During the battle, the 80th Division destroyed 14 enemy tanks and captured more than 1,000 German soldiers. Four hundred soldiers from the 80th Division were killed or wounded.[30]

Soldiers from the 318th enjoy an accordion concert in the ruins of Argentan. *US Army*

27 Ibid., 20-21; After-Action Report, 610th T.D.s, August 1944.

28 "Argentan, the Baptism of Fire," in *The 314th FA Battalion in the ETO*, 9.

29 Orientation Section, "80th Division Ever Forward," 6; "Baptism of Fire," Summary of Actions of Company F, 2nd Battalion, 318th Infantry Regiment, August 44 to May 45, 3; 80th Infantry Division, Summary of Operations, August 3-31, 1944; After-Action Report, S-3, 317th Infantry Regiment, August 1944.

30 Adkins and Adkins, *You Can't Get Closer than This*, 18.

"First flag," presented by 318th Infantry Regiment, flies over Argentan town hall.

Army Signal Corps

In keeping with army tradition, 318th Infantry Regiment commander Col. Harry McHugh presented the 80th Division's "first captured town" American flag to the mayor of Argentan.[31]

By nightfall on August 20, the 80th linked up with the 90th Division and the French 2nd Armored. Combat patrols fanned out from Argentan along all routes toward Falaise and the town of Trun. The 305th Engineers were active demining the roads along the 80th's path. The division's 314th Field Artillery Battalion encountered a minefield as it was leaving Argentan along a main highway. As the 305th Engineers set out to remove the obstacle, one of their jeeps ran over a mine, causing several engineer casualties.

On August 21, the British 50th Division, arriving from the Caen sector in the north, relieved the 80th Division.[32] Along with hundreds of casualties in the 80th's infantry regiments, the fighting at Argentan had cost the 305th Engineers 2 dead, 13 wounded, and 2 missing.

The Allied operation at the Argentan-Falaise gap was successful in killing or capturing thousands of German troops who were caught in the pocket. Huge amounts of weapons, equipment, vehicles, and supplies were left on the smoldering battlefield. The 80th also captured a map depot and a dump with 27,000 tons of ammunition. The Allies took 50,000 prisoners, with the 80th Division alone capturing 5,000. Ten thousand German soldiers were killed in the

---

31 Tristan Rondeau, "Baptism by Fire in Argentan: The First Engagement of August 18-19, 1944," in *Normandie 1944 Magazine*, no. 6 (English translation by Dennis Adams, 2013).

32 American Battle Monuments Commission, *80th Infantry Division*, August 3-31, 1944.

fighting, and their bodies were strewn across the battlefield.[33] The battle would prove to be one of the bloodiest of the European war.

The 80th Division's first real combat left an indelible impression on the soldiers. One GI wrote, "That was my first impression of what war was really like. It was a frightening and gruesome sight."[34] Another said, "Most of all, I recall the stench. The smell of dead and burning flesh. An overwhelming smell of death. The smell of victory was not sweet."[35] According to a historian, "Everywhere there was a choked mass of smoking tanks, trucks, field kitchens, horse-drawn wagons. Apathy, despair, terror strained at the fabric of German discipline. Abandoned horses, some still harnessed, balked and reared in panic, plunging into ravines or over riverbanks and dragging with them their wagons, their gun carriages, their loads."[36] Even General Eisenhower was moved by the scene, and he wrote: "One of the greatest killing grounds of the war areas. . . . It was literally possible to walk for hundreds of yards at a time, stepping on nothing but dead and decaying flesh."[37]

Although the ultimate credit for sealing the gap went to the 90th Division and (attached to the Canadians) the Polish 1st Armored Division, the 80th's capture of Argentan helped to close the gap and crush the German Seventh Army and put an end to German hopes of containing the Allies in western France.

The success was incomplete, however. The gap wasn't completely closed until August 25.[38] In the meantime, German troops had been able to pour through the gap to the east across France. Chiefly because of indecision within the Allied command, an estimated 20,000 to 40,000 Germans were allowed to escape the pocket and retreat from Normandy, ready to fight again when the Allied armies advanced across France. These escaping troops, however, left almost all their equipment behind; according to one estimate, they kept only about 50 heavy

33 Martin Blumenson et al., eds., *Command Decisions* (Washington, DC, 1960), 416-17.

34 Elvis Mitchell, quoted in "Argentan, the Baptism of Fire," in Beard, *The 314th FA Battalion in the ETO*, 17.

35 Beard, quoted in "Argentan, the Baptism of Fire," in Beard, *The 314th FA Battalion in the ETO*, 17.

36 Charles B. MacDonald, *The Mighty Endeavor: American Armed Forces in the European Theater in World War II* (New York: Oxford University Press, 1969), 317-18.

37 Eisenhower, *Crusade in Europe*, 278.

38 Blumenthal, *Patton's Third Army*, 106.

artillery pieces and as many tanks.[39] But when the Wehrmacht made another stand at the Moselle River a few weeks later, those troops who had escaped the Falaise pocket formed the cadre of resupplied and reinforced divisions that made a stubborn fight. Some of the Germans who escaped the pocket may have prolonged the war for months, and the German Army would remain a real threat for the present.

When B Company left Argentan on the afternoon of August 22, the town was a ruin. The 80th was ordered to pursue the Germans and establish a defensive line along the Marne, but the operation was delayed when it was discovered the Germans had blown up all the bridges between Argentan and Paris, a distance of about 120 miles.

The company motored seven miles to Medvey, where it stayed through August 26. Frank wrote a letter to Betty on August 22, just after arriving there. With the action at Argentan over, he wrote,

> We've been kept a little busy with building fords so infantry vehicles and tanks could keep pushing, and also we've run into the usual mine fields and booby traps. Another fight is over with and I can't mention the names of the towns or anything like that, but if you watch the papers you may run across it cause newsreel and camera men were around.

On his last night in Medvey, Frank mused, "I imagine all of you people back home are going crazy about the news about Paris.[40] We picked up a broadcast from Rockefeller Center and it seems you all had quite a celebration. I guess we don't take it that way—it's good news but there's still plenty of dirty work to do here and on the march to Berlin." He added, "I guess everyone back home thinks it will be over with by winter, but I think they all have another thought coming. I think next spring and summer is more like it." Frank's predictions often came close to the mark.

Argentan had been traumatic to the newly arrived recruits. Their priorities had been irretrievably altered and they now found it hard to mentally leave the bloody Argentan battlefield behind them. Looking back, Frank wrote, "It's rather strange not hearing any artillery fire. For a while in the past week it was a continuous blasting all day long and through the night. You get quite used to it and you stop jumping when they go off." The GIs found their priorities had been realigned

39 Martin Blumenson, "General Bradley's Decision at Argentan," in Blumenson, ed., *Command Decisions*, 319.

40 Paris fell to the Allies on August 25, with the French 2nd Armored Division given the lead.

Maj. Gen. Manton Eddy, commander XII Corps (left) meets with French boys in a newly liberated village, August 16, 1944. *Army Signal Corps*

during a few scant weeks. As Frank explained to Betty, "Seems like another anniversary almost slipped by, and I just thought of it now. I'm sorry, but I guess I couldn't get my mind off certain things that are important over here."

At the end of the Falaise-Argentan Campaign, the 80th Division was relieved of its temporary assignment to the V Corps, First Army, and returned to the command of Third Army. The 80th was assigned to the XII Corps, commanded by Maj. Gen. Manton S. Eddy, a World War I veteran who had commanded American troops in North Africa and Sicily. The 80th would serve under Eddy for most of the rest of the war.

In turning the 80th Division over to XII Corps, V Corps commander Lt. Gen. Leonard T. Gerow wrote to General McBride, "I desire to express to you . . . my personal thanks and appreciation of the excellent manner in which they functioned under my command. The fight put up by the 80th Infantry Division in the Alençon-Argentan area was a most gratifying one, resulting as it did in the destruction of such a large portion of the enemy forces."[41]

By most measures, the Allies' Normandy Campaign was a success. Since coming ashore on D day, the Allies had killed 90,000 Germans in Normandy, and

41 Quoted in Orientation Section, "80th Division Ever Forward," 6.

the vaunted German Army was in complete disarray. By the last week of August, the final remnants of the German forces in the west were streaming across the French countryside. The route through France to the German border was clear, and the 80th Division took off in hot pursuit, using any vehicle they could find on the battlefield that could move.[42] For the foreseeable future, B Company's motor convoy constantly pushed from bivouac to bivouac in this pursuit. There wouldn't be much time for letter writing. The company's five-night stay in Medvey would be the longest in one place for some time to come.

In the days ahead, the Allies' ability to sustain their pursuit would be constrained only by fuel and ammunition shortages. Delays caused by supply problems would allow German forces an opportunity to regroup, dig in, and lay mines along Third Army's path, all of which would have serious consequences for the Allies during the fall and winter campaigns.

42 Craig, *The 80th Infantry Division*, 22.

CHAPTER 4

THE RACE ACROSS FRANCE: AUG. 27-SEPT. 4, 1944

ON August 25, the 80th Infantry Division was paired with the 4th Armored Division to spearhead Third Army's historic high-speed, long-distance pursuit of the Nazis across France.[1] Patton had banked on a short campaign, and it was up to his soldiers—including those of the 305th Engineer Combat Battalion—to end it quickly.

It would, however, be a long, hard march. Within a month, the Moselle crossings and the fighting in Lorraine would become heated battlefields for the Nazis and the Allies. For now, confident after their victory in Normandy and believing the enemy to be on the run, the 80th Division motored across the bleak French countryside. As one soldier noted, "The long race across France was the dustiest, most tiresome ride I ever had."[2]

The 80th Division had originally been ordered to move east from Argentan to establish a line along the Marne River at Chalons-sur-Marne, but the plan was altered when reconnaissance found that the Germans had blown the bridges east of Argentan from Le Mans to Paris. Instead, the division was ordered to head south through Le Mans and east along the north bank of the Loire River. In its haste, the division took all available vehicles, including any left by the retreating Germans, and abandoned them when they were no longer operable. They stopped just to

---

1 Orientation Section, "80th Division Ever Forward," 6.

2 Chet Rutkowski, "Keep Them Rolling to the Meuse," in *314th FA Battalion in the ETO*, 18.

Lt. Gen. George Patton crosses the Seine standing up in a jeep. *Army Signal Corps*

barter for food, eat, and gas up before reaching a point north of Orleans by nightfall.[3]

B Company of the 305th Engineers did reconnaissance along the route and was able to obtain valuable information from the French civilians. The company diary reports they were able to pinpoint a dozen mines in the sector. Although the soldiers occasionally found the French townsfolk to be unfriendly or even hostile, a 305th after-action report observed, "The attitude of the civilians here, except in one or two instances, have been cooperative and friendly and their attitude had a demoralizing effect on the Germans."

The 610th Tank Destroyer Battalion reportedly found this portion of the trip to be pleasant: "The natives along the route cheered the columns all the way, and arms began to ache from returning the waves and salutations. . . . The briefest stop was the signal for much bartering for bread, cognac, and wine, and as the convoy moved the French enthusiastically tossed apples, tomatoes, etc., into the vehicles. A steel helmet was a necessity, for a hard apple thrown at a speeding vehicle can be a deadly missile.[4] The convoy finally stopped in the small village of Origny-le-Sec, 70 miles southeast of Paris, on the afternoon of August 27. It had completed an all-day and all-night advance from Medvey into the heart of France's Champagne region, logging a long 330 miles. The 305th Engineers had closed in on the Seine River bridgehead. B Company's morning report noted the long mileage without

---

3 Craig, *The 80th Infantry Division*, 22.

4 Quoted in Harry Yeide, *The Tank Killers: A History of America's World War II Tank Destroyer Force* (Havertown, PA: Casemate, 2004), 155-56. For now, the 80th's advance to the Seine was rapid, since any German opposition had been eliminated by Free French forces.

80th raises flag over newly liberated French village. *Army Signal Corps*

comment and added, "Morale excellent, weather warm and clear, making reconnaissance on Seine River."[5]

On August 27, the division was ordered to attack to the northeast to capture a crossing of the Marne at Chalons.[6] The Seine and several smaller rivers (including the Aube, Somme, and Soude) stood between the 80th Division and this objective.

The 317th and 318th Regiments, hitchhiking on tanks, set off on August 28 and made good progress. The 318th crossed the Seine on a pontoon bridge and traded fire with German defenders at the Aube while the 305th built another bridge. By that evening both infantry regiments had reached the Marne. B Company built a timber bridge across the Marne to facilitate the crossing.[7]

The company arrived at Cheniers, 58 miles farther along the route, on August 28. While the main body of the German force had withdrawn across the Moselle, the company met determined resistance and was hit with artillery, small arms, and automatic weapons fire. The 80th Division responded to the German attacks with its own self-propelled artillery. The company diary for that day reports that B Company came out ahead in the ensuing exchange, taking 30 Nazi prisoners and escorting them to an enclosure.

The enemy had mined the narrow and winding roads, which were now clogged with rubble and roadblocks—logs, abandoned vehicles, booby traps, and any debris the Nazis could find as they retreated. Engineers from the 305th helped keep the roads open as the 80th Division put more miles behind it. Although combat engineers landed in Normandy with knowledge and skills honed through many months of training, they now added hard-won experience by bridging the rivers,

5   Morning Report, B Company, 305th Engineers, August 27, 1944.

6   After-Action Report, S-3, 317th Infantry Regiment, August 1944.

7   Craig, *The 80th Infantry Division*, 23.

streams, creeks, and canals that crisscrossed Third Army's route through northern France.

On August 29, the company logged another 44 miles and arrived at Vraux, where the 1st Platoon, including Sergeant Lembo's squad, built a treadway bridge over a channel. Treadway bridges could be built and surfaced for different loads or floated atop simple pontoons. In this case, B Company's treadway carried the 80th Infantry and its attached tanks over the channel. The 3rd Platoon bridged the same channel with a timber bridge.

On August 30, the 319th Infantry approached the Marne River and crossed on foot on the framework of a bridge that had been destroyed by the Luftwaffe.[8] Frank Lembo's B Company, meantime, moved a few miles from its bivouac west of Vraux to another site northeast of the town, where it stayed until August 31.

The short break gave Frank his first opportunity to write since B Company had started its rapid march across France. On August 31, he recounted, "I had to run around and find out what day and date it is. Time is so compressed out here and this is the first breathing spell we've had in a while." The engineers were surprised to see a Messerschmitt Bf-109 (Me-109) fighter overhead. Frank told Betty, "A German plane came over a few minutes ago and everyone went diving into the bushes. We don't see too many of them. A couple came over the bridge we worked on yesterday but *ack ack* chased them away."

He was able to fill her in on recent events.

> The Heinies have been keeping us plenty busy. We've been chasing them pretty hard and they demolish everything in our way, so to keep the outfit moving we work. From the look of things, Adolf has sent all his young kids to the front because all that I've seen are pretty young. Captain Marshall ran into some the other day and four or five of them took 21 prisoners.

He added, "This march to Berlin has its good moments. The French are as happy as can be, and they keep throwing wine bottles and eggs at us as we come along. The other day our platoon was working where a bridge was blown out and we got about 160 eggs. They sure come in handy for breakfast." Regarding other events of the day, Frank mentioned, "Our truck radio went on the blink so we don't get any more news or music. I guess one of these days we'll get it fixed." Keeping up to date with the news was important to Frank, and music and news frequently

8 Ibid., 24.

accompanied him in his truck. Fortunately, the engineers were always resourceful in finding or fabricating whatever they needed to get things up and running again.

Anxieties about mail delivery grew as the distance back to the Normandy ports increased. Frank noted, "Just moving too fast for mail to keep up with us." He bemoaned, "I think that from now on our letters will be getting scarcer than all hell." He kept Betty apprised of the number of letters he'd received, actual and expected delivery times, the censors, airmail stationary, and V-mail. Packages were of primary concern; he advised Betty to abandon plans to knit him a sweater because it wouldn't arrive before spring, given what he saw as a two-plus month mail delay.[9] He wanted Betty to get what he needed started on its way to Europe as quickly as possible: wristwatch straps (scarce in the field), razor blades, chocolate-covered Brazil nuts, and a bottle of ink.

By the end of August the 305th had logged an extraordinary 684 miles since landing on Utah Beach just a few weeks earlier. The days they spent on the road had been grueling but exhilarating—Third Army's movements were making historic headlines, and the opposition was still relatively light and intermittent.

But as Third Army neared the district of Lorraine, it began to encounter serious supply shortages, particularly of fuel. An 80th Division history called gasoline "the lifeblood of a fast-moving army" and noted that since August 26, Third Army "had been running on borrowed time."[10]

The shortages were particularly evident to the engineers: "Toward the end of August ominous entries had begun to appear in the journals of the engineer combat groups of First and Third Armies. Gasoline was running short, as were certain items of bridge-building equipment. The armies had outrun their supply depots, which were far to the rear, most of them at the original invasion beaches."[11] Indeed, the 305th noted, "The further east we traveled from the beach we landed upon, the more critical our supply problems became . . . especially gasoline."[12]

Patton's high-speed push had strained the logistics capabilities of the 6,000 trucks of the Red Ball Express, a special service that utilized one-way roads and 24-hour-a-day operations to expedite fuel deliveries. It was impossible to sustain

9 Betty apparently ignored this suggestion; her sweater for Frank arrived in late December.

10 Craig, *The 80th Infantry Division*, 24.

11 Alfred M. Beck et al., *The Corps of Engineers: The War Against Germany* (Washington, DC: Center of Military History, U.S. Army, 1985), 390-91.

12 "Historical Journal of Supply," 305th Engineer Combat Battalion, August 1944.

American MP cheers on Red Ball Express trucks. *US Army*

the drive, even if Third Army's requests for fuel had received the unequivocal support of the high command.[13]

In fact, Third Army's supply problems had been exacerbated by the high command's balancing of competing SHAEF priorities. Not only did Courtney Hodges's First Army require supply, but British Gen. Bernard L. Montgomery, commander of the 21st Army Group, was given the green light for his combined armored-airborne assault through Holland, codenamed Market Garden. Allied airlift capacity was temporarily devoted to the British sector. Patton's supply flow was temporarily shut off so supplies could go to Monty.

Patton vehemently disagreed with the reallocation of fuel to the Brits. He wrote,

> Everything seemed rosy, when suddenly it was reported to me that the 140,000 gallons of gas we were to get that day had not arrived. . . . I later found that . . . the delay was due to a change of plan by the High Command, implemented, in my opinion, by General Montgomery. . . . I presented my case for a rapid advance to the east for the purpose of cutting the Siegfried Line before it could be manned. . . . It was my opinion then that this was the momentous error of the war.[14]

Back in the field, B Company examined its own logistics support needs and compared them to its dwindling supplies. The company tried to adapt its procedures to the world of scarcity. When its own transportation became

---

13 Green and Brown, *Patton's Third Army*, 122; Hugh M. Cole, *The Lorraine Campaign*, U.S. Army in World War II (Washington, D.C: Historical Division, Department of the Army, 1950), 22.

14 George S. Patton, *War as I Knew It* (Boston: Houghton Mifflin, 1947), 115.

problematic, the company was forced to search for trucks in other units of the division, borrow trailers from the infantry, and free up transport space by doubling up and even looking for novel ways of carrying equipment, including their vital assault boats.[15]

GIs also became creative in tracking down and utilizing stores abandoned by the fleeing Germans. On September 1, men from the 80th Division captured some Nazi supply points, including one in St. Julien that included 25 railway tank cars of gasoline—about 100,000 gallons.[16] One soldier from the 80th recalled:

> Somewhere near Chalons our trucks were so low on gas that we would be unable to move the next day. Capt. Benford told me to go to a blown-up rail yard that had just been captured that day and where there were several carloads of gas in drums. The railroad cars with the gasoline were about 50 or 60 feet from the road and separated from it by an iron fence and a six-foot ditch. Finally, in total darkness, [our driver] turned our truck around, pushed over the iron fence, eased through the ditch, slowly bumped over four sets of rails and stopped right up at the side of the car.[17]

In addition to fuel, the company was able to obtain German radios, generators, and essential electronic supplies. The battalion's after-action report noted, "At one time we secured several thousand German pencils, and distributed them throughout the division."[18]

At the start of the drive across France, the only real opposition came from small rearguard units that were trying to slow the Americans enough to disengage and set up a defensive line on the high ground east of the Moselle River between Metz and Nancy. At the time, German field commanders were reporting in despair to Hitler about the state of affairs.

> The retreating troops . . . had few heavy weapons and were mostly armed with carbines and rifles. . . . The eleven German Panzer divisions originally in France would have to be refitted before they could equal the strength of as many regiments; few had more than five

---

15 "Historical Journal of Supply," 305th Engineer Combat Battalion, August 1944.

16 "Periods for Historical Reporting, 1 September to 30 September 1944," After-Action Report, G-4, 80th Division.

17 Frank Lankford, quoted in "Keeping Them Rolling to the Meuse," in Beard, *The 314th FA Battalion in the ETO*, 19.

18 "Historical Journal of Supply," 305th Engineer Combat Battalion, August 1944.

to ten tanks in working order. The infantry divisions possessed only single pieces of artillery.[19]

Patton wrote on August 29, "It was evident at this time that there was no real threat against us." He ordered the XII Corps, under Maj. Gen. Manton Eddy, to advance on the town of Commercy, and the XX Corps to advance on Verdun.

On August 31, B Company traveled 48 miles to Revigney-sur-Ormaine, where it operated in support of the 1st Battalion of the 318th Infantry The company later followed behind the battalion as it traveled another 36 miles, reaching Euville on September 1. On the same day, the remainder of the 80th marched in the direction of Commercy, near the banks of the Meuse River. General Eddy had previously been given permission to halt based on the risk the tanks might run out of gasoline if they continued advancing. Believing "it was mandatory to get crossings over the Meuse," Patton called Eddy and "told him to continue until the tanks stopped and then get out and walk."[20] Somehow, "through a campaign of cajoling higher headquarters, meticulous scrounging of captured German resources, and just plain stealing the supplies of neighboring armies," Third Army continued to make slow, methodical advances.[21]

The 80th Division's first incursion across the Meuse took place on the night of September 1, when engineers from the 305th ferried light vehicles across the river and consolidated their position on the far bank. At this time the division's positions around Euville and Commercy were bombed and strafed by enemy aircraft. The 305th Engineers continued to find and destroy mined and booby-trapped roadblocks in the vicinity of the Meuse.

The XII Corps then ordered the 80th Division to relieve the 4th Armored Division on the high ground east of Commercy. The 80th, with the 319th Regiment leading the way, seized St. Mihiel, where it met resistance from artillery and small arms, and it also seized Bar-le-Duc.[22] After crossing the Meuse, Combat Teams 317

---

19 Cole, *The Lorraine Campaign*, 39.

20 Patton, *War as I Knew It*, 116.

21 Henry G. Phillips, *The Making of a Professional: Manton S. Eddy, USA* (Westport, CT: Greenwood Press, 2000), 162.

22 "Reports After Action Against Enemy," 319th Infantry Regiment, September 1945, l.

and 318 occupied a bridgehead in the vicinity of Commerce.[23] Combat Team 319 reached the west side of the Meuse near St. Mihiel and reconnoitered the river for possible crossing sites. The 319th Infantry crossed the Meuse on September 2.

The next day the three combat teams strengthened and expanded the Meuse bridgehead.[24] Ahead lay the province of Lorraine, which along with adjacent Alsace had changed hands between the Germans and French for centuries. For Third Army, the happy days of joyriding 50 miles or more a day amid the cheers of friendly villagers were at an end. The soldiers of the 80th were introduced to the unaccustomed and unforgettable sights of rural provincial life—manure piles in front of houses, animals living in a room connected to the family kitchen, and curbside toilets on public streets. One soldier described the latter: "A metal shielding that was built over a part of the sidewalk and out over the curb and about as high as your head with a door at each end. You could see feet as people stood there relieving themselves."[25]

Gasoline shortages, the stirrings of the German Army, the worsening weather, and the Lorraine countryside all conspired to slow Patton's advance. As one analyst pointed out, "The rolling farmland was broken by tangled woods. . . . Third Army would have to cross numerous rivers and streams . . . and would have to penetrate two fortified lines to reach Germany. . . . The Americans could not even count on the unqualified support of Lorraine's inhabitants."[26] The 319th reported, "Civilian attitude is not enthusiastic about American occupation and cooperation does not exist as it has in the past."[27] Nevertheless, "the Lorraine gateway was so invitingly open, it was unthinkable to Patton that Third Army should be halted in midstream."[28]

The 80th Division also confronted its first evidence of German atrocities as it moved forward. Retreating Germans had burned village after village to the ground,

23 80th Infantry Division, "Preparations for and Crossing the Moselle, September1-15, 1944," 1.

24 Ibid.

25 Lankford, "Keeping Them Rolling to the Meuse," in Beard, *The 314th FA Battalion*, 18.

26 Christopher R. Gabel, *The Lorraine Campaign: An Overview, September-December 1944* (Fort Leavenworth, KS: Combat Studies Institute, U.S. Army Command and General Staff College, 1985), 3.

27 "Reports After Action Against Enemy," 319th Infantry Regiment, September 1945, 3.

28 Gabel, *The Lorraine Campaign*, 4.

and fields were filled with murdered civilians. The Americans were beginning to see the cruelty of their enemy more clearly.

Frank Lembo did not write about this experience during the first days of September, but he told Betty something of the horror when he was finally settling down between the two Moselle crossings. It was always difficult for him to find words to describe his disturbing experiences to someone dear to him who would be quietly reading his letter back in the States. His anger was still at a fever pitch when he wrote about it from Fey-en-Haye on September 11:

> I got a chance to see some major brutality. They took one town, burned all the houses, cut the kids up and then put all the people in one house and burned it. One kid with a broken leg sought safety in a church, but they shot him there. It makes you madder than hell and I just hope this war doesn't end until we get on German soil. A little destruction there may teach them something, but surer than hell they've got to be taught something and we might as well do it while we are here.

B Company stayed in Euville, near the Meuse, until September 3, temporarily halted by the fuel shortage. Frank told Betty, "Things are normal as hell, and the last few days have been uneventful. I went out on a mine field job [at] two o'clock in the morning, but we couldn't find a thing." He continued, "We've been chasing the Germans all over this country and can't quite catch him. They are usually at your fingertips, but just stay out of reach. I'm sorry I can't tell you where we've been because it would amaze you to see how far we've come—but alas censorship."

He looked inward and sensed the multitude of changes that had taken place during the previous month in France. The young GI who had recently sailed across the Channel was now an experienced soldier. As he confided to Betty, "I don't think I'll get bitter and hard, but you see a lot of things you'll never forget." His buddies were similarly affected by what they saw. Frank's words about his friends' morale grew more cautious as the days passed. "Scotty and the rest are all around yet, except one, and they are healthy as ever and just beat up a little. I guess that covers it completely."

But at the end of his September 3 letter he got back down to basics, confessing, "I'm still thinking of the day we'll get married and settled down to raising a family. It's about the only thing you fight for, to get back home and lead a normal life. The other bull goes in one ear and out the other."

Worsening weather and worries about the coming months began to undercut morale as September got underway. Frank complained to Betty, "The weather has been pretty damp and chilly and winter is on its way. Our heavy clothing is in storage way back so I hope we get it soon. This march to Berlin is supposed to end

[by] Christmas so I hope it's true." He added, "I'm trying to think where I can get me a few extra blankets for the coming winter. I had a couple awhile back that was lying next to a blown-up jeep but we used it to cover the dead. I guess if everyone else can manage I'll be able to also."

As the start of September slipped by and the Moselle River loomed on the horizon, the 305th Combat Engineer Battalion intensified its review of river crossings with infantry and other elements of the division. The procedures were well established and had been thoroughly practiced in training and on waterways since entering France, but now last-minute reviews took place.

The engineers' boats typically carried a 17-man squad with equipment—14 riflemen, with 3 engineers to guide the boat. The engineers would shoulder the assault boats to the water's edge and ferry the infantry across in successive waves. Seventeen boats were required to carry a single rifle company.[29] In theory, crossings were carried out in darkness to gain an element of surprise. Engineers generally guided troops to the riverbank to board the boats, and everyone paddled to reach the opposite shore. Once across, the infantrymen would capture the area around the landing site. When the landing site was secure and free of fire, the engineers would build footbridges and then larger treadway bridges to allow more troops and equipment to cross. The infantry and engineers would work to simultaneously enlarge and secure the beachhead.

A river crossing seldom worked this smoothly in practice, and it certainly wouldn't work this way on the Moselle.

Continuing gasoline shortages left Third Army "virtually immobilized from 1 to 5 September," well short of the Moselle.[30] On September 3, 12th Army Group commander Omar Bradley relented and gave Patton half of his requested fuel allocation. Patton hoped this supply would permit Third Army to continue its drive across the Moselle and push toward the Siegfried Line, albeit at a slower pace than he wanted.[31] Finally, on September 4, the supply shortage started to break.[32] General Eisenhower, the SHAEF commander, clarified that he wanted to restart Third Army's advance: "I now deem it important, while supporting

---

29 Adkins and Adkins, *You Can't Get Closer than This*, 21; "Moselle Crossings: Engineers," Interviews with Representatives of 1117th Engineer Group, 557th Heavy Ponton Battalion, 248th Engineer Battalion, 167th Engineer Combat Battalion, and 305th Engineer Combat Battalion.

30 Cole, *Lorraine Campaign*, 52.

31 Patton, *War as I Knew It*, 117.

32 Cole, *Lorraine Campaign*, 52.

[Montgomery's] advance on eastward through Belgium, to get Patton moving once again so that we may be fully prepared to carry out the original conception for the final stages of the campaign."[33]

Eisenhower also showed that the Allied high command still believed the Germans were defeated and only one more push was needed. "For some days it has been obvious that our military forces can advance almost at will. Resistance has largely melted all along the front. . . . The defeat of the German armies is complete, and the only thing now needed to realize the whole conception is speed."[34]

Patton and Eddy shared Eisenhower's view that the Germans were finished.[35] But the slowdown in operations created by the supply disruption had wasted precious time and given the Germans an opportunity to catch their breath, reorganize, and prepare strong defenses on the east side of the Moselle.

The German First Army had retreated across the Meuse with nine battalions of infantry and only 10 tanks. But under the radar of Allied intelligence, it had since been reinforced with two veteran Panzer divisions from Italy and still more reinforcements (in the form of two *Volksgrenadier* divisions and a Panzer brigade). The army had only a shadow of the units that had first fought in Normandy, but the Germans were again a real fighting force capable of giving stiff opposition to the Americans.[36]

Every day brought challenges for the 305th as operations resumed. The troops had been marking time during what must have seemed like an endless four days of waiting, especially since they had little understanding of the political gyrations that tied their generals' hands.

The Moselle would be the engineers' first major contested crossing of the war. A tributary of the Rhine, the Moselle ran more than 300 miles through France, Luxembourg, and Germany. To date, the 305th had crossed over fords in places where bridges had been blown and bridged innumerable creeks and canals, as well as the Seine, Aube, Marne, and Meuse Rivers, but they had never faced a river the size of the Moselle in the face of heavy enemy resistance.

---

33 Dwight D. Eisenhower, diary entry, September 5, 1944, quoted in Cole, *Lorraine Campaign*, 53-54.

34 Cole, *Lorraine Campaign*, 53-54.

35 John Nelson Rickard, *Patton at Bay: The Lorraine Campaign, September to December, 1944* (Westport, CT: Praeger, 1999), 56, 60, 78. For example, Patton stated at a press conference on September 7, "You can't have men retreating for 300 or 400 miles and then hold anything," citing a "psychological result in long retreats."

36 Cole, *Lorraine Campaign*, 47.

If the fight at Argentan had been the baptism by fire of the 305th Engineers, the Moselle Campaign introduced them to the horrific realities of extended warfare in unforgiving terrain against a determined enemy. They quickly discovered the Germans would vigorously defend the territory at and just east of the Moselle for the next three months. After their ride across France, the Americans—generals, officers, and enlisted men alike—would never expect the operation would go on for as long as it did or that the struggle would be as painful and costly as it would be.

On September 4, while headed toward Pont-à-Mousson and the river, B Company's advance was impeded by unexpected pockets of German resistance along its route. A squad from the company's 3rd Platoon drove 12 Germans out of the town of Jaillon.[37] Then, after reaching a bivouac area near Manon-eu-Court, another 46 miles forward, the company received intelligence that a dozen Germans were holed up in the nearby town of Villey-St-Etienne. This time, two squads from the 3rd Platoon, which had gone to the town to reconnoiter bridges over the Moselle, surprised not 12 but about 50 enemy troops and engaged in an intense firefight. Overwhelmed, the platoon commander called for reinforcements, and the 2nd Platoon, led by company commander Robert C. Marshall, joined the fight. The engineers seized the town and were able to tenuously hold it until they received an order to withdraw. Seven Germans were killed in the fighting, and both sides suffered wounded. One enlisted man from B Company's 3rd Platoon was killed.[38]

Squads from B Company performed reconnaissance of the former Moselle bridges in the vicinity of Manon, to see if any could be rebuilt.[39] Combat engineers from the 305th also seized and held the lone bridge that hadn't been destroyed by the Germans. There was only light resistance.

B Company waited impatiently for word to jump off on the Moselle operation. The men had been on edge, waiting and preparing for days, knowing that the order could come at any time. Frank wrote on September 4, "Things are normal with hell due to pop." He reflected, "I'm glad our platoon is with the combat team as usual. Every time the company moves they run into artillery fire or something a little too big for them—I guess someone sticks his neck out a little too far." He noted, however, with pride, "The division has been doing rather well and I could tell you some of the towns they have taken, but it will all have to remain until after the war."

37 Morning Report, B Company, 305th Engineer Combat Battalion, September 4, 1944.

38 Ibid., September 5, 1944.

39 Ibid., September 4, 1944.

CHAPTER 5

FIRST ASSAULT ON THE MOSELLE: SEPT. 5-6, 1944

WHEN Maj. Gen. Manton Eddy, XII Corps commander, looked at the forces immediately available to make the assault on the Moselle, his eyes settled on two divisions—the 80th Infantry and the 4th Armored. This force was admittedly thin, but Patton and Eddy wanted to move quickly now that fuel was again flowing. There were other reasons to rush ahead with the crossing, even under less than optimal circumstances. Patton believed the window was still open to attack into territory thinly defended by demoralized German troops, and he wanted to catch the Germans before they had more time to ready their defenses.[1] The American generals counted on surprising the Germans and completing the crossing with a quick thrust, as had been done successfully at the Meuse.

Eddy's initial plan called for one regiment of the 80th Division to establish a bridgehead at Pont-à-Mousson, halfway between Nancy and Metz. Once the bridgehead was secured, the tanks of Maj. Gen. John Wood's 4th Armored Division, reinforced by an infantry battalion from the 318th Regiment, would pass through and attack Nancy from the north. The 80th's 317th Infantry Regiment was designated as the lead element for the assault, and the 80th's organic engineers, the 305th, would support the lead infantry units.[2] Eddy planned for the 80th to cross the Moselle on a broad front. Night patrols, aided by engineers from the 305th,

---

1 Patton, *War as I Knew It*, 117.

2 Ibid., 125; Cole, *Lorraine Campaign*, 57-58; Albin Irzyk, "8th Tank Battalion's Daring Moselle Crossing," in *World War II Magazine* (September 1997).

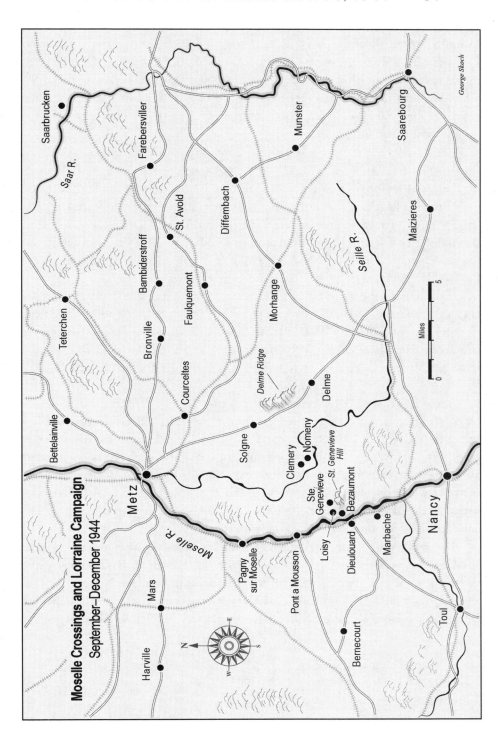

Moselle Crossings and Lorraine Campaign
September–December 1944

George Stoch

identified three possible crossing sites that appeared unprotected—one near Pagny-sur-Moselle, to the north of Pont-à-Mousson; another south of Vandières in the center; and a third in the vicinity of Dieulouard, at the southern end of the target area.[3] Although patrols reported the approaches to all of these sites could easily be observed by German troops on the east side of the river, plans for the assault went ahead unhindered.

Eddy's plan called for the 317th's three infantry battalions cross at two of the sites. The 1st Battalion would cross in assault boats east of Blenod-lès-Pont-à-Mousson and swing around to take Mousson Hill; the 2nd Battalion would ford at Pagny, on the north end of the operational area, and seize Hills 385 and 358; and the reserve units from the 317th's 3rd Battalion would follow the 1st Battalion after it secured a foothold at Pont-à-Mousson. The 4th Armored would follow behind with units from the 318th Infantry Regiment after the crossing site at Pont-à-Mousson was secured.

It turned out the terrain at the Moselle was more difficult than anything the engineers, infantry, and intelligence specialists had expected. The 80th would need to cross the 50-foot-wide Rhine-Marne Canal and surmount an eight-foot dyke (similar in shape to a hedgerow) before reaching the river. The smooth canal and snakelike Moselle, backed by high, rolling hills, formed a double obstacle.

According to the plan, the troops would cross over the canal in assault boats or on footbridges, scramble over the dyke, and make their way a few hundred feet across an open floodplain before they were in place to finally cross the river. At that point, the engineers would be responsible for moving the assault boats into the water again and carrying the infantrymen over the 150-foot-wide Moselle. In places the river was more than eight feet deep, and the incessant rains of the previous summer had soaked the ground, raised water levels, and increased the flow. The banks of the dyke and canal were slick with mud.

The 318th, minus one battalion, was to undertake an assault across the Moselle at Marbache, and the 319th, attached to the 4th Armored, would engage the Germans in the vicinity of Toul, with the mission of attacking at Nancy.[4]

Although the Allied commanders believed at the start of the operation that the Germans had largely abandoned the fight and were retreating to the safety of the

---

3 Summary of Interviews, "Moselle Operations, 80th Infantry Division," Interviews with Lt. Col. L. F. Fisher, Maj. J. D. Hayes, Capt. S. A. Ford.

4 80th Division, "Initial Crossing of the Moselle River," 3.

Siegfried Line, the delays caused by Third Army's shortages of fuel, supplies, and ammunition had given the Germans time to dig into the heights on the far bank of the Moselle, which overlooked the plain below. From there they observed the approaching 80th Division and the lead elements of the 4th Armored. German artillery was on the ready on the east bank of the river well before the 80th's arrival, and snipers were in place with clear lines of sight.

Elements of the 80th Division reached the river on September 4, but rest and preparation for the first major assault crossing of the war weren't in the cards. With gasoline allocations for the 80th and the 4th Armored once again flowing, Eddy immediately ordered the 317th Infantry Regiment to make a reconnaissance on the river north of Nancy to provide an assessment of enemy strength. Although the scouting parties didn't identify significant opposition, the emphasis on speed precluded a thorough reconnaissance in daylight, so detailed intelligence on the terrain and opposition was necessarily scarce. The troops from the 317th would go in without knowing what lay ahead of them.[5]

Frank Lembo found little time to write letters now that the operation was upon them, and the engineers needed to intensively patrol the riverbank at the edge of enemy territory. Letters became much scarcer over the following two weeks.

Eddy decided not to risk a night crossing on the evening of September 4, instead opting for what he hoped to be a surprise attack after daylight the next day. This, too, was a miscalculation, as the men of the 80th wouldn't even have the cover of darkness to mask their movements.

The assault by the 317th's three battalions jumped off on the morning of September 5, but Frank's B Company was still frustrated in its attempts to join the operation. The company's motor convoy, which had been held up when fighting erupted along the route, was still on the final leg of its trip to the river when the assault began. The 305th's convoy had left its bivouac in Euville at 4:00 a.m., motored 30 miles to a new area near Premy, and then traveled the final 11 miles to reach Fey-en-Haye, about four miles west of Pont-à-Mousson, at 11:00 a.m. on September 5.[6]

Upon its arrival at the river, B Company began to support the 2nd Battalion of the 317th, which was preparing to cross the river in the vicinity of Pont-à-Mousson.[7] The 2nd Battalion made its way across the Marne canal, assisted by

---

5 "The Bridging of the Moselle River by the 80th Division," Interview with Maj. J. D. Hayes, 1.

6 B Company Morning Report, 305th Engineer Combat Battalion, September 5, 1944.

7 Ibid.

Soldiers from the 317th stare across Moselle River before assault,
September 5, 1944. *Army Signal Corps*

the 1st squad of B Company's 3rd Platoon. The German defense, however, on the high ground east of the river, by now extended from Pagny to Millery, and the battalion had been closely observed as it advanced toward the riverbank. The infantrymen came under bombardment and became paralyzed in the flats between the canal and the river.[8] B Company planned to ferry platoons from the 2nd Battalion across the river in assault boats, but the six rubber boats assigned for the operation were destroyed by enemy artillery before they reached the water. The mission was aborted and the soldiers withdrew with substantial casualties, which included 20 engineers.

The 317th's 1st Battalion fared no better when it attempted to force a crossing with assault boats near Blenod. The battalion's assault was supposed to be preceded by both an artillery bombardment and an air attack on Mousson Hill, but neither happened.[9] Engineers from the 305th carried assault boats to the edge of

8 "Moselle Crossing," Interview with Maj. Charles Croker, 305th Engineer Battalion; "The Bridging of the Moselle River by the 80th Infantry Division," Interview with Maj. J. D. Hayes, 317th Infantry Regiment.

9 "The Bridging of the Moselle River by the 80th Infantry Division," Interview with Maj. J. D. Hayes.

the canal and paddled them across in preparation for the river crossing. The infantrymen were able to cross the canal over a partially demolished footbridge, assisted by the engineers. But after they had moved only about 200 yards toward the river, enemy machine guns began to sweep the troops on the exposed flats. Heavy mortar fire destroyed most of the rubber boats intended for the river crossing.[10] The 1st Battalion fell back toward the canal and took shelter behind a railroad embankment before withdrawing under fire.[11] The entire battalion was shaken and demoralized, and staff reported back to headquarters that further action by this unit would be out of the question in the near future; the battalion's commanding officer was replaced shortly afterward.[12]

Despite the failure of the first two crossings attempted by the 317th's 1st and 2nd Battalions, Eddy and other Third Army commanders insisted on another wave. The remaining elements of the 317th's three battalions were ordered to regroup and prepare for additional crossings that same day.

The 1st Battalion was ordered to retrace its steps and attempt a second crossing at Blenod, where it had come under fire early in the day. The battalion was once again stopped when the Germans opened fire on them in the flats between the canal and river. The 1st Battalion's crossing was aborted again, with significant casualties.[13]

The 317th's 2nd Battalion had withstood withering fire at Pont-à-Mousson earlier in the day, but Eddy ordered it to force another crossing, this time at the northern end of the 80th's operations area, at Pagny-sur-Moselle. The 2nd Battalion struggled to take the town of Pagny on its way to the river, but it was hit by heavy artillery fire from the hills east of town. The plan was for the 305th to carry the 2nd Battalion across the canal in 20 rubber boats, but the engineers were unable to force their way through to the canal and get the boats into the water. After hours of close fighting, the 2nd Battalion's assault at Pagny-sur-Moselle was also aborted.[14]

Despite its losses, the 317th's 2nd Battalion had more work to do that day. It left Pagny when the crossing failed and went south, with supporting engineers

10 "Moselle Crossing," Interview with Maj. Charles Croker, 305th Engineer Battalion.

11 "Summary of Interviews, Moselle Operation," Fisher, Hayes, Ford Interview; Follow-up Interview with Hayes.

12 "Moselle Operations, Assault Boat Crossing," Second Interview with Maj. J. D. Hayes.

13 80th Division, "Initial Crossing of the Moselle River," 5.

14 Ibid.

from the 305th, to try another crossing at the small town of Vandières. Infantrymen and engineers went out to reconnoiter the canal and river at the new site. The engineers built a footbridge in place of a bridge that had been destroyed by the Germans, using two barges they'd found on the bank as a foundation. That night the troops used the barges to cross the canal and made their way toward the river under cover of darkness. As the men prepared to cross the river in the 305th's assault boats, the sound of a command in German alerted them to an impending attack. The soldiers from the 2nd Battalion were able to fall to the ground just before their position was hit by machine gun bursts.[15] The 305th Engineers also fell back from the line of fire.

One company from the 317th's 2nd Battalion was able to withdraw, but the remainder of the battalion survived a night of heavy mortar and artillery fire only by clinging to the muddy bank of the canal. They were not pulled out until the next afternoon. An officer from the 2nd Battalion recalled, with their bodies partially submerged in the canal, "A few mortar shells arced their way through the night in our direction and the machine guns fired interdiction fire. There was nothing we could do but lay there until daylight, and it was one miserable long night. Some of the men began to panic and started to run and swim the canal. . . . Some of the men who tried it couldn't swim a stroke. They drowned before anyone could get there to help them."[16]

The 317th's 3rd Battalion, which had been in reserve earlier in the day, was ordered to make a frontal attack on the German position on Mousson Hill from Pont-à-Mousson. Men from the 305th ferried infantry across the Moselle in rubber assault boats, paddling against a strong current, and landed part of the battalion, reportedly nine assault boatloads, on the enemy bank. There were heavy casualties, however, and at least 38 of the 64 assault boats were riddled by artillery and small arms fire or pulled downstream by the current.[17]

Engineers made three trips to bring the wounded from the 3rd Battalion back to the west bank before their boats were destroyed by enemy fire. Boats also went

---

15 Adkins and Adkins, *You Can't Get Closer than This*, 25.

16 Ibid., 26-27.

17 Croker Interview, Moselle Crossings; "Moselle Operations, Assault Boat Crossing," Second Interview with Maj. J. D. Hayes; 80th Division, "Initial Crossings of the Moselle River," 4-5.

awash when the enemy opened a dam above the crossing site, wildly increasing the water level and flow. The engagement caused 11 more engineer casualties.[18]

In order to help the 317th's 3rd Battalion hang on to its small foothold on the east bank at Pont-à-Mousson, remnants of the 2nd Battalion and all other available troops were ordered to reinforce the 3rd Battalion's fragile position. Before the reinforcements arrived, however, the Germans counterattacked in force. In a chaotic rout, the Germans left their foxholes along the riverbank and attacked the Americans with bayonets, grenades, and machine pistols. The position of the 317th's 3rd Battalion was quickly wiped out, and the remnants of the battalion withdrew to the west side of the river with heavy losses. Many others were taken prisoner.[19]

Finally, on September 6, after failure after failure, Eddy called off all further attempts to cross the Moselle that day.[20] The 317th withdrew piecemeal to the woods on the western bluff overlooking the river. The men from the 305th withdrew to the relative safety of the west bank as well.[21]

While all of these actions by the 80th's 317th Infantry Regiment transpired, the 319th was able to establish a bridgehead at Toul in the face of fierce resistance. The infantry was soon turned back, but the 319th's operation was nevertheless considered to be one of the 80th's most successful of the day.[22] C Company of the 305th was in support of the 319th.[23]

The initial attempts to cross the Moselle were costly in terms of men and equipment. The 317th Infantry, in particular, experienced severe losses from the fruitless assaults on September 5 and 6. The first Moselle crossings were also disappointing for the engineers of the 305th. While engineer casualties weren't as heavy as those of the infantry, their attempts to cross the 80th's elements using fords, footbridges, and assault boats had ended in frustration. They had seen fellow

---

18 Croker Interview, Moselle Crossings.

19 "Moselle Operations, Assault Boat Crossing," Second Interview with Maj. J. D. Hayes.

20 Major Hayes stated General McBride on the morning of September 6 had come down to the 3rd Battalion command post to order all the troops across. During this meeting, the bridgehead was wiped out and attack plans were cancelled. ("Assault Boat Crossing," Hayes Interview).

21 Croker Interview, Moselle Crossings.

22 Craig, *The 80th Infantry Division*, 26.

23 Morning Report, Company C, 305th Engineer Combat Battalion, September 6, 1944.

soldiers die, suffer wounds, or taken prisoner at the canal and river and had lost most of their equipment, seemingly to no avail.

The commander of the 305th's supply section had his own take on the events that occurred over the preceding few days. In the 305th's after-action report for the month of September, he reported they had "supplied fourteen boats, assault, for a river crossing. The line companies who were responsible for the return of these boats and the pole type trailer, upon which they were hauled, never did return them, due to the situation. Some were destroyed during the action that occurred at the river crossing, and as these boats were considered a critical item in the Engineer Depot, it prompted me to go on a scavenger hunt for assault boats. The hunt resulted in securing sixteen assault boats, fourteen of which were slightly damaged and easily repairable and ready for the next assault."[24]

The failure of the first attempts at the river crossing shattered the widespread belief among the high command—and many people on the U.S. homefront—that Germany was defeated and that the war in Europe might be over before the end of the year.

There was a long list of deficiencies to review and remedy before the 80th would be ready for the next phase of the assault. Failure to allow adequate time for the exhausted soldiers to rest and regroup before the assaults began, the inability to reconnoiter the terrain and test enemy strength in daylight, the decision to make a daytime assault rather than cross under cover of darkness, the lack of essential air and artillery support, insufficient coordination, and misleading intelligence estimates all contributed to the breakdowns.

Commanders began planning another assault they knew had to be carried out in the face of entrenched enemy opposition. It would be a matter of days, however, before the details of the plan could be worked out.

24 Edward F. Packer, "Historical Journal of Supply," Summary of Daily Operations, After-Action Report, 305th Engineer Combat Battalion, September 1944.

CHAPTER 6

THE FINAL MOSELLE
BRIDGEHEAD: SEPT. 6-12, 1944

DURING the hiatus between attacks, Major General Eddy devised a more comprehensive plan that used XII Corps' 80th Division, 4th Armored Division, and the 137th Infantry of the 35th Division to cross the river and push through the German defenses in a concentrated attack on the town of Nancy. The 317th Infantry would again play a lead role in the assault, and the 305th Engineers would support the crossing and carry out tasks on the east bank. As these plans were formulated, the 318th and 319th Infantry continued fighting on the west side of the Moselle in the areas of Marbache and Toul, respectively. They ultimately captured the towns of Marbache, Liverdun, and Villey-le-Sec and mopped up west of the river.[1]

B Company stayed at its bivouac near Pont-à-Mousson until September 13, first in nearby Fey-en-Haye and then in Blenod-lès-Pont-à-Mousson. While action in the vicinity of the latter village was stopped to allow Eddy and other senior commanders time to develop their plan, engineers and infantry continued to scout and prepare for the next attempt to cross the Moselle. On September 7, B Company sent out a motorized patrol toward the canal and river, but enemy automatic weapons and artillery fire prevented the patrol from completing its mission.

---

1 "Preparations for and Crossing of Moselle R, 1–15 September 1944," 80th Infantry Division, 3; Summary of Interviews, Moselle Operations, Lt. Col. John G. Golden, former commanding officer, 2nd Battalion, 318th Infantry Regiment.

The failed September 5 attack had taken place at three crossing sites broadly arrayed along the twisted river from Pagny to Pont-à-Mousson and Vandières, but the commanders now engaged in a critical reappraisal of how and where the river might best be bridged. Patrols sent out by the 317th identified several possible crossing sites for XII Corps' next thrust, but planning soon focused on those around Dieulouard, a small town on the west side of the Moselle, about four miles downriver from the previous attempts at Pont-à-Mousson.[2]

Terrain was a crucial consideration in the selection of the Dieulouard site. While a crossing anywhere along the Moselle would be a major challenge, Dieulouard was seen as having the greatest likelihood of success. East of Dieulouard, the Moselle split into two arms around a several-hundred-foot-wide barren island, which was bisected by a macadam road. The road had the advantage of allowing tanks and other heavy vehicles to pass easily, but movements across the island would necessarily take place without cover. As before, an eight-foot dyke rose abruptly from the bottom of the barge canal that ran beside the river. The river was also surrounded by a wide flood plain under the sight of German-held hills in the east. Incessant rain meanwhile caused the river to surge and overflow its muddy banks.[3]

The new plan required infantrymen and engineers to cross three bodies of water—the canal and both arms of the river—as well as the island and flood plain, under close observation by the enemy, before reaching their objectives in the hills beyond. One scout from the 317th pointed out, "The ground formed a flat flood plain over a thousand yards wide without cover or concealment, giving the Germans excellent fields of fire for their automatic weapons."[4]

Eddy's evolving plan called for the 2nd Battalion of the 317th to cross north of the island, move over the flood plain, progress through the town of Loisy, and take the commanding Genevieve Hill. B Company's 1st Platoon would guide the initial assault waves from the 2nd Battalion across. The 317th's 1st Battalion would move up to the right of the 2nd Battalion and seize and secure Hill 381, northeast of

---

2 Summary of Interviews, Moselle Operation, 317th Infantry, Interview with Lt. Col. L. F. Fisher, Maj. J. D. Hayes, Capt. S. A. Ford, and Capt. J. E. Mullen).

3 Dieulouard River Crossing, 1; Moselle Crossing: Engineers, Interviews with Representatives of 1117th Engineer Group, 557th Heavy Ponton Battalion, 248th Engineer Combat Battalion, 167th Engineer Combat Battalion, and 305th Engineer Combat Battalion.

4 "Report for History, September 1944," S-2, 317th Infantry Regiment, 1.

Bezaumont.[5] The 317th's 3rd Battalion would cross south of Dieulouard, move across the island, and take the critical hill known as La Falaise. B Company and other units from the 305th Engineers would get the 317th across the canal and the river in 17 assault boats, since the engineers' ability to lay a bridge across the fast-moving, 150-foot-wide river was uncertain.[6]

The 317th was to be followed by armor and artillery and two battalions of the 318th Infantry, who would capture Mousson Hill and the surrounding hills on the east bank.[7] The 4th Armored Division would follow through the bridgehead and turn toward Nancy.

Eddy's plan also called for a division of labor between the division- and corps-level engineers. The 305th would cross the troops in boats and build footbridges for later crossings. The 167th Engineer Combat Battalion (part of the 1117th Engineer Group, now attached to the 80th) would bridge the canal and river with an infantry support bridge that would have sufficient capacity for half-tracks and heavy trucks. The 167th would also construct a pneumatic float bridge over the soft banks of the canal at the island as well as a heavy pontoon bridge. The latter was to be constructed later in the day, when the area would, it was hoped, be out of range of enemy artillery.[8]

An 80th Division after-action report clarified the roles of the various engineering elements. It noted, "The 305th Engr Cmbt Bn was responsible for crossing division foot elements, the 1117th Engr Group for the vehicular traffic. Co B, 305th, was to expedite construction of a foot bridge over the canal, guide the assault waves of the 2nd Battalion, 317th Infantry, across the ford north of the island, then follow-up by constructing a foot bridge over the Moselle."[9]

The plan for the crossing relied on surprise, so, for reasons of security, units from the 80th were given little advance notice of the operation. As one analyst explained: "Now a plan was adopted to confuse the enemy. The areas where the units were to assemble and jump-off for the attack were closed to all traffic. . . . No

---

5 Moselle Crossing Infantry, Interview with Lt. Col. Sterling Burnett, 1st Battalion, 317th Infantry Regiment.

6 Moselle Crossing, 305th Engineer Combat Battalion, Interview with Maj. Charles Croker.

7 80th Infantry Division, "Preparing for and Crossing of Moselle R., September 1-15, 1944," 6.

8 "Dieulouard Bridge Crossing," 1.

9 Ibid.; After-Action Report, 80th Division, September 1944, 1.

vehicles were allowed to be seen entering or leaving the area. All patrol activity was stopped in this area and a scene of inactivity greeted the enemy observer"[10]

Frank Lembo was able to get a few lines off to Betty on September 10, and by this time the waiting game was getting on the men's nerves. He wrote: "I haven't been doing very well in the past week. Things are more or less at a standstill. One of these days we'll be rolling again. We were out working this morning clearing a road the Germans had blocked, and everything came out all right. Their usual way of stopping us is to drop trees on the road and then sprinkle them with mines and booby-traps. It was fun watching our Air Force work on the Germans. Seems like things are coming to a climax over here and maybe this war will be over in the next four months. If it ends that soon I'll be satisfied."

The filth of the battlefield was always bothersome to Frank. As if, at the moment, this was at the top of his priorities, he told Betty, "There is a possibility of us coming back to get a shower today, it being the first in a month. It sort of makes me happy. I could stand some clean clothes."[11]

Late on September 11, the night before the next full-scale assault, B Company, with a platoon from C Company attached, motored with equipment seven miles to Blenod-lès-Pont-à-Mousson, closer to the Dieulouard crossing site. The company then covered the rest of the distance to the river on foot. The two assault battalions of the 317th also moved from Fey-en-Haye toward the banks of the canal at Dieulouard. In an attempt to achieve tactical surprise, soldiers of the 317th prepared in the woods for the assault under cover of darkness. Although most of the Germans were slow to recognize the emerging threat at Dieulouard, it didn't take long before they responded to the American incursion with force.

Starting before the break of dawn on September 12, American artillery fired a 15-minute concentrated barrage, mainly focused on the road south of Loisy, and at first light, aircraft zoomed in to bomb Mousson Hill.[12]

---

10 "Moselle Crossing, 317th Infantry Regiment Cont. [Continued]—Assault Boat Crossing."

11 Showers were a big production and most welcome among the troops. An officer in the 80th described the procedure: "The quartermaster bath and laundry units . . . would set up operations somewhere in our area. A few men at a time would be trucked to the bath and laundry point. There each soldier would turn in the clothing he was wearing, keeping only his weapons, helmet, boots, and personal belongings. After a hot shower, he would be issued clean clothing. His dirty uniform would be laundered and reissued to someone else. Often the fit of the 'new' uniforms was somewhat bizarre . . . but we made the best of such things by swapping clothing with one another. It was such a pleasure to get a hot shower and have clean clothing that no one complained." Quoted in Craig, *The 80th Division*, 46.

12 "Dieulouard Bridge Crossing," 2.

B Company engineers prepared to cross the first assault wave of the 2nd Battalion of the 317th Infantry Regiment over the canal and river very early that morning. Under cover of darkness, men from B Company went out ahead of the infantry in drizzling rain, hand-carrying their bridging equipment from the road to the bank of the canal. During the next four hours the engineers built a footbridge over the canal at a ford north of the island.[13] The men used four barges found along the bank to provide a firm base for the bridge. B Company engineers then hauled the assault boats to be used in the river crossing and 280 feet of footbridge from the road to the crossing site. The 2nd Battalion of the 317th and follow-on waves from the 317th's 1st and 3rd battalions and from the 318th were to cross over the footbridge during the next several hours.

Men from the 317th's 2nd Battalion jumped off north of the island at 3:15 a.m. and started over the engineers' footbridge half an hour later. The men pushed over the footbridge and covered the short distance to the riverbank.[14]

The sound of shells piercing the air and hitting the ground and river was deafening. German mortars hit the 2nd Battalion as B Company engineers were guiding it across the canal, and then artillery came in as the infantry crossed the open plain between the canal and river. The troops were forced to hit the ground in the face of the enemy shelling. A memoir reported, "Standing up, even tens of yards from the blast, was almost always fatal or nearly so. Several of my men were hit. It was almost daylight now, and we still hadn't crossed."[15]

When the 2nd Battalion of the 317th reached the river, the orderly execution of the crossing was further disrupted by chaos at the riverbank. Infantrymen arriving at the river failed to wait for the rest of their platoons to assemble, instead rushing directly onto the waiting assault boats.[16] B Company guided the men into the 17 rubber and plywood assault boats they'd moved across the canal to the river. Three engineers sat in the stern of each boat, guiding it across the river, while 12 infantrymen paddled. The river was swollen with rain, and the men struggled to keep the boats on course. The Americans fired 30 white phosphorus rounds at the town of Bezaumont on the east bank so that the blaze could be used as a marker to

13 Ibid., 1.

14 Moselle Operation–2nd Battalion, 317th Infantry Cont.; Interview with Captain Mullen.

15 Adkins and Adkins, *You Can't Get Closer than This*, 36.

16 Moselle Operation–2nd Battalion, 317th Infantry Cont.; Interview with Captain Mullen.

guide the boats through the darkness.[17] Fifty American machine guns placed on the forward slope of the Bois de Cuite on the edge of the woods, manned by engineers from the 167th and 248th, put a curtain of fire over the heads of the assault waves.[18]

An officer from the 317th recalled: "Enemy mortar fire had picked up the forward slope of the hill across the river and Company F lost men as a result of mortar fire during their crossing of the canal. The river was now being shelled by mortar and scattered artillery fire, and the first boat to hit the water had been met with machine gun fire. . . . There were about eight machine guns firing on us."[19] Another 2nd Battalion soldier reported "the air was filled with zipping bullets and screaming shells, some of which struck boats loaded with soldiers. When we discovered that the current was stronger than any of us expected, we all grabbed a paddle and pushed hard for the eastern bank."[20]

A contemporary account reported the enemy opened up with machine pistols when the infantrymen and B Company engineers reached the east bank in their assault boats. Artillery shells blasted the bank, but the German infantry was too thin to force the 317th back across the river.[21]

Two U.S. infantrymen triggered antipersonnel mines when they stepped onto the shore. Engineer demolition squads found 20 mines along the riverbank and 60 more later.[22] An officer of the 317th's 2nd Battalion recalled, "We knew the Germans had placed antipersonnel mines all over the place, and we could only hope the engineers had cleared all of them. A few days later, we learned the 305th Engineer Combat Battalion had removed 44 booby traps. The mines were blown in place by exploding the charges on top. God, I love those guys!"[23]

At the crossing site for the 1st Battalion of the 317th, B Company, aided by one platoon from C Company, constructed a 250-foot-long footbridge, taking only 45 minutes to complete the work. The bridge was hit by German machine gun fire as soon as the engineers began to push the 1st Battalion across. Sixty men from the 1st

---

17 "Dieulouard Bridge Crossing," 2.

18 Moselle Crossing, 1117th Engineer Group, Interview with Colonel Lovett, Commanding Officer, 1117th Engineer Group, 1.

19 Moselle Operation–2nd Battalion, 317th Infantry Cont.; Interview with Captain Mullen.

20 Adkins and Adkins, *You Can't Get Closer than This*, 36.

21 Moselle Crossing, 1117th Engineer Group, Interview with Colonel Lovett, Commanding Officer, 1117th Engineer Group.

22 Ibid.

23 Adkins and Adkins, *You Can't Get Closer than This*, 35.

Battalion were able to cross before the bridge collapsed, although others got across in seven assault boats manned by engineers from the 305th. B Company repaired the damaged footbridge under fire, and the remainder of the 1st Battalion subsequently used it to cross the river.[24]

The 305th's A Company guided the 3rd Battalion of the 317th over the canal and both arms of the river in the vicinity of the island.

The XII Corps' 1117th Engineer Group quickly began bridging operations to get vehicular traffic across the river and through the bridgehead while under artillery fire. Despite the conditions, the brass expressed frustration over perceived delays in constructing the heavy bridges, and Major General McBride ordered the engineers to bridge the canal and both arms of the river with heavy pontoon bridges immediately. The 1117th Engineer Group completed work on the canal bridge by 1:00 p.m. on September 12. It was difficult work, and the dyke and steep banks had to be bulldozed and filled before construction could proceed. Engineers from the 1117th then started work on the heavy pontoon bridges over the near and far arms of the Moselle. The bridging materials had been prefabricated in the bivouac area and trucked to the crossing site at Dieulouard. The bridges were continually targeted by enemy artillery while the work progressed.

Construction of the second heavy pontoon bridge couldn't begin until the canal bridge was ready, since bridging equipment had to be brought in. The 1117th completed the pontoon bridge over the near arm at 6:00 p.m. and the far arm at 8:00 p.m. on September 12, and tanks began crossing immediately.[25] Another heavy bridge was constructed farther downstream that night. Although it had been hoped the work on this bridge would escape the notice of the Germans, it was under continuous attack all night long. The men counted 25 artillery shells near the bridge the next morning.

The rest of the 80th's vehicles and equipment—field artillery, armor, and tank destroyers—started pouring through the bridgehead as soon as the heavy bridges were finished. The next day the infantry would have some armor support—and they would need it.[26]

Eventually, the engineering units put in five pontoon bridges, although some of these were later dismantled to provide materials for the final bridge over the far

---

24 Moselle Crossing Infantry, Interview with Lt. Col. Sterling S. Burnett, Commanding Officer, 1st Battalion, 317th Infantry.

25 "Moselle Crossing: Engineers."

26 "Dieulouard Bridge Crossing," 3.

arm of the Moselle. At the canal site, the engineers put in fill and constructed a wooden ramp. As one history of the 80th described it: "While the 317th was battering toward high ground beyond, the 305th Combat Engineers and the 1117th Engr. Gp. spanned the Moselle with ponton bridges, disregarding continuous hostile fire"[27]

Frank wrote to Betty on September 12 an account of what he had experienced crossing the Moselle. He only rarely let down his guard enough to write about his combat experiences, but on this occasion he told her: "Things sure did pop for us two nights ago. We had an operation to perform and we worked from ten at night to ten the following morning. We were in a valley and on one side of the water were the Germans and on the opposite hill on our side was all you could wish for. At a precise time in the dead of night everything we had opened up and the sight was something I'd never want to miss. For almost 1000-yard-wide line machine guns laid down fire, which turned everything to a red glare as far as you could see,[28] artillery did its share and it just can't be described. . . . Seems funny but then the infantry laid in the valley and the Engineers walked across the open field carrying equipment with bullets flying by hour after hour. Eddy had one plunk a rip in his field jacket. Scotty and I took a rest for a few minutes and sat under an iron tower, and one plunked off the tower above our heads. To tell the truth you get so tired and mad that you don't have time to get afraid, you just don't give a damn. Morning came the assault was over—a complete success, and we headed for a little rest. In back of us now is some heavy artillery and every time it lets go you seem to jump-off the ground from the jolt."

---

27 "Forward Eightieth," *Stars and Stripes* (Paris, 1945), www.lonesentry.com/gi_stories_booklets/80thinfantry/ (accessed February 8, 2017).

28 This was presumably a reference to the line of machine guns manned by engineers on the Bois de Cuite, mentioned earlier.

CHAPTER 7

THE FIGHT FOR THE HILLS: SEPT. 13-30, 1944

THE 80th Division was finally across the Moselle, but its ability to hold its position remained uncertain. By September 12, the 80th's three infantry regiments were advancing toward their objectives on the far side of the river, but over the next three days the Germans staged ferocious counterattacks determined to destroy the bridgehead and push the Americans back across the river. Engineers supported the infantry, consolidated and expanded the Dieulouard bridgehead, assisted with fortifications, and cleared roads of rubble and mines as the 80th fought its way forward.

The 317th Infantry's battalions pushed out from the Moselle toward their objectives on September 12, reaching them within hours of coming onto the bank. As night fell, soldiers dug in to their positions to await the inevitable counterattack.

Early on September 13, the enemy launched its first major counterattack against the advancing American troops and bridgehead.[1] Two battalions of the 29th Panzergrenadier Regiment attacked the American line at 4:00 a.m. in a coordinated infantry and armored attack.[2] The Germans concentrated heavy artillery, mortar, and small arms fire on the 317th's positions, targeting all roads leading in and out of Dieulouard, as well as the men who were by now driving east to the hills.

---

1 "Dieulouard River Crossing," 6.

2 Summary of Interviews, Moselle Operation, Lt. Col. L. F. Fisher, Maj. J. D. Hayes, Capt. S. A. Ford, Capt. J. E. Mullen, 317th Infantry Regiment.

The scene at the bridgehead was deadly and chaotic. The enemy forced the advancing infantrymen back to the riverbank, and some even ran back across the bridge toward Dieulouard. It was a rout and a slaughter. German artillery and mortar fire prevented the evacuation of the dead and wounded to the hospitals in the rear. Bodies littered the ground. The Germans kept the momentum following their counterattack and came close to completely overrunning the bridgehead, before American P-47 fighter-bombers, dispatched by the 19th Tactical Air Command, intervened.

Once again, the 317th's 2nd Battalion played a central role in the action and took heavy losses. It seized its objective, Ste. Genevieve Ridge, the high ground opposite Dieulouard, on its first thrust out from the river, but the Germans forced a retreat after little more than an hour. The Americans and Germans struggled for control of Ste. Genevieve throughout the day on September 13. The 2nd battalion was able to restore its position in the town with the help of Shermans from the 80th Division's attached 702nd Tank Battalion, but it lost it again shortly afterward. The 80th Division again forced a reversal after the first tanks from 4th Armored Division crossed over the Moselle on a pontoon bridge with the 318th Infantry, which had just arrived from Toul.[3] By noon on September 13, the 2nd Battalion had retaken Ste. Genevieve. The Germans withdrew from the area at the sight of the tanks, and the 4th Armored ran them back to Loisy.

Other units from the 317th Infantry Regiment also fought hard to gain and regain ground after the enemy counterattacked. The 1st Battalion seized its objective in Bezaumont, directly across from Dieulouard, and advanced east toward Landremont, a few miles distant. The 1st Battalion was able to hold Landremont despite two strong German counterattacks. Meanwhile, the 317th's 3rd Battalion seized its objective near Loisy, holding off a crippling counterattack. Later in the day the 318th Infantry arrived in the 317th's sector and installed roadblocks to tighten the perimeter defenses.

The 317th actively patrolled the enemy positions during this period of intense combat. The 305th Engineers' B Company supported the actions of the infantry, clearing mines, abatis, and rubble from the roads. Late in the day on September 13, B Company moved from Blenod-lès-Pont-à-Mousson on the west side of the Moselle to a position near Jezainville on the east side. For the moment, the company was chiefly concerned with setting up a defensive position along the river to protect their foot and pontoon bridges.

---

3 Cole, *Lorraine Campaign*, 85.

The next day, September 14, got off to the same start as the day before, with savage counterattacks on the bridgehead and advanced positions. During a series of early morning counterattacks, the Germans were able to retake Ste. Genevieve, Atton, and Mousson Hill with the aid of approximately 30 tanks and self-propelled guns (SPGs). The 2nd Battalion of the 317th, now operating with little more than half its normal strength due to casualties, lost and regained Ste. Genevieve yet again.

The engineers protecting the bridges were forced back by enemy artillery fire. In addition to their struggle to establish and expand the bridgehead, engineers stepped in as infantry in the fighting at Dieulouard, Ste. Genevieve, and Loisy. Later in the day, the 305th's 3rd Platoon moved forward and removed mines from the roads near Loisy, and the 2nd Platoon removed mines, booby traps, and wrecked vehicles from nearby roads. The 305th experienced light casualties from exploding booby traps.

German armor cut through the positions held by the 317th and 318th Regiments as the second day of fighting progressed, leaving some units, including squads from B Company, isolated and unable to communicate. An officer from the 317th reported that, despite perimeter defenses set up by engineers at the bridgehead,

> The Germans were able to run tanks down the roads and valleys between units and cut them off on the surrounding hills. Engineers around the river were defending their bridges, with the enemy to their front between them and the remainder of their infantry regiments. From this the idea fixed itself in the mind of the defending engineers that the infantry had been wiped out.[4]

An account from the commander of the 317th's 2nd Battalion captured the emotions of the men who were separated from their units and without communication:

> The engineers were deployed there along the river, and told us that everything had been wiped out across the river, and that they were prepared to defend to the last man. . . . Germans were in Bezaumont, Loisy and everywhere. Enemy tanks had run into the CP of the 2dBn, and the 318th infantry was wiped out. We found a platoon of Tank Destroyers and went into Bezaumont. No one there knew the exact location of the 2dBn. Germans

4 Summary of Operations, Moselle Crossing, 80th Infantry Division, Interview with Lt. Col. L. F. Fisher.

who were placing direct fire on the town fired upon us, so we started another way and ran into our own artillery fire. A shot-up tank almost ran into us as we went up the draw. We pulled up a little onto the hillside and saw it pass, the dead crew hanging out of the turret. It exploded far below. In Bezaumont we found what was reported to be all that was left of a tank platoon, one American tank. Nevertheless, we tried to find the 2dBn, and in so doing contacted elements of the 1stBn.[5]

When the German counteroffensive finally stalled on September 15, the third day of intense fighting, the 2nd Battalion of the 317th had been able to end the day occupying Ste. Genevieve with a sizable force, including reinforcements from the 318th. The Americans also found themselves in possession of the surrounding objectives, but they had taken a beating and their ranks were depleted.

On September 16, B Company took on the responsibility of maintaining the security of the bridges over the Moselle. The 2nd Platoon dug in on the east side of the river and set up defensive positions while the 3rd Platoon set up positions on the west side. The enemy shelled both positions around the clock. The engineers eventually were ordered to withdraw and traveled 15 miles back to their bivouac area in Jezainville.

As the 317th and 318th were mired in fighting around Dieulouard and in the hills across the river, the 319th Infantry seized territory along the Moselle in the vicinity of Toul and went on to do a reconnaissance in force toward Foret de Haye, with the mission of attacking toward Nancy. A task force, named for its commander, Brig. Gen. E. B. Sebree of the 35th Infantry Division, was formed with the 134th Infantry Regiment and the 319th Infantry. On September 15, Task Force Sebree entered Nancy and took it easily, since the Germans had abandoned the town the previous day.[6] C Company of the 305th supported the 319th, removing 40 trees and 150 mines from the infantry's path. Soon after Nancy was in hand, the 319th and elements of the 305th left the city and rejoined the rest of the 80th Division. The capture of Nancy marked the start of what the army called the Rhineland Campaign, which would last until March 21, 1945, when the Allied armies finally crossed the Rhine River into Germany.

Fighting off strong enemy opposition at the Moselle crossing sites and the hills beyond continued unabated throughout September, but Patton remained confident the Third Army could regain its momentum and drive through the

---

5 Moselle Operation, 317th Infantry, September 12-15, interview with Maj. J. D. Hayes.

6 "Reports After-Action Against Enemy," 319th Infantry Regiment, September 1944, 1-2.

German defenses to the Rhine. But it was soon clear to everyone that the Third Army would be stuck in extended combat in Lorraine for the foreseeable future. The 80th Division would continue to battle over the hills east of the Moselle throughout September and into October. The memoir of a soldier in the 318th noted, "The next several days would see the worst artillery barrage yet, some of the most bitter fighting in the entire European Theater of Operations. ... The Infantry fought fiercely, hill by hill, tree by tree, clawing their way back to regain land only to lose it again, and then begin the exhausting struggle all over again."[7]

The bad weather experienced by the GIs during the first weeks of the Moselle operation stayed with them after they reached the east bank. Frank got a chance to write a letter on September 18 from his bivouac in Jezainville:

> Things have been rather rugged over the past week, enemy resistance and the weather have made life pretty miserable. We were ready to go to sleep last night and the creek washed down on us. We had put our tent down there because of the shelling, but I wish I had put it up on higher ground now. Artillery moved in right in back of our truck, so every half hour or so you were jarred off your feet. I'm getting a little sick of all this noise. (There it goes again.)

The towns and villages surrounding the Moselle had been reduced to rubble after weeks of artillery fire by both sides; there were some towns in which no buildings still stood. One report noted the soldiers moved from "one heap of rubble to another."

The B Company motor convoy was on the move throughout September, although it never went very far from the bridgehead. On September 19, the trucks left their bivouac in Jezainville and went another 10 miles to Atton, where the men stacked timber and removed antitank and antipersonnel mines.

The engineers were under constant fire as they supported all three infantry regiments of the 80th Division. One of the 305th's companies had been relieved of engineering work and become fully committed as infantry despite its light weapons load. Meanwhile, other engineers patrolled roads, installed roadblocks, hauled rock and cinders, and built bypasses. Engineers also buried dead cattle and removed obstacles to keep the supply lines open.

All of the engineers worked on demolitions. The Germans had heavily mined the riverbanks and roads, and engineers had to go out to clear them every day. B

---

7 Elvin, *Box from Braunau*, 15.

Company's diary focused increasingly on the threat of mines and booby traps as the month of September progressed. On one mission, men from the company found 44 booby traps and two Teller antitank mines, each of which could blast the tracks off a tank.[8] On another mission, while the engineers were removing mines and booby traps near Blenod-lès-Pont-à-Mousson, one of the booby traps exploded, causing casualties among the engineers. Friendly mines also posed a threat. The 305th had to develop a policy for minefields placed by Americans because some units neglected to report them.[9]

One of the engineers' responsibilities was to quickly lay their own minefields, which involved laying down the mines, pulling the pin to activate them, and "running like hell." Engineers often laid hasty minefields as they retreated to slow down or stop enemy tanks "or whatever is chasing you." The other type of minefield, called deliberate, was usually laid out in a grid, and the mines were camouflaged with dirt and grass. When deactivating the minefield, each mine had to be dug up using a bayonet and the pin slid back in, straining the demolition man's nerves.

Bulldozers were a critical piece of equipment in the engineers' arsenal, but tank dozers, utilizing Sherman tanks, were exceptionally useful in clearing roads of almost everything, including dangerous mines. A heavy-duty bulldozer blade was attached to the front of a Sherman tank, which helped clear obstacles and minefields and also gave them a way to repair roads while under fire. Eisenhower lauded this versatile piece of equipment when he explained, "Some imaginative and sensible man . . . solved the problem by merely converting a number of Sherman tanks into bulldozers. . . . From that time on our engineering detachments on the front lines began to enjoy a degree of safety that actually led them to seek this kind of adventurous work." Eisenhower said the person who came up with the idea should have "by acclamation, received all the medals we could have pinned on him."[10]

Meantime, the grueling combat and frustratingly slow progress took a toll on the soldiers' morale. On September 20, Frank wrote Betty, "I'm not much in the mood for writing, but I haven't dropped you a line in quite awhile, and heaven only knows when I'll be able to write again. There hasn't been anything happening to

8 Craig, *The 80th Infantry Division*, 28.

9 "Summary of Daily Operations, September 1944," 305th Engineer Combat Battalion.

10 Eisenhower, *Crusade in Europe*, 202.

cheer me up so I guess it's just another dull letter. Weather has been poor as hell and things not as hot, war is sure hell in all ways." He added, "Don't worry about the sweater being small. I've lost about 25 pounds so it should fit snug as a bug. It sure will come in handy and thanks a lot." Frank was slim to start with, and 25 pounds was a considerable weight loss in only two and a half months in Europe.

He was always concerned that Betty didn't know where he was or what he was doing or, seemingly, what was happening in the war. He told her, "One of the wives of the boys in my squad knows who we are fighting with and something about the 80th so she's going to write you a line and give you some dope. Being a Pennsylvania division the papers there carry quite a bit of news, so in three or four weeks you can expect something. My tongue is tied here."

Frank fretted about money and Betty's spending habits. It may have only been September, but he predicted, "Soon you'll be running around doing your Christmas shopping and getting in debt again (as usual.) I won't have no shopping to do this year, but maybe next year I'll be able to enjoy the Christmas spirit for a change." On September 21, the company moved six miles from Etton to Autreville-sur-Moselle.

In a September 22 letter Frank let Betty know in the clearest terms what he thought about loudmouths back home who didn't know anything about the war.

I guess it was quite a jolt to all you people back home at the considerable slowness our armies are now moving. We sort of knew all the time it wasn't going to end so fast as newspapers back home were having it. It sort of hurts when you're in the midst of carnage, and you see some American boys wounded and killed and then pick up something and read where they are planning for the celebration and other things back home. What the hell do the people back home have to celebrate? They haven't lived like dogs, they haven't been shelled, they haven't had the stink of dead around, nor have they lived in hell. I guess the day it's over instead of turning toward God and saying a prayer, they'll head for the nearest bar. I'm sorry for the blow off but it stores up in you and you have to let go. It's the same story for everyone here, every time mail and newspapers come." Frank added, "I haven't been feeling so good lately. I don't know what it was, but I just seemed to be run down. I couldn't eat and everything else seemed to be wrong.

B Company's convoy moved to Millery on September 23. The next day Frank mentioned to Betty that he was moving alongside infantry. In support of the 318th, B Company engineers marked roads, constructed bypasses, and put in culverts, specifically in the vicinity of Morey. A dozer was used to clear the mud from the roads. On September 25 the company moved its bivouac from Millery to Villers-les-Prud'hommes and sent out patrols for reconnaissance. Two days later, B

Company moved with the rest of the 80th to Dieulouard and Pont-à-Mousson, where they had begun the month. They stayed in Pont-à-Mousson through the end of September. The company put in defensive positions near the town under fire on September 27 while operating in support of the 319th Infantry Regiment.

The soldiers had no way to know this, but the period known as the "October pause" or "October lull" had begun. At least for the time being, priority was once again given to British Field Marshal Bernard L. Montgomery's army group in the north, not just in the wake of its failed Operation Market Garden, but to force open the port of Antwerp, which was essential to the continuation of Allied operations in France.[11] In a September 22 meeting with his top commanders, Eisenhower said there would be no major advances by the American army until Antwerp was under control. Patton's increasingly long supply lines from the Normandy beachhead could no longer meet operational needs. Before the final advance into Germany, access to an established port closer to the front was a necessity.

The Third Army's approach to the Siegfried Line slowed during this period but didn't stop altogether. The 80th Division's infantry went out on a limited number of local missions, in part to secure jumping-off points for future operations. Patton won this concession from Bradley when the October lull was put in place. Bradley outlined in a letter to Eisenhower that he had ordered Patton to assume a defensive stance. "At the same time, however, I have authorized George to make some minor adjustments in his present lines. There are about three localities just in front of his present position which he assures me he can take from time to time as ammunition becomes available on his present allotment, and which will save many casualties in the long run."[12]

But Bradley's leniency was not enough to permit the major operations that Patton wanted to pursue. Once again, logistical shortfalls caused by the diversion of supplies to Montgomery's 21st Army Group had brought the Third Army "to an abrupt halt."[13] Always irreverent, Patton observed, "Going on the defense and

---

11 Bradley, *A General's Life*, 336. Like the previous decision concerning Falaise, Bradley described this slowdown as "yet another poor decision. . . . Stopping Patton, a proven ground gainer, to favor Monty, who wasn't, made no sense at all."

12 Cole, *Lorraine Campaign*, 259.

13 Gabel, *Lorraine Campaign*, 21.

British Field Marshal Bernard L. Montgomery and American Lt. Gen. George S. Patton.

Army Signal Corps

having our limited supplies cut still more is very discouraging. Bradley and I are depressed. We would like to go to China and serve under Admiral Nimitz."[14]

Patton gave his generals a series of priorities to secure "a suitable line of departure so that we can move rapidly when the Supreme Commander directs us to resume the offensive." One of these priorities was to seize the high ground close to the Seille River. This job would fall to the 80th Infantry Division.[15]

While they were able to undertake some operations during this period, including an approach to the Seille and initial probing attacks, one chronicler concluded, "Third Army was relatively dormant from 25 September to 8 November." But the army used the time effectively, using strict rationing to accumulate stocks of fuel and ammunition and rotating units out of the front line to allow them to rest, maintain equipment, and absorb replacements. When full-scale

14 Blumenson, *The Patton Papers*, 553.

15 Cole, *Lorraine Campaign*, 259–60.

operations resumed, the Third Army's troops were relatively rested, and substantial stockpiles of supplies had been accumulated.[16]

The October lull had its bright sides for many weary B Company GIs. Living conditions improved markedly once the company reached Pont-à-Mousson. It wasn't quite like home, but it wasn't bad, as Frank's squad finally got out of the rain. Frank reported to Betty that the squad had been "taking it easy last night, and I must say our living quarters are rather enjoyable. We are in a large public building and we have beds and mattresses." Many other men in the 80th were not so fortunate in finding indoor quarters.

The persistent rains made many of the roads impassable. Some were covered with mud, and others had been flooded out. The 305th Combat Engineers built new roads and constructed plank roads to maintain the flow of traffic along the main supply routes (MSRs). At the bridgehead, men, vehicles, and equipment were mired in the muddy banks of the canal and river and were stuck in traffic jams on narrow roadways. Large numbers of Germans were now surrendering, adding to the problem of moving men and equipment over the limited road network.

On September 30, B Company's engineers reinforced the defensive position by constructing an abatis 400 yards long, laying a hasty minefield with 62 antitank mines, and adding 17 antipersonnel mines and barbed wire. All the while the men were under automatic weapons fire. The men built dugouts and observation posts (OPs) and, as usual, took on the burden of burying dead cattle.

Frank closed his correspondence for the month with a September 30 letter to Betty. He happily reported, "News is very scarce today. We still are living in buildings and there hasn't been too much woe. It seems to come in spurts." Given the importance of mail to Frank, it's laudable that he added, "Since the question of either mail or supplies has come up, we are doing without mail, which we gladly agree with. All our mail is back at some coast port, and it really must be stacked up."

Throughout the summer and fall, many people, including some servicemen, thought the war might be over by Christmas. Frank never thought this was likely. He attached to his letter a clipping from a GI newspaper that portrayed a cynical attitude toward the home front, a view that Frank seemed to share. The cartoon of two people clicking their heels with glee and trumpets blaring was accompanied by the following text:

16 Gabel, *Lorraine Campaign*, 22.

Some of the nation's department stores have already sent directives to their personnel on how to behave on V-Day. Most call for closing the store, removing merchandise from show windows, boarding up the windows. Employees of Milwaukee's famed Boston Store got the curtest note. 'Finish waiting on your customer: then get out and celebrate.' Those people back home are with us all the way, aren't they? Hope we haven't delayed their celebrations too long.

Establishing and holding the Moselle bridgehead during September 1944 was a critical contribution to the success of the Allies' ground war in Europe, but it cost the 80th Division about 3,000 casualties, including more than 1,200 killed or severely wounded and another 500 missing or captured. As would be true during most of the war, the 317th and 318th Infantry Regiments suffered the overwhelming majority of serious casualties. In September, the 305th Engineers suffered their bloodiest month of the war, with 22 killed or seriously wounded.[17]

17 Robert Murrell, "80th Losses in Action, September 1944." http://www.80thdivision.com. AfterActionReports /80th_LossesInAction_Murrell.pdf (accessed March 14, 2017).

CHAPTER 8

THE SILVER STAR AT THE SEILLE: OCT. 1-NOV. 9, 1944

AS October began, the 80th Infantry Division continued to consolidate its hard-won positions east of the Moselle, from Pont-à-Mousson in the north to Monteney in the south. At great cost a firm bridgehead over the Moselle had been established. Early October saw B Company still at Pont-à-Mousson, providing security at the bridgehead and patrolling, keeping roads open, clearing and laying mines, and digging emplacements.

The 80th Division and XII Corps were ready to move on to the Seille River, a tributary of the Moselle and the next natural barrier between the Third Army and the Rhine. It also meant another difficult assault crossing for the engineers. The Germans had taken advantage of the heights since the Americans first approached the Moselle in early September, and they still held the high ground between the Moselle and the nearby Seille.

Patton was itching to move, but the Third Army had been fighting fuel shortages since before the Moselle crossing, and its ranks had been depleted in the few months since Normandy. While XII Corps had been bloodied at the Moselle near Nancy, its neighboring XX Corps had suffered heavy losses trying to hammer in the German-held fortress network around Metz. For now, while the army awaited resupply and replacements, only occasional probing attacks were permitted.

On October 2, the 317th Infantry attacked the town of Sivry, about 12 miles southeast of the B Company bivouac at Pont-a-Mousson. The Germans placed a heavy concentration of artillery fire on the town and launched a counterattack with a battalion of infantry, cutting through the 317th and disrupting communications.

American units were battered by heavy artillery as well as machine guns and small arms.

But only a few hours after the 317th achieved a toehold in Sivry, 80th Division commander Horace McBride ordered the soldiers to evacuate, which cost them additional casualties. The Germans immediately reoccupied Sivry. The 2nd Battalion of the 317th once again took heavy losses in the engagement—half of its attacking force was lost. One of its companies returned with only 40 of its 193 men. The ill-advised attack attack on Sivry and hasty evacuation led Patton to rebuke McBride for misusing resources.[1]

After the attack on Sivry, the battered 2nd Battalion, which earlier had led the two assault crossings of the Moselle and secured the bridgehead, would be manned chiefly by replacements. A history of the 317th Infantry commented on the new recruits: "Some were in their mid-forties and others scavenged from rear area units. Some were the 'sad sacks' of their units or orderlies who lacked basic infantry skills."[2]

The acute losses and replacement of these losses with a haphazard group of poorly trained recruits put an end to the 317th's cohesion, which had been developed in training and fortified in the field. During their pause, the 317th's battalions worked hard to instill in the new men basic infantry and survival skills as well as a sense of unit cohesion. One officer said, "By this time, the 317th was really a regiment of replacements. . . . What we lacked was the fine sense of camaraderie which the regiment had built at Camp Forrest and during the various maneuvers. We tried to design the training to recapture some of that camaraderie and also to teach the new recruits how to survive in combat."[3]

Interviews with several 80th Division veterans highlight the various ways replacements could reach the rifle companies. At times soldiers assigned to noncombat positions were eager to join the fight. Staff Sergeant Bob Burrows had been assigned to XII Corps headquarters as a driver for civil affairs, coming ashore in Normandy a few days after D Day. Several of his requests for reassignment were turned down, but after the Ardennes offensive, he told his commander, "I know

---

1 Cole, *Lorraine Campaign*, 284-85.

2 Dean J. Dominique, "The Attack Will Go On: The 317th Infantry Regiment in World War II," Thesis submitted to the Graduate Faculty at Louisiana State University (2003), 47.

3 Quoted in Dominique, "The Attack Will Go On," 47.

you can't turn me down now." General Eddy approved his request and he joined the 2nd Battalion of the 317th on Christmas morning.[4]

Corporal Charles Parker was originally assigned to an antiaircraft battery, a type of unit that exceeded requirements and was frequently dismantled for reassignment. Much of his unit was reassigned to the infantry in April 1944, but he was retained for a few months as part of the training cadre. He was eventually reassigned in October. His training unit included "guys from Quartermaster, guys who had been in the Aleutian Islands for two years, everyone you could think of." He ultimately joined the 2nd Battalion of the 319th Infantry in January 1945, a few days after Company G had taken more than 40 casualties. "My group was a full 6x6; there may have been other trucks. They told most of the guys to go upstairs and rest, but a platoon commander grabbed a few of us and within a few minutes after I arrived with the company, I'm out on guard duty."[5]

At other times soldiers were drafted and assigned to fill understrength units. PFCs Burt Marsh and Charles Faulconer both joined the 319th Infantry in January 1945 after being drafted and going through an accelerated 16 weeks of basic training.[6]

Throughout the so-called October lull the 80th Division waited for resupply, contenting itself with occasional probing attacks. The lull, however, was sometimes broken by artillery exchanges and periods of combat that led to significant casualties for the infantry and engineers. The 305th Combat Engineer Battalion suffered 24 killed or severely wounded during these October engagements.

Engineering work continued through the early days of the slowdown. For example, B Company's engineers made a reconnaissance of the roads leading to the 318th's command post on October 5. The next day, the company diary reported that squads from the 2nd Platoon removed three wrecked German tanks from a road, dispatched patrols, and marked the forward edge of a minefield in the vicinity of the defensive position. Lieutenant Henke's 1st Platoon dug in an advance command post with the aid of a dozer.

The pause in combat operations gave Frank an opportunity to write home frequently, though he rarely wrote about combat and the ways it affected him. He was well aware of the censors (he would censor letters himself one day), so much of

---

4 Interview with Rishi Sharma, September 14, 2017.

5 Interview, September 16, 2017.

6 Interview, September 14 (Marsh) and 16 (Faulconer), 2017.

what he was experiencing was off-limits in letters. Frank wrote to Betty nearly every day during the lull—writing home was a welcome relief from the tedium—but there was less and less real news to report. His letters focused on bright spots in his daily life, like good food, packages from home, being with his buddies, and time to dream.

Sleeping in the field was cold and wet, so indoor accommodations and other comforts at Pont-à-Mousson were a favorite topic of correspondence. Frank wrote his first October letter to Betty from comparatively comfortable quarters on October 2, 1944: "We are still living in buildings and today they fixed the generators, so we have electric lights. It is strange seeing them because it's the first time in three months that such a thing has happened." The men spent two days clearing out a room so they could move the kitchen in from a barn. Rations had also improved considerably. He wrote, "A few of the boys are out butchering a heifer so we'll be eating steak and other meat tomorrow. Chickens seemed to have disappeared from here and the same of hogs."

On the downside, Frank noted the miserable weather: "I guess we'd have been a lot further if weather had been with us since D day." A few days later he added, "The weather hasn't been too good lately. I don't mind the cold but it's wet—brrrr."

He spent a moment looking back on his experiences in France and thought of the vacations he and Betty would take after the war. He wrote, "In the past I visited Argentan, Orleans, Chambois, Commercy and Bar le Duc. The French towns are so different than ours but I imagine a peacetime visit to France would be so much different."

His October letters were filled with updates on his buddies. He wrote with disappointment that Scotty "left us to have his hernia taken care of so another friend is gone. I doubt if he'll come back to us. I'll have to look him up after the war. He sure was a good friend." Frank had lost friends already, but Scotty had been his closest pal since training and was in a different category altogether. A few days later he reported: "Scotty has been gone for a week now. . . . I miss seeing him around but he's better off back of the front lines." He mentioned other buddies in letters from early October as well. "The craziest things happen over here. The other day I found out that Bill Miller's outfit is attached to the division, and ever since we came to France, I must have passed him many a time. I'm going to try and see him as soon as I can."

Frank also thought about other men he knew from the States who had gone off to war in different theaters, and he wondered whether they were faring well. He mentioned his neighbor and friend, Sup, who had gone into the navy and been out

Third Army Commander Lt. Gen. George S. Patton talks with 80th Division commander Maj. Gen. Horace McBride. *Army Signal Corps*

of touch since Frank had gone overseas. He was thinking also of Betty's older brother: "By the way, if Leslie is still floating around the South Pacific I guess he wants to get home too. Needless to say that is the one thought that remains in our minds. You think of coming home, settling down and enjoying civilian life again."

Home and the end of the war still seemed far off to Frank. In his letters he was always pessimistic about when the war would end (and he turned out to be right). On October 4, he presciently wrote: "I don't look for the end of things here until next springtime. Events of the last month sort of showed a trend that 'Ike' says 'Berlin by Christmas,' but it seems way off." A short time later, he wrote, "The winter chill is setting in and I guess we'll have to be contented with victory next spring that is unless a breakthrough is made somewhere."

On October 5, General McBride finally decided it was time to follow up on Patton's September 25 priorities to seize the high ground west of the Seille and drive the Germans beyond the river. The mission was to be accomplished in two phases. The first objective would be Mount St. Jean, and the second would be Letricourt. McBride issued a field order directing the 80th Division to attack on October 8 to push the enemy back across the Seille.[7]

7 Cole, *Lorraine Campaign*, 285; Craig, *The 80th Infantry Division*, 32.

Frank was incredulous that the army, in its wisdom, had finally gotten around to issuing passes now that the fighting was imminent. He told Betty, "Of all things, a few of the boys received passes the other day and went to visit Commercy. A few in my squad went and there wasn't very much doing. Food is hard to get and liquor is all that you can buy. They can have their passes, I'll wait for my good time when I get home and spend it with you." Frank was nevertheless envious of the lucky few who got some time away from the front lines, confiding to Betty, "I would like to visit some cities of France, but I don't think I'll get a chance until the war is over. Some of the boys went on pass, but I didn't get a chance."

On October 7, B Company left the comforts of Pont-à-Mousson and the west side of the Moselle for good. The motor convoy moved three miles to Ville-au-Val in preparation for the upcoming attacks. The company stayed at Ville-au-Val until October 11.

That night, on the eve of the division's first heavy fighting in weeks, Frank wrote to Betty:

> I don't have much time but I want to get this letter in now because I may be busy for the next few days. We moved out of our rather comfortable buildings and in a few more hours I'll be sleeping in my pup tent again. It was nice while it lasted but then all good things come to an end. I sewed myself a rather warm canvas bedroll with my blankets. I'm awaiting winter. I guess it will be pretty rugged and all I hope is that spring rolls around fast.

On October 8, the Third Army followed through with the "limited, probing" attacks that had been authorized by the high command. The 80th Division, the 35th Infantry Division, and parts of the 6th Armored Division participated in the attack. The 80th Division's objectives were to secure the area around the town of Manoncourt, secure Mounts St. Jean and Toulon, and clear the Bois de Fourasse.[8] Mounts St. Jean and Toulon were the commanding hills between the Moselle and the Seille. It was hard fighting, but with the help of a squadron of P-47 Thunderbolts, Mount St. Jean fell quickly to the 318th Infantry. Units from the 317th, along with the 6th Armored Division, took McBride's second objective, the village of Letricourt. The 318th moved up and took Manoncourt, fighting off fierce opposition; B Company operated in support of the 318th during this engagement. The 319th attacked and seized Mount Toulon.

---

8 318th Infantry, "History October 1944."

The Germans fiercely defended the territory and counterattacked the 80th Division's riflemen with automatic weapons, mortars, and artillery. As the infantry advanced slowly through mud, rain, and enemy opposition, casualties mounted and lack of replacements forced the infantry to consolidate its positions. One officer of the 318th said that October 8 was the 80th Division's bloodiest day of the war; approximately 115 soldiers were killed that day.[9]

There were times when the GIs reflected on the war and their fallen comrades, whose numbers continued to rise. Frank disclosed on October 10, "Things have been pretty rough the past few days and I've lost some very good friends. It hurts deep when your own buddies go. Well it's no sense in keeping thinking about them, may the dead rest in peace and the wounded get well again." He added, "No, I can't say when this will be over with. We fight yard-by-yard now and then fight to hold every yard. Maybe something will break one of these days, but the going is going to be slow."

As it turned out, the October 8 attacks were only a short, brutal interruption in the October lull. Inactivity resumed after these attacks and continued for the rest of the month.[10]

There was always engineering work to do, however. The Germans had laid minefields in their wake as they backed away from the Moselle, and these, along with other booby traps, dotted the countryside between the 80th Division's positions and the Seille. The Germans also planted mines in their defensive positions on the east side of the river. The U.S. engineers would have to clear mines from both sides of the Seille before the start of the impending assault by the infantry and armor.

The company diary notes, for example, in the morning hours of October 9, that a squad from the 1st Platoon, with Lieutenant Henke in charge, moved out by truck to remove mines and booby traps south of Benincourt. On October 11, engineers from B Company removed 12 S-mines and 7 Riegel mines while on a mission south of Les-A-Fers.

B Company left Ville-au-Val on October 11 and moved to Serrieres. Frank wrote a chatty letter to Betty from there on October 13, observing, not for the first time, "Another letter, and with it more wet weather and mud. I've never seen a place like this for damp weather. We are quite used to it, but it still brings on quite a

---

9   Elvin, *Box from Branau*, 77.

10   318th Infantry "History October 1944," 5; Cole, *Lorraine Campaign*, 289-90.

bit of cursing." He added, "I'm glad to hear my sweater is finished and on its way. I'm sure I'm going to get a lot of use out of it. I thought maybe we might get them from the army; new men coming to the front get sweaters instead of blouses. You're supposed to get a lot of things over here, but somehow they never reach us."

He confirmed Betty's guess about his location was on the mark—a sort of relief to him since he was prohibited from sharing this information in a letter home. "In your letter of October 2 you mentioned a couple of cities over here, and you were right in believing what you did, right smack in the center. Gen hit it on the nose too so I was wondering how you get the information. I can't mention a darn thing."

He offered other miscellaneous bits of news and opinion in this letter: "Right now we are listening to Glenn Miller and the sound is pretty good. I get a kick out hearing he's a Major. No army but ours could rank a man as a Major for having an orchestra—some laughs." Regarding his own team, he wrote, "By the way, I never mentioned that I have a new Corporal. He's a swell fellow and we get along fine."

On October 14, the company's motor convoy moved to the heights of Ste. Genevieve, a village overlooking the Seille. The company bivouacked there until October 31, the final day of the Third Army's October lull. By now the town—that is, a church and a few small houses—was in ruins, and other towns had been destroyed during American artillery preparation as well. An after-action report for the 808th Tank Destroyers, attached to XII Corps, lists some of the targets that were taken out: "The direct fire missions: the town [of] Moivron, church steeple at Moreville, pillbox on Mt St Jean, town of Benincourt, water tower at Rennaissance Farm, church steeple at Manoncourt, all fire was accurate and effective."[11]

Intelligence improved during the 80th Division's period of rest. More important, the Intelligence staff learned the Germans were withdrawing units from Lorraine. Their situation was so diminished that even panzer units were partially dependent on horse-drawn transport. Nevertheless, the assault on the Seille was expected to be a fierce fight.

On October 15, Frank wrote, "I'm in a rather good mood for a change and to tell you the truth it's an exception. Today is Sunday and it's sort of been like a Sunday back home. I woke up this morning, took a bath in a bucket, washed clothes and then enjoyed a delicious dinner. We moved into buildings again

---

11 After-Action Report, Headquarters, 808th Tank Destroyer Battalion, 25 September-31 October 1944, www.tankdestroyer.net/images/stories/ArticlePDFs/808th_TD_Sept_25-Oct_31_44_AAR.pdf.

yesterday and I hope we stay awhile. We have one room to sleep in, and a barn we use as a kitchen. It's dry and we make it rather comfortable. It would be nice spending a winter like this."

He added something about his squad's cooking: "We had six chickens (I can't say where we got them—lend lease, I guess) and they were delicious. We had bread, butter, mashed potatoes and cookies. You should see some of these boys cook. Tonight we are having chicken with noodle soup." Later, he told Betty, "We are still living in buildings and going through some humorous experiences. A couple days ago we slaughtered a hog and we've been enjoying ham, sausage and tenderloin. That with the apple pie we've been baking have made the past couple of days a feast."

As the October lull deepened and the Third Army continued to allow its units to rest and recuperate, additional men were able to get away on passes. A lucky few went to Paris, which had recently been opened to American troops, but Frank's bad luck in drawing a pass did not change. On October 17, he confessed, "I'd like to be able to get to Paris to buy some things. I thought I'd be able to get some perfume for you but it looks like we'll never get a chance to go back. They are leaving to go to a certain city now but from what I hear you don't have such a good time."

He concluded the October 17 letter by reassuring Betty of his love, telling her, "That double picture I have of you is standing up rather good. It's in my left hand pocket and has always been there since I arrived in France. The smaller one I always have in the right pocket."

Although division-level combat ceased after the October 8-9 attacks, the 80th Division commenced an aggressive series of nighttime patrols to prepare for the inevitable Seille crossing. The 318th's history for October described these patrols: "During the last two weeks of the month each of the front-line battalions sent at least one, and often as many as three combat patrols across the River almost every night. Patrols made penetrations of over 1000 yards inside the enemy lines." Squads from the 305th went out with the infantry patrols to guide the boats, gather technical information, analyze enemy strength, and identify potential crossing sites. The 318th history noted, "Most of the patrols crossed the Seille in rubber boats supplied by 305th Engineers.[12]

---

12 318th Infantry Regiment History, October 1944.

Sergeant Lembo and some men from B Company went on one of these patrols on October 18, and on this mission behind enemy lines, in the early morning hours of October 19, Frank's actions earned him a Silver Star.

Lembo's Silver Star citation provides information on the general circumstances of his mission:

> The President of the United States of America, authorized by Act of Congress July 9, 1918, takes pleasure in presenting the Silver Star to First Lieutenant (Corps of Engineers), [then Second Lieutenant] Frank T. Lembo (ASN: 0-2010358), United States Army, for gallantry in action while serving with the 305th Engineer Battalion, 80th Infantry Division, in connection with military operations against an enemy of the United States on 19 October 1944 in France. While deep in hostile territory, Lieutenant Lembo's patrol was subjected to severe enemy fire and forced to withdraw. Alone, he voluntarily remained in exposed and hazardous territory to hold the hostile forces while his men moved to a position of safety. Lieutenant Lembo's gallantry and devotion to duty saved his comrades from possible injury or capture and were in keeping with the highest traditions of the military service and reflect great credit upon himself, his unit and the United States Army.

Frank said his superior officer lost track of the paperwork for his Silver Star, which is why it was awarded months after the event occurred. And it's also why the citation mistakenly terms him a lieutenant, which he later became; on the day of the patrol, he was a sergeant. Unfortunately, Frank refused to talk about the action during his lifetime. Specific details died with him, as he intended.[13]

Frank, however, was undoubtedly alluding to the operation, in typical GI fashion, when he wrote on October 21, two days after the incident, "Went out on a mission the other night and four of us had the time of our life. Dumb luck ran us right into a German outpost, and they threw up a few shots at us. We didn't get our job done though and no one was hurt. After the war I'll tell you about it all, it's rather humorous."

---

13 The battalion journal provides a few more cryptic details about the mission. The weather apparently was miserable, as it was most of the month. Furthermore, the mission was almost canceled. In a series of messages transcribed in the battalion journal, the patrol reported to battalion S-2 (Intelligence) at 1:20 p.m., "Weather not favorable for flying. Will wait to see if weather clears." At 3:10 the patrol reported: "Impossible to make flight. We will return to CP." Finally, at 4 p.m., "Disregard last msg. We are going ahead with mission." Finally, at 4:20, a staff officer at battalion headquarters instructed B Company, "Deliver targets to vicinity of [one code-named site] instead of [another code-named site]. See Serial 6, 7, 8, 9, 305th Engineer Combat Battalion Journal, 18 October 1944.

Frank told a story later in life about a senior commander ordering his party to move down a lane; Frank's instincts told him it was a trap and that his men would be annihilated by enemy fire. He disobeyed the order and managed to get his men back safely. Frank only said, "Somebody really screwed up." He may have been referring to the action that won him the Silver Star, but that's only speculation.

On October 20, the day after Lembo's Silver Star mission, the company settled into engineering work around the divisional and regimental command posts. Lieutenant Henke's 1st Platoon maintained roads in the 80th Division's CP area, while the 2nd Platoon repaired and maintained roads in the 319th's area. The next day, the 1st Platoon went to Mount Toulon to prepare dugouts for CPs, and one of Company B's dozers was used to dig gun emplacements for field artillery.

While Frank was writing in the hours between dusk and dark, "something didn't come up." His letters diligently recounted the lighter side of GI life. The men did whatever they could to make the time go by while Patton was waiting for authorization to move forward. Along with his usual words of love and hope, Frank's main enthusiasm was food. Shortly after telling Betty about taking fire on his harrowing mission behind enemy lines, he resumed a breezy tone: "We've got roast beef cooking and mashed potatoes and peas with it for supper so I'm sitting here starving. I lost my baker so now I'll have to find another or start in myself. I've got biscuit making under control."

He indulged in another rare pleasure during the enforced slowdown of Third Army operations. Near the close of an October 21 letter, he wrote, "I almost forgot the other day we saw Marlene Dietrich in person, and the show was very good. It was about two hours long, we had perfect seats and I really enjoyed myself. It was rather raw and everyone had a good laugh."[14]

Frank added, "We are still comfortably located but we keep busy. A lot of our work has been removing German mines from roads. All in all, I'll be glad when this is all over with. I think I'll go on a pass after payday. I may be able to buy something for you. I think a visit to some town would do me good. I've got to stop in a city long enough to see something."

The October lull was gradually ending. On October 21, the Third Army received orders from Bradley that it was to resume offensive operations around November 10. With the addition of replacement troops and several new divisions,

14 It is worth noting the Marlene Dietrich show took place the afternoon of October 19. Frank attended the show less than 12 hours after returning from his Silver Star scouting mission. See Serial 1, 0843 hours, October 19, 1944, 305th Engineer Combat Battalion Journal.

Marlene Dietrich poses with 80th division soldiers. *Army Signal Corps*

Third Army's strength was up to 250,000 troops (as opposed to fewer than 90,000 opposing forces). Supply levels were high and the existing units were well rested. Patton's ultimate objective remained the Rhine River, but now Third Army was ready to take on the first major obstacle in its path: the Seille.[15]

Third Army's advantage in troop strength was tempered by the impact of horrible weather on offensive operations. It rained 20 days during October, with a total of seven inches on top of already wet roads. The weather virtually grounded the air forces, which had been instrumental in supporting earlier Third Army advances. The incessant rain made the roads slippery with mud, so engineers had to keep the main supply route open by continuously maintaining existing roads, constructing plank roads, and repairing bridges. B Company hauled and spread gravel, scraped mud, and cleared roads of rubble and debris. Platoons cut logs for

15 Gabel, *Lorraine Campaign*, 24.

dugout covers, drained gun emplacements and dugouts, and dug command posts, which were frequently moved during the month.

The company's morning reports state that B Company destroyed bazooka duds, worked on snake demolition charges, and destroyed an enemy mine dump. As usual, B Company had the job of burying dead livestock. On October 25, the 1st Platoon held a school in demolition in Morey, while the company held a school in snake demolition. The 3rd Platoon cleared roads from Sivry to Serrieres and also cut and hauled logs to the 2nd Battalion of the 318th.[16] The engineers took some of the infantry back to the Moselle to practice river crossings.[17] The 305th engineers also joined with other 80th Division units in enlarging and improving the Moselle bridgehead to speed the flow of supplies.

The 305th's informal stopover at Ste. Genevieve—extended as it had been—was formalized when the division was ordered into reserve from October 24 to October 28. Frank and the rest of the men of the 80th Division were given a modicum of warmth, showers, and winter clothing.

By the end of October, Frank was as sick as a dog. The company had gone into reserve at a convenient time. On October 27, he wrote: "Haven't been doing very much lately. I was busy for two days and then yesterday I didn't feel so good so I slept most of the time. I caught cold somewhere and it's a lulu, head, chest and throat, but I feel much better today, so in a couple of days I'll be up to snuff."

During the last few days of October, B Company cleared numerous enemy and friendly minefields that dotted the Seille Valley and laid trip flares. A squad from the 1st Platoon went out to Hill 340 on a mine-clearing mission on October 28 and came back with 75 Riegel mines. Road repair continued in the vicinity of Manoncourt, Sivry, and Serrieres.

In the meantime, Frank was finally off on another mission. He took a few days away from his squad and made a long-anticipated trip to Paris, which he had been dreaming about for months. He wrote on October 27: "By the way, you won't get any mail for about five days cause I'm going to Paris on a pass, so don't worry. I guess it will do me some good to get away from here for a few days." He may have still been suffering from his cold, but some things were more important.

As soon as he returned from his journey, Frank wrote about his impressions of the first foreign city he had visited. Betty must have read Frank's October 31 letter

16 Morning Reports, B Company, October 23-28.

17 Elvin, *Box from Branau*, 79.

with mixed emotions. She couldn't have avoided feeling jealous, as Frank undoubtedly intended.

My Paris trip is over and I hope I can tell you all about it.

After quite a long drive we arrived in Paris, 16 of us, and there we were received with open arms by the Red Cross. We got our room in one of the biggest hotels and it was perfect, three men to a room, private bath and a large balcony overlooking the city.

Our meals were served in the hotel restaurant with excellent service. For awhile everything seemed like a dream and fantastic. The bathtub caught plenty of hell, and anything you wanted was at your command. The Red Cross arranged a tour for us with English speaking guides. We toured the city for three hours and to me it seems to be the prettiest place in the world. The Arc de Triumph, Napoleon's Tomb, and all the other places were beautiful. I should say so beautiful that they can't be described. I attended Mass at the Cathedral of Notre Dame and it was amazing. It was built in the year 1100 and the beauty of it can't be conceived.

Paris itself is untouched by war, the fashions and stores are up to date and the prices are fantastic. A blouse costs $60.00 and dress $120.00. We didn't get a chance to do much shopping because the stores are closed on Sunday and Monday. We went to Montmartre, the Greenwich Village of Paris, and had loads of fun. Monday we got a rather pretty guide from the Red Cross information center and she took us to buy perfume. There are French girls who speak English so we were able to get along okay. I hope you like the perfume. I guess it will be quite awhile getting to you. We even got to ride the subway, and to tell the truth, I think it's going to be hard getting used to civilian life again.

The time came to leave for the front again so with sad faces we left gay Paris. After 44 perfect hours, all I can say is I'll always remember my trip there, and I hope someday we can both go to the city once more. Its wonderful sights and the atmosphere are things everyone should see.

Back here things are normal and today is payday, just as well because I borrowed $34.00 for my Paris trip. My cold is still with me and I'm hoping it leaves me soon.

It didn't take long for Frank to settle back into his routine when he returned to Ste. Genevieve. By November 1 his trip to Paris was all but forgotten, if his letter to Betty is to be believed. Boredom set in and his previous day's exuberance disappeared. He continued to write frequently as the dreary November days wore on. He reported on happy moments but also let his discouragement show: "Another letter and there isn't much news. Nothing seems to happen lately, and although we are kept busy there's nothing to write home about. Winter seems to be settling in here. The mornings are rather chilly. I don't mind the cold too much, but since I've had this cold I really feel it. But colds are commonplace here so it doesn't make much difference."

He continued: "I think you'd faint if you could see me now. My hair has been growing and growing, so I finally got it all cut off. I take a lot of kidding but I feel good. . . . I haven't received much mail in the last eight days. I'm wondering if I should switch to v-mail. They claim weather conditions are cancelling a lot of plane trips."

He wrote again on November 3 and told Betty about an adventure that was probably a measure of the men's desperation for something novel to do: "We went down to the river and caught us some fish while there. We dropped a couple blocks of T.N.T in the river and the concussion killed enough for the whole platoon. The boys had a fish fry but I didn't indulge." He apparently meant it when he wrote, "Another day, another dollar, and still in the army. I guess it will be like that for a while, but there'll come the day."

He became sentimental during the turn of the season to Thanksgiving, since he and Betty had gotten engaged, amid a big family celebration, on the holiday the year before. In a November 3 letter, he wrote, "Thanksgiving will be coming soon and I wonder if we'll get turkey. I don't think I'll ever forget last Thanksgiving I was home with you. We were just engaged and both of us were happy. Yet darling a year later I love you all the more." Thanksgiving wasn't the only holiday on his mind. He told Betty that he was going to write out Christmas cards for his friends, and by the next day he reported, "I wrote out all my Christmas cards so all I have do is mail them when the right time arrives."

Frank continued his updates on his squad's culinary experiments on November 4, including a new dessert on the menu: "Outside of spending the afternoon making pudding I haven't done very much." A day later he was pleased to announce, "We were experimenting with pastry this noon and I stuffed myself trying different things we thought up. I guess you're going to have trouble after we're married with my presence in the kitchen."[18] Experimenting with food had an extra benefit: "I think in the last few weeks I've gained back the weight I lost. We've been eating very good and more like a home life atmosphere. We set a table for ten and eat out of chinaware. The boarding house reach is used, so when I get home

---

18 Frank eventually took full responsibility for grocery shopping and cooking, but not until many years later, after he retired.

you'll understand when I grab for something. Occasionally I'm going to make one hellava grab for you. I guess you won't mind that."

Despite his regular letters, Betty apparently felt Frank was being inattentive, although it may have been the Paris trip that made her uneasy. He unnecessarily wrote to convince her that his feelings hadn't changed. "I'm glad honey you are making plans for our future. I may not mention anything in that line and I guess it's because of the kind of life you lead over here, but there are many times when I think of them and all I can say it isn't going to take us long to get hitched."

He let her know he was once again increasing the allotment of money he was sending home because "you know money is useless here." He reassured her, "I don't gamble anymore because all the old gamblers are gone." Later he told her he was increasing his allotment even more, reminding her that "as much as we save will help us later on. We should be able to settle down initially. I've got about $1500.00 altogether and beside what more comes in it should be sufficient. If no jobs are available my father will be good for $45.00 a week and possibly more. Just to end any fears of my not thinking about the future I'll say I'll do plenty of thinking and figuring."[19]

Betty shared information on her own winter woes, predictably worrying Frank. Although he was ironically the one in harm's way, he temporarily forgot his surroundings and took time to write, "I hope you are well enough now to keep from running to the doctor every so often. You sure do worry me, you better get some resistance and get rid of your sickness before I get home, but then again I'll be able to take care of you. By the way, on the subject of 'double' or 'twin.' you know with me it's 'double'." Later he wrote, "There isn't any doubt that you'll be able to make me happy after this war is over with, as for when it will be over I can't say, but I'm hoping it's Berlin by Christmas."

While he may have hoped for Berlin by Christmas, Frank was clearly planning for winter in Europe. He was using the time to see to his cold-weather clothes:

I'm awaiting your sweater and hope Mom's wool socks arrive soon. I guess when I get all my clothes I'll keep warm, but I'll look like a polar bear. Today we weren't busy so I sewed together a few blankets to form a bag and made myself slippers to fit into my boots. It will be nice getting back to civilization where you won't have to make what you want. We are also awaiting our sleeping bags which are G.I. issue, they'll come in handy with winter settling in.

19 Frank's savings were worth slightly more than $23,000 in 2020 dollars, and his hoped-for $45 weekly income would now be worth $657.

The army did its best to reduce the burden of unrelenting boredom—the men were more accustomed to adrenalin-fueled action than leisure. "Of all things yesterday we were issued a liquor ration. One bottle of vermouth and one bottle of brandy for the squad. Heaven only knows what the Army will do next." He found out soon enough. The next day he was moved to remark, "Of all things another liquor ration and I believe in the phrase 'to the victors belong the spoils.' It's Heine liquor and pretty good at that."

Betty attentively kept track of Frank's army career in "His Service Record" since he left for basic training, but around this time she began to keep a separate scrapbook of newspaper articles and maps that described the progress of the 80th Division and other Third Army units. She read the newspapers carefully and maintained the scrapbook conscientiously up through the German surrender in May 1945. The earliest dated clipping was a November 4 "Somewhere in Europe" article from Stars and Stripes, with an update on XII Corps activities.

In one of her letters, Betty's curiosity got the better of her. She asked Frank what awards and citations his unit had earned. Despite his own heroic actions and pending recommendation for the Silver Star, Frank's reply on November 6 was sharp. Bluntly he said, "In answer to your question, we are entitled to wear the ETO ribbon, at least one star, and possibly two. I can't tell you what battles. But from previous letters you should know where and when. We at the front don't worry about ribbons and stars. Our job is cut out for us, and we let the men stationed in Paris and such wear the ribbons, all we care for is to kick Heine in the pants and get the hell home. We'll do it too, like Patton says 'Hold him by the nose and kick him in the —.'" Another of Frank's rebukes must have been harder for her to swallow: "No, OCS is out completely, and it has been since we left the States. I don't care too much now, I'm happy as I am." As much as he knew and loved Betty, the questions must have stung.

The next day was November 7, and the national elections were at the forefront of Frank's mind. "Another day and with it another letter to you, also being Election Day, I hope we have the good news that Dewey is elected. Most of my boys feel the same so we're hoping. I guess we'll hear Wednesday morning who won the election."

Dreams about the better life that awaited him kept him going. He wrote, "I got to thinking of getting married in the damnest place the other night. Abe and I had to dive down because more fire was coming in on us, and I just started thinking about walking down the aisle with an organ playing. One dropped forty feet away from us and then my thoughts turned to different things. I sure do miss you honey and about one hour relaxation in your arms would be worth a million dollars to me right now. I hope this ends soon."

The November 10 start date specified in Bradley's October 21 order was finally at hand, and the Third Army was told to recommence its attack on Metz. This time, instead of driving directly against the fortress town, Patton encircled it with the XX Corps to the north and the XII Corps to the south. First, however, the 80th Division and XII Corps needed to cross the Seille River, and after more than a month of waiting, the Seille crossing was set for November 8. Earlier, Field Order No. 14 was issued, stating the 80th Division would take part in the Third Army's attack to envelop Metz and then dash to the German border.[20] A suddenly happy Patton told reporters, "Sometime ago, I told you we were going to be stopped for a while, and I was correct. Now we are going to start again."[21]

Every night coordinated patrols were sent behind enemy lines to reconnoiter German positions, the approaches to the river, and the opposite banks. A soldier from the 318th Infantry wrote about a November 3 patrol and recalled that nerves were on edge when the patrol climbed into the rubber boats and crossed into German territory. As the patrol reached the town of Rouves, the enemy suddenly opened fire from all directions. The men from the patrol ran back to the riverbank under heavy mortar and machine gun fire, but when they got to the river, the rope used to pull the boat broke and came loose. Some of the men waiting on the bank panicked as the Germans closed behind them, and they jumped into the water and tried to swim. Many were swept under. The remainder of the patrol finally reached the opposite bank and friendly territory. The leader of the patrol from the 318th reported, "It was a foolish, foolish patrol. . . . But it was standard procedure."[22]

The division's positions were battered by constant rain while the men made their final preparations. When the downpours finally ended, they were recognized as the worst rainfall in decades. On November 7, Frank wrote in a real understatement, "The weather around these parts is still rather miserable with rain the outstanding event. I hope that this winter we put the clinker on the Heine's."

With all the rain, the Seille had grown several times its normal width and had spilled over its banks. Floodwaters also washed out bridges back at the Moselle at a

---

20 Robert T. Murrell, *Operational History, 80th Infantry Division* (Lewistown, PA: n.p., 2001), 76-77.

21 Blumenson, *Patton Papers*, 568.

22 Elvin, *Box from Branau*, 84.

time when Third Army engineers were engaged in heavy fighting and not free for bridging and repair work. Many soldiers developed trench foot in the damp.

The flooding led General Eddy to recommend delaying the Seille crossing, but Patton held firm, telling Eddy to name his successor, because the attack would go on. Patton wrote in his diary, "The attack will go on . . . I know the Lord will help us again. Either He will give us good weather or the bad weather will hurt the Germans more than it does us. His Will Be DONE."[23]

One analyst noted, because of the drenching rain and flooding, "Almost all operations were limited to hard roads, a circumstance that the Germans exploited through the maximum use of demolitions, intensifying the engineers' operations to remove mines and booby traps. Third Army engineers built over 130 bridges during the month of November."[24]

The 80th Division's assault crossing was set to jump off from the towns of Clemery and Nomeny, about seven miles east of the Moselle crossing site at Pont-à-Mousson.[25] In advance, B Company's engineers went out on reconnaissance missions and assembled and prepared the equipment they would be bringing across by foot.[26] On November 7, B Company's motor convoy left Ste. Genevieve and traveled five miles under blackout conditions to Benincourt, near the banks of the Seille. The convoy arrived at its destination at 2:00 a.m.

The November 8 attack began with an intense 60-minute artillery preparation.[27] The shelling suppressed enemy fire from east of the river, although counterattacks by artillery and small arms were sometimes vicious. One fortunate consequence of the rain was that the Germans didn't expect the Third Army to attack until after the awful weather had lifted. The crossing wasn't easy, but it could have been worse. Reports by the 80th Division and the regiments all observed the surprise of Germans, "who never dreamed a human being would attempt to cross the flooded Seille River."[28]

Each of the 80th Division's three infantry regiments made separate crossings, always with great difficulty and significant loss of life.

23 Blumenson, *Patton Papers*, 570.

24 Gabel, *Lorraine Campaign*, 24.

25 After-Action Report, 80th Infantry Division, November 1944.

26 Summary of Daily Operations, November 1944, After-Action Report, 305th Engineer Combat Battalion, November 1944.

27 After-Action Report, 80th Division, November 1944.

28 "Baptism of Fire," 8; see also *Ever Forward*, 12.

The crossings by the 318th's three battalions were supported by B Company's three platoons. The company's 1st Platoon, with Sergeant Lembo's squad, was responsible for crossing the 318th's 1st Battalion, the lead element in the attack. The 1st Battalion jumped off from a site southeast of Nomeny at 5:30 a.m. Lieutenant Henke's 1st Platoon was waiting at the river to help the battalion's first wave into the rubber boats and onto the footbridges. The 305th had prepositioned assault boats along the riverbank the night before, but the river had risen several feet (growing to a width of 200 to 300 yards) overnight, and the infantry had to wade through deep mud and waist-high water for about 100 yards before reaching the boats.[29] The engineers guided the assault boats across the rapidly flowing river while the infantrymen paddled. Once over the river, the battalion's mission was to take the heights along the Montigny Ridge and the town of Mailley, about a mile and a half north of the crossing site.[30]

B Company's 2nd and 3rd platoons were meanwhile crossing the 2nd and 3rd Battalions of the 318th, also in boats and over footbridges. The assault by these elements jumped off at Clemery. Snipers fired at the boats while the infantry paddled across.[31]

Despite the fact that tanks weren't able to join the infantry until that evening, the 318th's three battalions made good progress on the opposite bank and captured Rouves.[32] The nighttime patrols had paid off: "As the battalion had been in position in the area several weeks, they knew where the enemy gun positions were and their approximate strength."[33] Nevertheless, the infantry took heavy casualties. For example, the 2nd Battalion of the 318th, at the end of the operation, was left with "130 men, less than the equivalent of a company."[34] The 3rd Battalion also suffered serious casualties, including its commanding officer and about 75 enlisted men.

29 Lorraine Campaign (Seille and Nied River Crossings), Interview with Lt. Col. Glenn H. Gardner and others, June 21, 1945; Interview with Maj. Matthew L. Dwyer, 2nd Battalion, 318th Infantry Regiment, June 23, 1945.

30 After-Action Report, 318th Infantry Regiment, November 1944, 2.

31 After-Action Report, S-3, 317th Infantry Regiment, November 1944.

32 After-Action Report, 318th Infantry Regiment, November 1944.

33 Lorraine Campaign (Seille and Nied River Crossings), Interview with Capt. Edward E. Hueske, S-3, 1st Battalion, 318th Infantry Regiment, June 22, 1945.

34 "Baptism of Fire," 8.

Bailey Bridge across Seille, constructed by 305th Engineers. *Frank Lembo photo collection*

A battalion of the 319th Infantry took part in the assault, supported by a squad from the 305th Engineers. The 319th's 1st Battalion crossed the Seille over a small bridge built by B Company in the vicinity of Chenicourt, about four and a half miles southeast of Nomeny.

During the Seille crossings, the 317th Infantry met relatively heavy artillery and mortar fire. The 1st Battalion crossed in the general area of Port-sur-Seille, while the 3rd Battalion crossed just north of Morville-sur-Seille. The 2nd Battalion was held in reserve.[35]

When the 317th reached the opposite bank, the infantrymen pushed forward against well-entrenched German positions. A regimental report observed: "The Germans began shelling the approaches to the river where engineers had built small footbridges. Along the banks, the enemy emplaced hundreds of small wooden mines, called shoe-mines [schu-mines] which contained enough explosives to blow off a foot. On the far side of the river, the infantrymen followed the trail of dead

---

35 Lorraine Campaign (Seille and Nied Crossings and Reduction of Maginot Fortresses and St. Avold), Interview with Maj. A. C. Johnson, S-4, 317th Regiment, June 21, 1945.

and wounded through the minefields." All three battalion commanders of the 317th were killed or put out of action during this attack.[36]

According to the 305th's after-action report, the division's objective was "a maze of mines and booby-trapped vineyards."[37] Later, the engineers found a large mine works in a nearby field that held two types of mines previously unknown to the Third Army. According to the 305th's monthly intelligence summary: "The 305th Engineer Battalion was given credit for finding new enemy types of demolitions. Third Army, XII and XX Corps G-2 reports carried the accounts of our finding the new German 'TOPF mine A.' . . . Also, credit was given for finding four 250-lb. bombs, to which were affixed grenades covered with dirt. When the dirt was removed, the grenades would be set off, in turn detonating the four bombs."[38]

Bridge building over the raging river had been a challenge for the engineers, particularly heavy bridges for vehicular traffic. The 305th's after-action report noted, "Flood conditions prevailed even after the attack commenced, which forced us to abandon several bridges that were constructed but later flooded. . . . The problem of maintaining the roads, approaches, and bridges was enormous."[39] But before the end of the day on November 8, engineers managed to build bridges at Clemery and Port-sur-Seille.[40] The bridge at Clemery, however, collapsed from the heavy flow of water during the night.[41] By nightfall the 80th Division had built a total of 10 bridges across the Seille.[42] The 3rd Battalion of the 318th cleared out the village of Nomeny on November 9, "giving engineers a chance to build the bridge at Nomeny the 6th Armored Division used to cross the river."[43]

Firsthand information about the Seille crossing didn't filter home for a week, but the image of the fighting amid flooding and shelling was vivid to families

36 Dominique, "The Attack Will Go On," 54.

37 Intelligence Summary for Month of November 1944, 305th Engineer Combat Battalion.

38 Ibid.

39 Ibid.

40 After-Action Report, 80th Infantry Division, November 1944.

41 Lorraine Campaign (Seille and Nied River Crossings), Interview with Maj. M. L. Dwyer, 318th Infantry Regiment, June 23, 1945, 2.

42 Cole, *Lorraine Campaign*, 353.

43 After-Action Report, S-3, 318th Infantry Regiment, November 1944, 2.

waiting nervously back home. They would have received word of the operation from news reports but not letters from their sons or lovers who were fighting at the front.

When Frank had a chance to write again (on November 16), he filled Betty in on his experiences at the Seille: "Things were hot on and off, the night we crossed a river was about the hottest, but Heine threw his shells about 50 yards too far and that saved us. They shelled us out when we put a vehicle bridge in but later on we returned and got it in. If you could see my truck going to the river you'd thought we were going to a picnic, about twenty men hanging on a rubber float hanging on top and rolling merrily along. That night we slept in a barn, and then spent the next day working in a river getting a bridge out from under water[44] and some guns out. I was in the damn water for eight hours and shook about 20 pounds off."

---

44 This is a reference to the bridge at Clemery, which collapsed the night before.

CHAPTER 9

TO THE GERMAN BORDER: NOV. 9-DEC. 17, 1944

OVER the next few weeks the 80th Infantry Division battled the Germans in town after town in what became known as the Lorraine Campaign. The fighting took them from the Seille River to the Maginot Line, after which they were briefly put in reserve. In mid-December, however, just as the 80th Division was poised to assault the Siegfried Line on the German border, it was called back to join the Battle of the Bulge farther to the north, the enemy's largest counteroffensive of the war.

In early November, despite heavy casualties during the Seille operation, the 80th Division's infantry regiments were tasked with pursuing the next objective on the other side of the Seille: the high ground known as Delme Ridge. The promontory, which had loomed large ahead of the Blue Ridge Division since it first crossed the Moselle, was considered essential to controlling the area east of the river. Its importance was highlighted by the New York Times: "The ridge was one of the most important objects in LTG George S. Patton's attack and just had to be taken if the Metz-Nancy line were to be straightened."[1] Allied intelligence considered it the most strongly fortified German position in the area.[2]

As the 80th Division began to move out from the Seille bridgehead on November 10, B Company's 2nd and 3rd platoons brought the remainder of their engineer equipment across the Seille at Clemery and swept mines from the roads

---

1   Quoted in 80th Division, Ever Forward, 12.

2   Cole, *Lorraine Campaign*, 352.

on the east side of the bank from Clemery to Rouves and from there to the crossing site at Nomeny.

The division's infantry fought hard against stiff opposition the next few days. Within 48 hours after crossing the Seille on November 8, the division had captured five strongly fortified towns, advanced five miles across a 10-mile-wide front, and destroyed or captured many large pieces of enemy equipment. These gains, however, came at a high cost in men.[3] The prisoner count also soared as the 80th Division took over 1,200 prisoners between November 9 and 12.[4]

On November 9, the 319th Infantry's 1st Battalion fought off stiff resistance, and with the support of the 702nd Tank Battalion, took a succession of towns and set off for the Delme Ridge. As the 80th Division's infantry approached, they encountered "elaborate entrenchments," with obstacles and antitank guns. The 1st Battalion, 319th Infantry reported "extensive minefields and many booby traps had been placed along the forward slopes of Delme Ridge south of Liocourt. C Company lost three men and a number of Germans were also killed by their own minefields."[5]

On the left, the 317th Infantry at first took heavy casualties during the attack on Delme Ridge. Then, to the surprise of the Americans, the Germans abandoned their positions on the ridge after aircraft and artillery, plus tanks from the 6th Armored Division, pounded their positions.[6] The 80th Division occupied Delme Ridge on November 10.[7] During the ensuing hours, the GIs liberated the nearby towns, lost them again, and finally ended up victorious, but always burdened by heavy casualties. The situation east of the Seille was horrific. An account from the 1st Battalion, 318th Infantry, described "mud and water was waist deep. Casualties for the day included 100 men. . . . Stiff resistance had been met in the town of Nomeny. The CO of A Company was killed by machine gun fire from emplacements [on the Montigny Ridge] and his company, disorganized from the

---

3   After-Action Reports, 317th, 318th, and 319th Infantry, 80th Division, November 1944.

4   After-Action Report, 80th Infantry Division, November 1944.

5   Seille and Neid River Crossings, 1st Battalion, 319th Infantry Regiment, Interview with Lt. William P. Sweaney, Battalion S-3, June 27, 1945.

6   Cole, *Lorraine Campaign*, 352.

7   After-Action Report, 31 Regiment S-3, November 1944; Interviews with Capt. Edward E. Hueske and Maj. Matthew Dwyer.

heavy resistance, was cut off."[8] Radios didn't work because they had gotten wet in the crossing, and communications within the battalion fell apart, adding to the confusion.

Despite these setbacks, an 80th Division history summarized: "With the capture of Delme Ridge, the pathway to the Saar Basin, the Metz-Nancy line was secured. The battalion moved swiftly for the Maginot Line."[9]

B Company's 1st Platoon supported the 1st Battalion, 318th Infantry, as it moved out from the Seille while its 2nd and 3rd platoons operated in direct support of other infantry battalions from the 318th and 319th. The 305th swept the roads of mines and, as the company diary described it, "[did] a good job of it, building bridges, putting in culverts and removing mine fields and road blocks as they advance."

Meanwhile, the 2nd Battalion of the 318th advanced to Rouves in its first action east of the Seille River.[10] The enemy counterattacked with about 100 infantry supported by tanks, but the 2nd Battalion successfully repulsed the attack. Accurate artillery fire persisted until "elements of the 2d Bn. put a 57mm AT gun in a position at the cross roads and put several rounds of HE into the church steeples in the town." Numerous German prisoners were taken over the course of the day.

On the night of November 10, Lieutenant Henke's 1st Platoon left its bivouac at Benincourt and drove five miles to Nomeny, where the first waves from the 318th had come across a short time earlier.[11] The convoy made only a brief stop and immediately traveled eight more miles to Thezey-Saint-Martin. The next day, November 11, B Company followed the infantry to Foville and then started for Mancheux. Later that day the convoy moved again, finally stopping for the night at Tragney.

The 1st Battalion of the 318th, supported by B Company's 1st Platoon, quickly advanced over the Montigny Ridge and onto a hill overlooking Mailly. It beat back an enemy counterattack and consolidated positions for the night. The battalion met little resistance when it marched through Montigny, Philin, and Thezey-Saint-Martin with tanks from the 702nd Tank Battalion. B Company's motor convoy passed through with the infantry. The 1st Battalion continued the

8   Lorraine Campaign, Seille and Nied River Crossings, Interview with Capt. Edward E. Hueske, S-3, 1st Battalion, 318th Infantry, 1-2.

9   History, 2nd Battalion, 318th Infantry Regiment, 23.

10 Ibid., 22.

11 Ibid.

attack and took town after town against light opposition, but conditions in the field continued to be miserable. A report from the 1st Battalion observed, "All men had to wade through water crossing the Seille two days earlier and had not yet been able to get dry. The weather was very cold and damp. Some 35 men were evacuated that night with trench foot and blisters."

On November 11, the 1st Battalion pushed through to the town of Morville against the heaviest resistance it had yet encountered. The enemy cut through the battalion with several 75mm antitank guns and automatic weapons. The day's casualties for the battalion included the commanding officer of C Company, 3 other officers, and 15 enlisted men.[12]

Losses were taking their toll in the other infantry battalions as well. On November 11, for example, the 2nd Battalion of the 318th, which had been reduced to about 150 men, was reorganized as a rifle company.[13] By mid-November the division's fighting strength was sorely depleted, limiting offensive operations.

The Nied française, the next body of water in the infantry's path, temporarily halted the advance. By now the air was colder and the rain had turned to snow. The Nied française was the first and leftmost tributary of the Saar River. The second, on the right, was known as the Nied allemande. The 317th advanced to the Nied française on November 11, seized an intact bridge, and defended it against intense German counterattacks.[14]

On November 12, the 3rd Battalion of the 318th took control of the Nied française bridge, and the infantry expanded the bridgehead. The 1st Battalion of the 318th crossed over the bridge and successfully engaged the Germans in several neighboring towns. Then the 2nd Battalion crossed and, in conjunction with the 6th Armored Division, took Baudrecourt, Valimont, and other villages.[15] An 80th Division history noted: "The 3rd Battalion of the 318th had some good luck. . . . The troops captured a railroad bridge over the river and got across with dry feet."[16] The 317th, in reserve, guarded the bridge while the other two regiments advanced.

---

12 Lorraine Campaign, Seille and Nied River Crossings, Interview with Capt. Edward E. Hueske, S-3, 1st Battalion, 318th Infantry, 2-3.

13 Cole, *Lorraine Campaign*, 362; Lorraine Campaign, Seille and Nied River Crossings; Interviews with Lt. Col. Glenn Gardner, executive officer, 318th Infantry Regiment, 3.

14 Dominique, "The Attack Will Go On," 53.

15 After-Action Report, 318th Infantry Regiment, November 1944.

16 Craig, *The 80th Infantry Division*, 36.

On November 12, B Company's motor convoy pulled up stakes and traveled five miles from Tregney to Meville-sur-Nied.

On November 14, after an intensive artillery preparation, the 318th Infantry and attached armor units attacked the enemy at Thicourt and Thionville. The 80th took the towns and several hundred prisoners.[17] The 3rd Battalion of the 318th went on a tactical march through the towns of Arraincourt, Brulange, Thicourt, and Thionville and set up defensive positions with the 6th Armored. The 2nd Battalion of the 318th arrived at Thicourt and remained in reserve in the town until November 20.

Patton noted in a in a November 14 letter to his wife that it had been raining every day and that the men were "having a hell of a time with 'immersion' [trench] feet. . . . However, the enemy must be suffering more, so it is a question of mutual crucifixion."[18]

B Company moved to Baudrecourt on November 14 and stayed there until November 17. Frank was unable to write any letters between the Seille crossing on November 8 and November 14, but he jotted a quick note on the back of an army-issued "Merry X-MAS 1944" Christmas card: "Sorry I haven't written sooner but by the papers you can tell why. We've been rather busy, and I guess we'll keep up the same until the end. Once I told you we were at the bottom of the last hill, well we're half way up now and riding for the top. I hope you can spend your Christmas celebrating the holiday and victory!"

On November 16, the 318th's 3rd Battalion and the 6th Armored took Chemery after heavy opposition. A number of Shermans from 6th Armored were taken out and others were forced to withdraw, but here, too, the 80th Division was able to accomplish its objectives.[19]

General Eddy paused the entire XII Corps for two days, starting on November 16, to allow for refitting and consolidation. When action resumed, the 80th Division remained in a holding position until Patton ordered it to move again.[20] Attacks did not completely stop, but the offensive pace slowed considerably.

Frank took time out on November 16 to fill in Betty on his experiences at the Seille. He mentioned that, a few days after the crossing, "We took our first

---

17 After-Action Report, 80th Division, November 1944.

18 Blumenson, *Patton Papers*, 574.

19 After-Action Report, 318th Infantry Regiment, November 1944, 4.

20 Rickard, *Patton at Bay*, 202-6.

prisoners when we moved into a town, only the infantry didn't arrive yet so we had a helluva time. I guess it was the worst shelling I've seen or been near. The prisoners were afraid we were going to shoot them, and they cried like a baby—we should have shot them." He continued,

> Things have been rather hectic since a week or so ago. You probably know we are on the move and we've had quite a lot of work. Rain, snow, and mud haven't helped us any. Yesterday we had to clear a minefield and in one path we took out 88 mines. We put them in one pile and blew them up. It was 880 pounds going up and it blew hell out of everything, but we got a kick out of it.

He concluded, "We've been sleeping inside so far and sometimes it's in barns, other nights in rooms with French families, they in one part of the house and us in the other. Personally it's a hell of a life and I hope it ends soon. I'm getting a little tired, and slowly wearing out."

As the November days went by, B Company's motor convoy continued its pace of a few miles a day. Between November 10—when the company crossed the Seille—and 17, the engineers' convoy moved through Foville, Mancheux, Tragney, Meville-sur-Nied, and Baudrecourt. Frank dryly told Betty, "I'm hoping I'll get me a bath one of these days. This moving around keeps you pretty filthy. I'm glad you can't see me sometimes."

The 1st and 2nd platoons moved out by motor convoy on November 18 from Baudrecourt and arrived at Brulange after traveling 10 miles. The company diary reports the town was shelled for 24 hours, but there were no casualties. Frank was able to get in a few lines on November 18 from his billet in Brulange. He let Betty know the letter would be a quick one "and a shaky one, every time the artillery goes off we jump about ten feet and it jars everything." He also noted a rare appearance by the Luftwaffe: "Heine came flying over us again and the barrage that went up was deafening. They took off like a bat out of hell."

B Company engineers were grateful they were finally in one place long enough to be reached by mail—the first in a week, but they found the distinction between themselves and the people living comfortably back home was sharp. They lived in two worlds that grew further apart as time passed. Frank probably mirrored the sentiments of the others in B Company when he told Betty, "I see in today's paper you people are having strike trouble again. I guess the best thing is to ship us home and let the people at home who forget the war come over here and get a taste of this. It may change their minds."

With yearning, Frank remembered it was their one-year anniversary—they were engaged on Thanksgiving the year before and had a turkey dinner with family to celebrate. He wrote with regret, "I guess we'll pass up turkey this year. But next year I'll be enjoying your cooking on Thanksgiving day."

Frank was able to mail a handful of Christmas cards to Betty, most showcasing GI humor. He must have mailed the cards to her at the same time he sent the rest of his Christmas cards to family and friends. One of the cards was a cartoon of a soldier running up the gangplank of the USS America, with the message "Merry Christmas—It won't be long now." Another shows a soldier and his sexy sweetheart under bed covers and crowned with mistletoe, champagne and cigarette in hand. A third is a cartoon of two soldiers dancing arm in arm. Each card contained a loving, handwritten Christmas message. Future and better Christmases with his sweetheart were at the forefront of his mind as he remembered happy Christmases past and pondered the cold winter that awaited him. Always stoic, Frank closed his letter, "Darling I hope you're keeping up morale on the home front and if there isn't any mail it's because we're trying to get this war over with."[21]

Frank wrote again from Brulange the next night, November 19. He was in a rare melancholy mood.

> "Well honey—I feel good after a hot bath, a shave and a change of clothes, but I wonder for how long. I got a little homesick today and it really hit me hard for a while, but I guess everyone is entitled to get blue. I was thinking today what a Christmas it would be . . . back in civilization again. No floors to sleep on, dishes to eat from, a chance to wash every day, not having to wear the same clothes for a month, so many things can pop into your mind, and yet so much to look forward to. You'll have to get used to my strange behavior at times. I guess you'll still be able to enjoy your Christmas without me, you have so many people running in and so many things to go through. It would be nice to spend it with you but we'll have to make the best of things. You have the advantage over me. I'll probably be busy working, but now no day has any special importance to me.

The 80th Division arrived at the next obstacle, the Nied allemande, on November 19. The 317th Infantry was in the advance and discovered the Germans had destroyed the bridge. They put patrols across the river.[22]

On November 22, the 305th helped the infantry over the Nied allemande, again under enemy fire, by building footbridges, operating ferries, and supporting

---

21 The home front was apparently thinking about Christmas as well. The battalion adjutant noted in the journal for November 29 that "mail is beginning to include a lot of Christmas packages."

22 Dominique, "The Attack Will Go On," 57.

raft bridges. The engineers also put Class B Bailey bridges and wooden trestle bridges over the river to accommodate heavier traffic. High water only complicated their work, but the infantry established bridgeheads across the river.[23]

B Company left Brulange on November 21, motoring 10 miles to the town of Faulquemont. Other units in the 80th had reached the town on November 20, where troop movements were halted while new plans were developed for the next phase of the offensive against the Maginot Line and to the German border. On November 22, orders were issued for the 80th to attack the Maginot Line three days hence.[24]

One of B Company's platoons built a 50-foot-long Bailey bridge in Faulquemont while Lieutenant Henke's 1st Platoon cleared mines, built culverts, and maintained the roads. Engineers had to repair a blown bridge before vehicular traffic could pass. Numerous craters had to be filled, and two very large ones required 25 truckloads of rock each. Rubble from nearby demolished buildings gave the engineers a ready source for the material. A newspaper article commented that residents of the town tossed planks and ladders to assist the Americans in the river crossing.[25]

B Company motored two miles to Cites Des Charbonnage on November 24. While there it reached a milestone—Capt. Edward Sebago relieved Capt. Robert Marshall as commander of B Company of the 305th Engineer Combat Battalion. Marshall had been a mainstay of the company and had held the 305th together during many hard days. He was now assigned as Battalion S-3 (chief of operations), but he later returned as commander of B Company on January 29, 1945. Marshall's transfer was occasioned by the wounding and evacuation of the battalion's executive officer, Major Croker, which required a succession of officer reassignments. Marshall was moved up to replace the S-3, and Captain Sebago was moved up from command of the battalion's headquarters and service company.[26]

Frank looked on the bright side, as usual, and reported, "Yesterday was Thanksgiving and we were able to get some chicken cooked. Our kitchen isn't set up so each squad does its own cooking. We didn't have any pots or pans so we let the lady in whose house we slept cook them. It was a fairly good meal, but it didn't

---

23 After-Action Report, 80th Division, November 1944.

24 Craig, *The 80th Infantry Division*, 37; Dominique, "The Attack Will Go On," 57.

25 Robert Cromie, "Civilians Help Patton's Army Capture Town," *Chicago Tribune*, November 28, 1944.

26 305th Engineer Combat Battalion Journal, November 24, 1944.

matter much what we ate. I'm not that concerned over food. . . . We moved into rooms in some pretty fancy houses yesterday and they weren't beat up at all. Artillery knocked the roof off one across from us this morning but they missed us. A couple shells came screaming in and then you see a scramble." He added, "The day has been pretty miserable. I went out this morning to finish a job we started last night but the infantry arrived there and chased us out. We beat them to it last night. They always get scared when we come around for some reason or other. I guess it's because we make too much noise."

Betty apparently had a recent get-together with Scotty's wife, and Frank wrote, "It was good to hear you had a nice time in New York with Tess. I haven't heard any news from Scotty in some time. . . . Once they leave us we don't get news from them."

On the morning of November 25, after a 30-minute artillery preparation, the 318th's 2nd and 3rd battalions, along with the 610th Tank Destroyers, launched a coordinated attack north of Bambiderstroff on the Germans entrenched in the Maginot Line emplacements.[27] The Maginot Line was a line of French fortresses built during the 1930s to defend the frontiers against a German attack. By this time, the fortresses had been neglected since 1940, and most of the heavy artillery pieces (which had faced east, toward Germany) had been removed. Nevertheless, they provided shelter for Germans armed with machine guns and were heavily defended by barbed wire and minefields. Despite their weaknesses, they were a serious obstacle for the U.S. infantry. At each turn, the GIs faced barbed wire, prepared lanes of fire, dugouts roofed with concrete and sod, foxholes, and breastworks improvised from cordwood.

The 80th drove forward across a wide front through wooded terrain to occupy the high ground, but German grenadiers proved to be resourceful fighters in the woods. The Germans in the Maginot forts placed "murderous fire" on the troops of the 3rd Battalion of the 318th as they swooped across the open stretches of terrain in front of the German positions.[28]

By November 25 the Maginot Line had been breached across the entire front of the 80th Division, and the infantry captured nine forts.[29] Many of the defenders

27 After-Action Report, 318th Infantry Regiment, November 1944, 6; After-Action Report, 319th Infantry Regiment, November 1944.

28 After-Action Report, 318th Infantry Regiment, November 1944, 6.

29 After-Action Reports, 80th Division, 317th, 318th, 319th Infantry Regiments, November 1944.

Maginot Line prisoners taken by the 318th walk out of Bambesch Woods near Bambiderstroff.
Army Signal Corps

had withdrawn by the time of the 80th's arrival, and the pillboxes were manned only by troops with machine guns. American tank destroyers penetrated the pillboxes with the newly arrived 90mm guns, which were able to punch through the five-to-six-foot-thick reinforced concrete walls.

A captured German battalion commander defending a sector of the Maginot Line said the 80th's attack was "almost perfect" in its use of maneuver to expose his flanks and in cooperation between infantry and armor. By 5:00 p.m. on November 25, he confessed to an American officer, "My battalion is no more."[30] More and more Germans surrendered. An officer of the 3rd Battalion of the 318th noted "this was the first evidence on the part of the Germans of any willingness to surrender and also this was the first appearance of the Hitler youth.[31]

On November 26, B Company left its bivouac for Bambiderstroff, a town near the Bambesch woods. Troops from the 318th and the 702nd Tank Battalion had cleared the enemy from Bambiderstroff the previous day, and November 26 was

---

30 After-Action Report, G-2, 80th Infantry Division, November 1944.

31 Lorraine Campaign (Seille and Nied River Crossings); Interview with Lt. John Bier, S-3 (Operations staff), 3rd Battalion, 318th, then S-2 (Intelligence staff), 4.

marked by mop-ups of the Maginot pillboxes and attacks and counterattacks in the vicinity of Longeville-les-Saint-Avold. One of 3rd Battalion's companies had 20 men taken prisoner, and others from the battalion were wounded. The 1st Battalion cleared the Longeville woods.[32]

B Company worked in and around Bambiderstroff from November 25 to 27. Local historian Simon Petitot reported the company built two Bailey bridges and two treadway bridges in and near the village. Other engineering chores included filling in an antitank ditch dug by the Germans (two engineers from B Company were wounded while reconnoitering the ditch) and filling in numerous craters in the roads. The company journal noted the 1st Platoon built a footbridge and several infantry support bridges on November 25 and put in culverts and cleared mines on November 26. The 2nd and 3rd platoons filled in craters, put in a bypass around the antitank ditch, and filled in segments of the ditch to allow vehicular traffic.[33]

The engineers weren't always sensitive to local concerns. On one occasion the bulldozer operators shoved a wagon and its contents—two disabled jeeps and the rubble from at least one house—into the craters as fill material and confiscated much of the town's supply of cut wood for the winter to construct a bridge. When a citizen complained, an engineer replied, "We're winning the war." Petitot pointed out that many damaged houses were rebuilt using their same materials after the war, but if the rubble had been pushed into one of the craters, the owner couldn't rebuild.

On November 27, the 318th's 1st and 3rd battalions consolidated their positions near Longeville-les-Saint-Avold. The infantry fought its way into Longeville and set up roadblocks on the roads leading into the town.[34] B Company followed the infantry to Longeville, where a demolition crew used 80 pounds of TNT to blow a hole in a steel emplacement for an artillery command post. During the afternoon a bridge stretching from the Bambesch woods to the high ridge to the right of the battalion sector was installed to enable vehicles to cross.

The day before, November 26, the 80th Division approached St. Avold, a large communications center near the German border. The Americans initially met

32 After-Action Report, 318th Infantry Regiment, November 1944, 6.

33 B Company Morning Reports, November 25-27, 1944.

34 After-Action Report, 318th Infantry Regiment, November 1944, 7.

Engineers take road materials from a stone wall. *Army Signal Corps*

heavy resistance, but the German defenses crumbled as the Americans advanced toward and through the town on November 27.[35]

Each of B Company's platoons supported one of the 318th's infantry battalions during the St. Avold engagement. The capture of the town by the 319th on November 27 was a critical milestone in the division's drive from the Moselle to the Rhine. The 80th was now at the German border.

Division commander McBride clearly considered St. Avold to be unfriendly territory; he issued an order that personnel should not converse with civilians in the town, must be armed when they were in town, and should stay in groups of four or more.[36]

Engineers from the 305th were forced to perform the full range of engineering duties in St. Avold. Demolitions set up by the Germans before they left had done

35 Summary of Operational Interviews Obtained from 80th and 6th Armored Divisions Concerning Lorraine Campaign, After-Action Report, 80th Infantry Division, November 1944.

36 Combat Battalion Journal, 305th Engineer, 2230 hours, November 27, 1944.

considerable damage, blowing up much of the town's infrastructure, including the railroad station, town square, and several important crossroads and culverts.

The engineers apparently had time for a short break as well. A *Chicago Tribune* reporter observed, "In a wrecked café in the main street a group of GIs belonging to the 80th's 305th Engineers was crowded around a piano being played by Pvt. Frank Foster, Anderson, Ind."[37]

B Company operated in close support of the 319th Infantry Regiment in St. Avold on November 28, clearing the roads of mines, filling craters, and removing abatis. The 319th, meanwhile, pressed the attack to the east, clearing Hambourg Haut and seizing the villages of Betting and Benning.[38] The next day, November 29, B Company resumed support of the 318th Infantry Regiment. Lieutenant Henke's 1st Platoon continued to scour St. Avold for mines and booby traps.

The engineers remained in the vicinity of St. Avold, moving between Bambiderstroff, Longeville, Guenville, and St. Avold through the end of November 1944. In her scrapbook, Betty kept a map summarizing the known locations of 80th Division units that had been published in the New York Daily News on November 30.

The 80th also encountered a new type of weapon in St. Avold that gave the war-hardened soldiers a serious case of the jitters: time bombs.[39] A resident reported to the 319th the Germans had hidden these devices in town, concealed in buildings that had been formerly occupied by the Nazis. The informant said there were about 30 devices, but he didn't know where they were or when they were set to detonate. The story was confirmed when a device with a time clock and 200 pounds of TNT was found in some rubble. McBride ordered the 80th—meaning engineers from the 305th—to find and remove the bombs. The battalion's new S-3, B Company's former commander, Capt. Robert Marshall, ordered B Company to "check very thoroughly all buildings in St. Avold. . . . Time bombs are being found. Put an officer in charge."[40]

The 305th's after-action reports indicate the battalion spent a considerable amount of time checking public buildings and utilities. The engineers found a few of the time-bomb devices, but not all of them. Several blew up on December 3,

37 Cromie, "Civilians Help Patton's Army," 3.

38 Lorraine Campaign, Seille and Neid River Crossings, 1st Battalion, 319th Infantry Regiment, Interview with Battalion S-2.

39 Craig, *The 80th Infantry Division*, 37-38.

40 Combat Battalion Journal, 305th Engineer, Serial 5, 1155 hours, November 28, 1944.

destroying some buildings where American soldiers were billeted. The explosions caused pandemonium as the soldiers first ran into the street and then took refuge with the locals. The time bombs caused many casualties in the 80th.[41]

During this time, engineers from the 305th fought a fire that was started by an explosion and cleared rubble left by the detonation of other bombs. Victims were rescued, bodies were extricated, and equipment was salvaged from the blown buildings. Before leaving St. Avold, the engineers destroyed and cleared "aerial time bombs (used as explosives)," duds, and a large quantity of explosives and ammunition.

The threat of the time bombs was so unnerving that the Third Army shelved its plans to move its headquarters from Nancy to St. Avold. An 80th Division report noted, "Psychologically it affected every unit in the Third Army during these days of bitter fighting."[42] The troops were reportedly glad to be on the road again when they finally cleared the St. Avold's area.

Shortly after leaving the town on November 28, the 317th encountered heavy resistance in the village of Farebersviller. This was a German stronghold, and its defenses included several Tiger tanks. The roads were too muddy for American tanks to be called up, so the infantry attacked without them. The 317th drove the Germans out of town after a nasty fight. That evening the Germans counterattacked and took several prisoners, but the 317th seized the town again. The Germans counterattacked twice on November 29, but the infantry repulsed both.[43]

The 317th Infantry Regiment's after-action report for November described the action: "3d Bn advanced to and entered Farebersviller, meeting heavy enemy SA, arty and mortar fire. Received counterattack at nightfall. 29 November—1st Bn on Pos received SA fire. 2d Bn received two counterattacks of five tanks and infantry, both repulsed. 3d Bn continued house to house fighting in Farebersviller."[44] A *Stars and Stripes* reporter wrote about this fight, and the article played a part in Frank's correspondence with Betty.

---

41 After-Action Report, 305th Engineer Combat Battalion, Intelligence Summary for Month of November 1944.

42 St. Avold Time Bomb Incident.

43 Dominique, "The Attack Will Go On," 60-62.

44 After-Action Report, S-3, 317th Infantry Regiment, November 1944.

On November 30, troops from the 80th stood at the German frontier. Several days earlier, the 314th Field Artillery Battalion fired the first 80th Division shells onto German soil. PFC Francis Neighly remembered that the crew put the shell on a table and everyone signed their name on it. "We then took it back to the gun and shot it into Germany. It was quite a thrill."[45]

But the 80th couldn't enter Germany in force yet because of a renewed shortage of supplies, particularly fuel, which again had been redirected to Field Marshal Montgomery's operations in the north. Personnel shortfalls were also acute. Many soldiers had been killed or wounded in the November campaign, and others suffered from trench foot or combat fatigue. Replacements hadn't yet arrived or were green. Patton's Third Army offensive ground to a stop at the German border.

Many veterans remember the November campaign as one of the most difficult periods of sustained combat of the war.[46] Third Army troops had won only a small amount of ground, and every inch was hard fought. In 28 days of fighting, the 80th Infantry Division and the 6th Armored Division had advanced only 55 miles from the Seille near Nomeny to the Saar River. This was after advancing almost 400 miles in just two weeks after Normandy. As one 80th report indicated, "The 28 days of fighting were marked by a stubborn delaying action on the part of the Germans and extremely bad weather conditions."[47]

The 80th took 4,000 prisoners but suffered over 3,000 casualties during November's fighting.[48] Especially worrisome were the infantry regiments, who took 98 percent of the division's casualties. A total of 1,351 infantrymen were killed, severely wounded, or missing/captured during November, a total that doesn't include minor wounds. The 317th Infantry Regiment was hit particularly hard, suffering nearly half the division's total casualties.[49] Further, a study of the Lorraine Campaign noted, "Noncombat casualties, most due to trench foot, roughly equaled combat casualties for the month of November." Worse, 95

45 Quoted in Beard, "Through Fire and Water and Mud—To the Siegfried Line," The 314th FA Battalion in the ETO, 48.

46 Craig, The 80th Infantry Division, 38.

47 Summary of Operational Interviews Obtained from 80th and 6th Armored Divisions Concerning Lorraine Campaign.

48 After-Action Report, 80th Infantry Division, November 1944; Murrell, "80th Losses in Action," November 1944.

49 Murrell, "80th Losses in Action."

percent of the trench foot casualties were out for the long term, "at least until spring."[50] The 305th Engineer Combat Battalion fared better during the month—only 1 enlisted man was killed and 12 were wounded.

Casualties were so severe among infantrymen that the traditional replacement system couldn't keep the regiments at full strength. Worsening the situation was that, at the time of Europe's maximum need for replacement troops, the War Department cut back the ETO's allotment to increase the flow of soldiers to the Pacific.[51] Patton began to "draft" rear-area corps and army troops and train them as infantry. Even non-infantry combat troops, such as the engineers, were "taxed" to provide manpower for the infantry. Some unneeded combat units, such as antiaircraft and tank destroyer unitsn, were also broken up to supply the constant demand for riflemen.[52]

After the war, the 305th Battalion's newspaper, *Fire in the Hole*, reported of the November campaign:

> The month of November will always have a very important place in the memory of the 305th Engineers. We suddenly found ourselves in work that seemed to have no ending. The enemy had ample time to lay minefields, build roadblocks, and strengthen their fortified positions to such an extent that at every turn of the road we encountered a new obstacle. Under heavy fire we established bridgeheads over the Seille and Nied rivers. The Seille experienced a flash flood the day before our crossing and greatly hampered the operation. The records indicate that the Alsace Lorraine sector was probably the toughest we had to crack. . . . November will be remembered as a month when a working day meant everywhere from sixteen to twenty-hours.[53]

Despite Patton's rosy prediction in August that the war would be over quickly, his men fought in Lorraine for three months before the campaign was over and took heavy losses. Patton wrote to the War Department in disgust: "I hope that in the final settlement of the war, you insist that the Germans retain Lorraine, because I can imagine no greater burden than to be the owner of this nasty country where it

50 Gabel, *The Lorraine Campaign*, 30.

51 Bradley, *A Soldier's Story*, 446-47.

52 Gabel, *The Lorraine Campaign*, 30.

53 *Fire in the Hole*, July 21, 1945, 1.

rains every day and where the whole wealth of the people consists in assorted manure piles."[54]

The division's original plan was to move east from St. Avold and establish a bridgehead east of the Saar River, between Saarbrucken and Saargemund. This assignment evolved and shifted to the north, requiring the division to move toward Forbach due to the presence of other friendly forces in the vicinity and heavy enemy opposition.

The 80th Division had taken St. Avold in the final days of November, but pockets of resistance remained. The engineers withstood enemy attacks as they operated in St. Avold for several more days. On December 3, the Germans shelled the town with heavy artillery, and a round fell into the billeting area of B Company's 2nd Platoon, wounding 4 enlisted men. Elsewhere in the 80th's position, an explosion in the antiaircraft platoon's headquarters caused 50 casualties. As troops began to leave St. Avold, B Company went ahead of them to fill craters and shell holes and clear rubble.

B Company's bivouac remained in St. Avold until December 6, awaiting the order to advance against the Siegfried Line (as the Allies called it), also known as the West Wall (as the Germans called it): a barrier of concrete fortifications, trenches, and tank dugouts along the German border. The men of B Company had time at St. Avold to rest and write home to their families while anticipating the next attack.

Frank caught up on his correspondence, writing often to Betty, friends, and family. He was as upbeat as ever. On December 2, he wrote from St. Avold: "For once in a long while we are no longer at the front, and I must say it's amazing just to hang around doing nothing. A few days ago we were pulled back and I guess we'll go up in awhile again."

Things didn't change, and two days later he wrote, "We had it rather easy the past few days and it seems funny to just loaf around. We were at the front yesterday but it was a quiet day. We worked for us for a change, and that's unusual for us." He continued, "We are in a rather large city and living in what was formerly Gestapo headquarters. The past two days we have been working on a gas motor we found and soon we hope to have electricity."

He gave Betty an update on his squad's enterprise later in the week: "We got our electricity plant going and all of a sudden the damn thing flew apart and with it

---

54 Quoted in Steven Zaloga, *George S. Patton: Leadership, Strategy, Conflict*, Command, no. 3 (Oxford, UK: Osprey, 2010), 29-30.

went three days of hard work, but undaunted in the morning we'll try again. It's fun anyway."

Frank wrote again the next day, on a rainy evening, happily telling her, "woe and behold, the Army came through with medium heavy wool sweaters today. Now when I get yours too I needn't worry about the cold, we also have bedrolls on the way so I'll be able to shed some blankets. Needless to say we are really loaded down, four blankets, rubber boots, overshoes, sweater and other items.

"After the war I think I'll go into the unloading trucks business. The past few weeks we've been hauling rock and other material, so out comes all our tools, clothing and everything else. The boys bitch but I take all their griping with a grin and their gripes go in one ear and out the other. If you'd listen to all the personal gripes you'd go batty, so I usually refer to the plight of the infantryman in a quiet voice and that's all."

The extended billeting at St. Avold meant mail deliveries were back on schedule. He wrote, "I received a letter from Scotty and he'll be back with us soon from what he says. I hope he hits this outfit again because the old boys just can't be replaced and we can use every one of them, anyway. I'll be glad to see him again."

As if he didn't already have enough on his mind, Betty apparently gave Frank hell for what she saw as his lack of appreciation for everything she did for him. She didn't think his words of thanks made the grade. But Frank was ever patient and always reassuring, whether he thought Betty's complaints were reasonable or not. He wrote in apparent seriousness, "I never do thank you for the air mail stamps you send me but honey if it slips my mind I just want you to know they are well appreciated, in fact everything you do is well appreciated, the letters you write, the things you send and just being plain you. Being so far away makes it hard for me to show what I think of you but time will come when this all will be a thing of the past and our future will be together."

A day later he continued in the same vein: "Well darling what have you been doing with yourself? I hope you've been feeling better and also that you don't let your nerves run away with you. Someday I'll be home to take care of you." He assured Betty his day wasn't all "blood, sweat, toil and tears": "The boys found a couple bottles of rather good cognac and we're saving a bottle for Christmas, the other one is making the rounds. I'd like to know how much liquor the armies have consumed since D day."

On December 4, the 318th and 319th attacked entrenched German positions to the northeast of Farebersviller, Theding, and Kochern. Engineers from B Company constructed a treadway bridge during the early hours of the attack, which allowed tanks from the 702nd Tank Battalion to accompany the infantry. The

318th described the operation as "one of the most successful this regiment has ever undertaken."[55]

On December 7, the 305th was ordered to move to Helleringen to go into reserve with other units from the 80th. The 80th was slated to play a major role in the upcoming assault on the West Wall, so it received priority for rest and recuperation until orders arrived. The 80th had been in continual contact with the enemy for 102 days.[56]

The men used their free time to train, repair equipment, and prepare winter clothing. Engineering crews were trained in the use of acetylene welding as an expedient way of sealing pillboxes, and they retrained infantrymen in the specialties they'd need in the field, including the assault of fortified positions and the use of explosives and demolitions. They also repaired roads in the division headquarters sector. Basically, the men were granted an unprecedented period of rest and relaxation, courtesy of the army. They seemed to take advantage of it.

In his next letter, Frank voiced his opinion about civilians who run their mouths about the war: "From the clipping you sent me, the papers make it rather simple to take a town, but it's not the whole story. Oh well let's forget the war, I am for a few days." To illustrate the realities confronted every day by the 80th, Frank sent her his own clipping, headlined, "A Village Lies Still in Death After War Hurtles Through." The article, written by *Stars and Stripes* journalist Jimmy Cannon, began: "The dead hold Farebersviller now. Once the enemy did and then we came. But they returned, and so did we. Today only the dead are there."[57] Cannon's description was based on a fight by the 317th Infantry Regiment.

Above the article was a photo with the heading, "Rolling to the Rhine, Not Through it." The caption reads, "Trucks of the Third Army plow through hub-deep water on a flooded Lorraine road, under weather conditions typical of those encountered in General Patton's current smash toward the Rhine."

The period in reserve did give the men of the 80th Division time to think of things other than war. Frank wrote to Betty on December 8:

55 Organizational History, 318th Infantry Regiment, December 1944, 3; Organizational History, 80th Infantry Division, December 1944, 3-5.

56 After-Action Report, 305th Engineer Combat Battalion, December 1944, sec. 1.

57 Jimmy Cannon, "A Village Lies Still in Death After War Hurtles Through," *Stars and Stripes*, n.d. After the war, Cannon became a well-known sports columnist.

I'm just loafing now and I enjoy it, at least you'll sit down and do something without worrying about running out to do a job. Just finished the pots and pans and while Sinatra and Crosby thrash it out on the radio I'll buzz you a few lines. Received two letters from you yesterday so all in all I'm in a good mood. Our company mess is now set up and that saves us from preparing our own meals. I like the idea because it gives us a break. Trying to cook your own meals as we've done the past four months gets pretty discouraging at times.

On December 10, the men let down their guard and did something that would have been unthinkable during the autumn campaign: they attended a battalion party in the liberated town of Merlebach. As Frank described it to Betty:

Yesterday we went to a show our battalion put on for us in the next town and we had a rather nice time. The Division band played, they had an amateur show and finally a movie at nine o'clock. The Red Cross Girls served coffee, doughnuts and cake. When we got back to our 'house' we had coffee and apple pie. The women had baked them for us. Tonight we are all going to a dance and it should be a riot. Hardly any of the boys speaks French or German and I guess the girls don't speak English. I wasn't going, but everyone else is going, so I guess I'll tag along.

The dance apparently lived up to everyone's expectations because a few days later Frank gave Betty a glowing report. Some unnamed individuals rounded up a number of French girls to entertain the GIs, or as Frank described it, "The dance the other night was a riot. There were about 800 G.I.s and three hundred girls, and hardly anyone could speak. The boys would reach out and grab a girl when they wanted to dance and some couples went through four hours of dancing and yet neither spoke. The girls didn't dance very well and when it came to jitterbugging it was a sad sight. It was a good laugh." It's doubtful Betty got a good laugh, however. Frank's "oh it was just a big joke" descriptions of his encounters with English and French girls must have made Betty nervous.

The dance wasn't the only social event on the engineers' calendar. On December 12, Frank wrote, "Tomorrow is our beer party and I imagine all concerned will have a good time. I haven't had any French beer but from what the boys say it's something like our beer."

B Company continued to wait in Helleringen for the division to get its orders, and Frank got a chance to interact with some French citizens during the long wait. He related, "We have the cutest boy next door, he's two years old and blonde headed. We talk to him in English and he repeats what we say to him. This town is full of babies (young ones) and the boys kid with them all, they are crazy over chocolate." He added, "If I knew we'd be here for a while, I'd start looking for a

Christmas tree. We'll have to have a little Christmas spirit and that's the best way to get it. Probably we'll be fighting Heine again at that time."[58]

If Frank's exuberance over his activities while in reserve gave Betty pause, she found a way to needle him by suggesting she couldn't even recognize him in a photo. Still at Helleringen on December 15, he wrote, "In answer to your question about the picture taken in Paris I'm standing in the rear with a mackinaw on. I must have changed a lot if you can't pick me out. Probably your mom and dad are right."[59]

On December 15, the 305th Combat Engineer Battalion officially reorganized in accordance with the most recent U.S. Army Table of Organization and Equipment (TOE) in order to push as many personnel as possible into the fighting units from the administrative and support positions. This came as B Company was soon to end its two-and-a-half-week-long rest at St. Avold and Helleringen.

On December 18, the division received the order to move out. The 305th joined other 80th units that were already in position to attack the teeth of Hitler's West Wall, the Siegfried Line. This fortified defense system extended for more than 392 miles along the German border, with more than 18,000 bunkers, tunnels, and tank traps. As during previous offensives, B Company moved out to clear the roads ahead of the infantry. The infantry, however, had just commenced the assault on the Siegfried Line when, on December 18, the 80th Division received a sudden change in orders. All hell had broken loose on the First Army's front to the north, in the Ardennes.

---

58 That prediction turned out to be more correct than Frank imagined.

59 Initially, Betty's parents didn't consider Frank a suitable match for their daughter. One of the proudest moments of Frank's life came many years later, when Betty's mother, who had moved in with the Lembos, called Frank upstairs and said, "I did not approve of your marriage to my daughter and I want you to know I was wrong. You have been a wonderful husband to my daughter and father to my grandchildren."

CHAPTER 10

THE BATTLE OF THE BULGE: DEC. 18-31, 1944

TAKING advantage of a period of overcast skies, which kept Allied airpower at bay, on December 16, Hitler unleashed a huge offensive in the Ardennes along an 85-mile front, from Monschau, Germany, in the north, to Diekirch, Luxembourg, in the south. Hitler had secretly been building up troop levels and weaponry in the forested area for months, away from the eyes of Allied intelligence.[1] Twenty-five German divisions, consisting of crack SS and panzer troops and new recruits from very young to old men, broke through a lightly defended gap in U.S. First Army's line. The highly mechanized German assault force caught the Americans by surprise as they settled down to anticipate the Christmas holiday.

The objectives of the German assault were to seize the road network in eastern Belgium and then cross the Meuse River to seize Liege and Antwerp, which they intended to reach before the Americans could regroup and counterattack in force. The hope was to divide the British and American armies, both physically and politically.

The Americans missed many signals that an offensive was being prepared and at first thought it was just a diversionary attack. The Allied high command, however, reacted quickly upon receiving word it was indeed a major offensive. The

---

1 Hugh M. Cole, *The Ardennes: The Battle of the Bulge*, The U.S. Army in World War II: The European Theater of Operations (Washington, DC: Government Printing Office, 1965), 48-212; Steven J. Zaloga, *Battle of the Bulge* (Oxford, UK: Osprey, 2010), 6-7; Bradley, *A Soldier's Story*, 455-59.

Third Army's General Patton was ordered to quickly move a combat command of his 10th Armored Division, which was closest to the Ardennes region, toward the southern end of the German incursion. The Ninth Army's 7th Armored Division was simultaneously ordered to buttress the defensive shoulder in the north. Otherwise, Omar Bradley had few reserves to bolster his overextended forces in the Ardennes. At first, only airborne divisions were at hand in SHAEF reserve, so the 82nd Airborne was ordered to motor north to Werbemont (behind St. Vith) while the 101st Airborne was hastily trucked to the key communications hub at Bastogne.[2]

On December 18, as the Germans poured through the front, Bradley called on Patton to drop his existing plans and reorient the Third Army to help stem the enemy tide. Patton at first balked but quickly recognized the Ardennes was now the big show. He replied he could send the 4th Armored immediately toward Longwy and get the 80th moving the following morning to Luxembourg.[3]

Eisenhower realized, strategically, the German offensive represented an opportunity for the Allies to destroy the German forces in the open rather than continually attack their fortified positions. First, however, the Americans had to halt the offensive, and that required the Third Army to drive north and slam into the southern edge of the German bulge. At a December 19 conference in Verdun, Eisenhower asked Patton how long it would take to turn his army north and counterattack. Patton replied that he could attack with three divisions three days later, on December 22.[4] The historian who assembled Patton's papers termed this "the sublime moment of his career." Other generals present were skeptical. Patton's aide, Col. Charles R. Codman, reported, "There was a stir, a shuffling of

---

2 Bradley, *A Soldier's Story*, 465-67.

3 Blumenson, *Patton Papers*, 596.

4 Ibid., 599. What Patton actually said is reported somewhat differently. Barron, Bradley, and other sources say Patton initially said he could attack with three divisions in 48 hours (which would be December 21), but the consensus emerged he should attack no earlier than December 22 and possibly December 23. See Leo Barron, *Patton at the Battle of the Bulge: How the General's Tanks Turned the Tide at Bastogne* (New York: NAL Caliber, 2014), 60; Bradley, *A Soldier's Life*, 472. In his memoirs, Patton stated Eisenhower wanted him to attack with six divisions, and he replied he could attack with three divisions on the 22nd and that six divisions would take longer (Patton, *War as I Knew It*, 181). Cole supports the same view: "Patton replied that he could start a piecemeal attack in three days [December 22], a coordinated attack in six" (Cole, *Ardennes*, 487). Patton's aide, Col. Charles Codman, reported that Patton promised that three divisions could attack "the morning of December 22nd." (Charles R. Codman, *Drive* [Boston: Little, Brown, 1957], 232). Eisenhower does not address what Patton said; he wrote: "We estimated that Patton could begin a three-division attack by the morning of December 23, possibly by the twenty-second" (*Crusade in Europe*, 351).

feet, as those present straightened up in their chairs. In some faces, skepticism. But through the room the current of excitement leaped like a flame. To disengage three divisions actually in combat and launch them over more than a 100 miles of icy roads straight into the heart of a major attack of unprecedented violence presented problems which few Commanders would have undertaken to resolve in that length of time."[5]

Before he entered the meeting, Patton had ordered his staff to prepare three contingency plans for a northward turn, and he now put them into effect. The 80th Infantry Division, along with the 4th Armored and 26th Infantry divisions, were temporarily reassigned to the III Corps, commanded by Maj. Gen. John Milliken. By the time Eisenhower asked Patton how quickly he could respond, Third Army's momentum toward the Saar had already been stopped and the divisions were ready to move north.[6] The corps command staff and the 4th Armored had already begun the trek to Belgium. (Indeed, the G-2 staff of 4th Armored had already arrived there.) The 80th Division moved out on the same day as the Verdun conference. At noon on December 19, while the conference was still underway, Milliken issued a situation report stating all three divisions were on the move.[7]

The troop movement was very challenging: pulling out of fighting on an eastward-facing front, shifting direction, and motoring more than 100 miles north on unknown, frozen roads against strong resistance. The author of the most complete book on Patton's papers characterized the move as "astonishing, technically difficult, and daring." The entire army must make a 90-degree turn to the north, creating "logistical nightmares—getting divisions on new roads and making sure that supplies reached them from dumps established in quite a different context."[8]

B Company of the 305th Engineers was the lead element in the 80th's motor convoy as it did an about-face from the German border and drove north toward Luxembourg City and the flank of the German offensive. The 80th column advanced 165 miles from the Helleringen reserve area to Lintgen, Luxembourg, in

---

5 Codman, *Drive*, 232.

6 Craig, *The 80th Infantry Division*, 39; Cole, *Ardennes*, 487; After-Action Report, *80th Infantry Division*, December 1944.

7 Barron, *Patton at the Battle of the Bulge*, 58-61; Blumenson, *Patton Papers*, 596-98; Craig, *The 80th Infantry Division*, 39.

8 Blumenson, *Patton Papers*, 600.

36 hours.[9] One soldier from the 317th Infantry who was in the motor convoy recalled, that 25-30 men were in each truck as they "skidded over icy and crowded roads for the entire day and night."[10] The traffic was bumper to bumper on all roads. At first the trucks proceeded in blackout conditions, but Patton ordered them to use full beams and "for the first time since leaving the US, [the convoy] drove with lights on."[11]

The *New York Journal* praised this movement as "a feat as remarkable as any of Stonewall Jackson's foot cavalry."[12]

To add to the shock of the German incursion, there was a sudden change in weather that caught the American troops ill-prepared for winter, since most of them lacked winter clothing or boots. Temperatures plunged to -10°F during the cold days of December. The shoes of some men froze to their feet and had to be cut off. Frostbite became commonplace.

By December 21, B Company had reached Lintgen and started to dig in defensive positions for the 318th Infantry Regiment. The 305th had prepared for a crossing of the Sure River on its way to Germany, but with the adoption of the defensive posture, the Sure instead became a protective barrier. The engineers executed a rare order to blow up the intact bridge over the river to deny it to the Nazis.

There was yet another change in orders the next day, December 22, when the 80th was ordered to abandon its defensive positions and join the attack into the flank of the German salient.[13] One of B Company's platoons left its bivouac at dawn and moved out in support of the 318th while the remainder left Lintgen later that afternoon and drove eight miles to Chau de Birtrange, close to Luxembourg City, where the 305th's command post would remain for the next month.

Each of the 305th's engineer companies operated in direct support of a combat team as the 80th Division moved forward. The 80th attacked along the road northward from Luxembourg City to Ettelbruck, with the 317th Infantry Regiment

---

9 Craig, *The 80th Infantry Division*, 39.

10 Dominique and Hayes, *One Hell of a War*, 143.

11 Ibid.

12 Quoted in Craig, *The 80th Infantry Division*, 40.

13 After-Action Report, 305th Engineer Combat Battalion, December 1944, 2; Craig, *The 80th Infantry Division*, 40.

in reserve.[14] The Nazis had controlled Ettelbruck since 1940, but it had changed hands in September during the headlong Allied advance. The Germans regained control of the city just a few days earlier.[15]

On December 23, the 1st and 3rd battalions of the 318th were given the mission to retake Ettelbruck and prevent the enemy from using that main supply route, but initially they were unable to dislodge the Germans, in large measure because of the unfavorable terrain.[16] The ground was difficult to seize and hold; it was densely forested and marked with steep ridges, deep ravines, and twisting roads, which were covered in snow and ice.

The 318th Infantry initially faced a regiment of the 352nd Volksgrenadier Division, part of German Seventh Army, which had advanced on Ettelbruck from the other direction. There was bitter fighting as the 318th's three battalions struggled with the Germans for control of the city. The 318th fought the enemy house-to-house under artillery and small arms fire before regaining limited control.[17]

Engineers from B Company moved forward into Ettelbruck with other units of the 80th, and late on Christmas Eve, a detail of B Company's demolition men infiltrated enemy-held ground in the town and destroyed three guns and three prime movers. Additional engineer patrols were sent out to determine the condition of the bridges east of town. Casualties among the infantry continued to rise. That night, enemy artillery fire struck and damaged the company's billeting area in Chau de Birtrange.

The 80th's two other infantry regiments also saw action. The 317th advanced on Bourscheid[18] while the 319th attacked the town of Heiderscheid, which was situated along an important supply route to Bastogne. The 319th moved in at 2:30 a.m. on Christmas Eve and spent the rest of the morning engaged in savage house-to-house fighting, fending off several counterattacks by German infantry

---

14 Cole, *Ardennes*, 357.

15 Ibid., 224-27.

16 After-Action Report, 318th Infantry Regiment, December 1944, 2.

17 Craig, *The 80th Infantry Division*, 41; After-Action Report, 318th Infantry Regiment, December 1944, 2.

18 After-Action Report, 80th Infantry Division, December 1944.

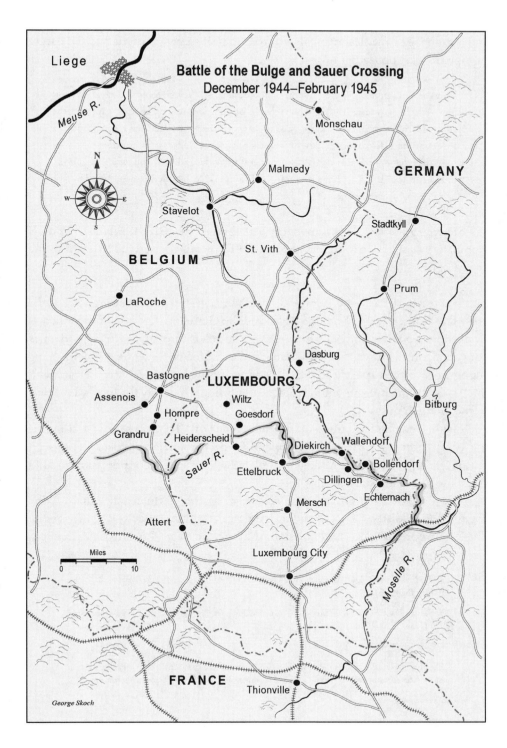

and armor.[19] The memoir of a captain from the 319th gives insight into the nature of the house-to-house fighting:

> When the [infantrymen] were quite near [the buildings], they signaled the tanks to stop firing. . . . They poured through holes made by the gunfire, and quickly captured the houses. Members of the 'Wreckin' Second' bragged that any time they could get into a house on both sides of a street, they could capture all the houses on that street. . . . They would throw a grenade through a window, let it explode, and then follow it through the window, firing at anything they saw. . . . It was a savage, cold-blooded assault, fueled by fear and an animal-like excitement.[20]

Shortly after the engagement in Ettelbruck, the 318th Infantry, with B Company's 1st Platoon in support, was given a new mission: aid the 101st Airborne at Bastogne.

The town of Bastogne, about 35 miles northwest of Luxembourg City as the crow flies, was critical to both the Allies and the Germans. The town functioned as a transportation hub, with all seven of the main roads through the lower Ardennes converging in the town. For the Germans, Bastogne was essential to maintaining supply lines as their spearheads advanced toward the Meuse. As was the case with the Allies, maintaining an uninterrupted supply line, especially for fuel, was critical to the German mission.

Major General Troy Middleton, commander of VIII Corps, now assisted by the 101st Airborne, ordered his troops to hold Bastogne at all costs.[21] Although Patton initially questioned Middleton's plan, he later said, "Your decision to hold Bastogne was a stroke of genius."[22]

The stakes were high and time was short as the German 5th Panzer Army encircled and isolated the town and the Americans within. Initially, Patton assigned the 4th Armored Division the mission of lifting the siege.[23] At the time, the 80th

---

19 "Reducing the Bulge," interview with Capt. George W. Harmon, S-1, 2nd Battalion, 319th Infantry Regiment.

20 George W. Harmon, "Memories of Heiderscheid," www.thetroubleshooters.com/ 702nd/maddog002.html.

21 Cole, *Ardennes*, 306.

22 Letter from George S. Patton Jr. to Troy Middleton, April 25, 1945 www.unit histories.com/units_index/default.asp?file=../units/3rd%20US%20Army%20letter.asp.

23 Cole, *Ardennes*, 356.

Division was still heavily engaged around Ettelbruck along the southern neck of the bulge.

The defenders of Bastogne were increasingly hard-pressed and let the approaching Third Army troops know of their urgent need for relief. On December 23, 101st Airborne commander Brig. Gen. Anthony McAuliffe sent the message, "Sorry I did not get to shake hands today. I was disappointed." A more succinct staff officer followed up with a message received by 4th Armored: "There is only one more shopping day before Christmas."[24]

On Christmas Eve, General McBride received orders from III Corps commander Milliken to provide two battalions to add an infantry punch to the 4th Armored attack. In response, McBride formed a task force from the 80th, and the 1st and 2nd battalions of the 318th were attached to the 4th Armored, even though the effective fighting strength of the 2nd Battalion had been reduced to 200 riflemen[25] and the 1st Battalion was also significantly below strength. Moreover, all of the 1st Battalion's officers, including the commanding officer, had been killed or wounded in the previous days' fighting, and the battalion had taken more than 100 casualties.[26] Basically, McBride was assigning companies to do a battalion's job.

B Company's 1st Platoon was assigned as the engineer complement for the 2nd battalion on their mission to Bastogne. As a 1st Platoon squad leader, Sgt. Frank Lembo was a critical leader in the detachment, which was tasked to clear roads, set up roadblocks, and sweep mines from the snow-covered ground. The 22nd Field Artillery Battalion, the 8th Tank Battalion, and a company of the 10th Armored Infantry Battalion also supported the 4th Armored.

The contingent from the 80th left the front lines near Ettelbruck on Christmas Eve, after disengaging with some difficulty. During the night, the men from the 80th's task force climbed onto trucks and traveled 40 miles in the bitter cold over icy roads to join the 4th Armored Division. A guide from the 4th Armored met the column and led it north through the towns of Arlon, Attert, and Martelsange.

As events transpired, the 318th's two infantry battalions were given separate objectives. The 2nd Battalion was to be the principal infantry element engaged in

24 Quoted in ibid., 531.

25 History of Second Battalion, 318 Infantry Regiment, 26.

26 After-Action Report, 318th Infantry Regiment, December 1944, 2; Action of the 1st Battalion of the 318th Regiment in the Drive Toward Bastogne," Interview with Maj. George Connaughton, January 29, 1945; Barron, *Patton at the Battle of the Bulge*, 244.

the relief operation. Lembo's platoon was attached to this battalion in support of the action at Bastogne.

The 318th's 1st Battalion, attached to Combat Command A (CCA), was initially able to advance through thickly wooded and mountainous terrain and reach its first objective, Tintange, despite stiff opposition. The CCA commander stated the battalion would probably have to fight to get to its line of departure, and he was correct.[27] The battalion was accompanied by tanks from the 35th Armored Battalion.[28]

Despite strong resistance, the understrength 1st Battalion seized Honville on December 26. But the perceived slow advance incurred the wrath of headquarters. Undoubtedly fueled by impatience from higher-ups, Col. Lansing MacVicker, the commander of the 318th, relieved the 1st Battalion's newly appointed commanding officer of his command (the previous commanding officer had been killed at Ettelbruck) just after the battalion occupied Honville.[29]

The 318th's 2nd Battalion, with the 305th's 1st Platoon and Lembo's squad, joined up with Combat Command B (CCB) of the 4th Armored at Fauvillers, about 11 miles from Bastogne, shortly after midnight on the early morning of December 25.[30] Its mission was to drive a wedge through the enemy lines and continue on through the nearby villages to Bastogne.

Infantrymen from the 318th jumped off into the Lambay Chenet woods early on Christmas morning. They met fierce opposition from the reinforced German 5th Paratroop Division, which was well dug in there. The men from the 318th fought hand-to-hand with bayonets and hand grenades in their approach to the besieged city. The 318th's 2nd Battalion was continuously exposed to machine gun

---

27 After-Action Report, Annex 1, Covering Operations of the 318th Infantry Minus, During the Attachment to 4th Armored Division; Interview with Maj. George W. Connaughton, former commanding officer, 1st Battalion, 318th Infantry, 3; Barron, *Patton at the Battle of the Bulge*, 260.

28 Barron, *Patton at the Battle of the Bulge*, 243-54; Cole, *Ardennes*, 548-49; Interview with Maj. George W. Connaughton.

29 History, 318th Infantry Regiment, December 1944; After-Action Report, Annex 1, Covering Operations of the 318th Infantry Minus, During the Attachment to 4th Armored Division; Interview with Maj. George W. Connaughton, 4.

30 History of Second Battalion, 318th Infantry Regiment, 26.

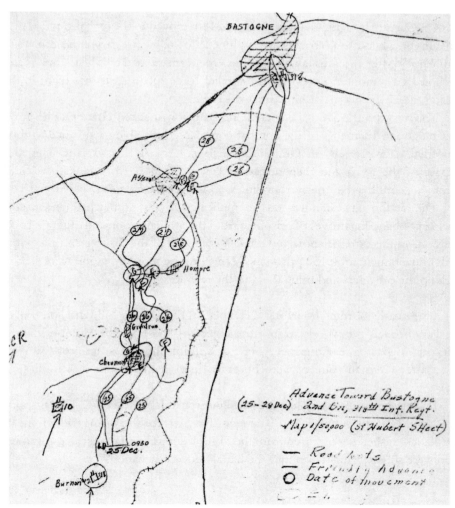

Hand-drawn map showing 2nd Battalion's approach to Bastogne.[31] *Prepared for 2nd battalion after action report.*

and small arms fire and suffered heavy casualties, further weakening its already reduced fighting strength.[32]

31 After-Action Report, 2nd Battalion, 318th Infantry Regiment.

32 Action of the 2nd Battalion, 318th Regiment, in the Bastogne Salient; Interviews conducted January 25, 1945; Cole, *Ardennes*, 548-49.

On Christmas night, infantry from the 318th moved to the high ground east of Chaumont while the Germans were pinned down by fire from the 8th Tank Battalion.[33] After a vicious tank battle, the Americans cleared out the Germans and occupied Chaumont.[34] The men on the relief force spent Christmas night in the village and enjoyed a makeshift Christmas dinner.

The next day the 318th's depleted 2nd Battalion attacked Grandru, just north of Chaumont. Elements of the combat command were able to advance to their objective, a crossroads on Grandru's outskirts. An attack company feigned a bypass of the town and then turned and, with support from tanks, took it.[35] Firefights continued in the surrounding woods over the next day.

The action at Grandru was complicated by a somewhat unexpected problem—handling droves of prisoners from the 5th Paratroop and other German divisions in the extreme snow and cold. A company of the 318th's 2nd Battalion, with only 50 men, took 150 prisoners. Men from the mortar platoon were sent to pick up the prisoners and bring them to the rear area.[36]

In the early morning hours of December 27, the 318th's 2nd Battalion fought its way through the woods to its next objective, the town of Hompre on the outskirts of Bastogne. American troops moved into houses on the road west of town after German soldiers were observed leaving the woods and infiltrating them.[37]

By this point the skies had cleared, and the GIs observed C-47 transports overhead, airlifting supplies into Bastogne. They watched in dismay when one of the planes crashed nearby. Men from the 318th went forward to rescue the airmen, who were subsequently taken into the battalion for evacuation.[38]

---

33 Cole, *Ardennes*, 539.

34 Annex 1 to 318th Infantry Regiment After-Action Report for December 1944; Action of the 2nd Battalion, 318th Regiment, 80th Division, in the Bastogne Salient.

35 Action of the 2nd Battalion, 318th Regiment, 80th Division, in the Bastogne Salient, interviews with Lt. Col. Glenn Gardner et al.

36 Annex 1 to 318th Infantry Regiment After-Action Report for December 1944.

37 Cole, *Ardennes*, 551; Green and Brown, *Patton's Third Army*, 201; Action of the 2nd Battalion, 318th Regiment, 80th Division, in the Bastogne Salient, interviews with Lt. Col. Glenn Gardner et al.

38 Annex 1 to 318th Infantry Regiment After-Action Report for December 1944; Action of the 2nd Battalion, 318th Regiment, 80th Division, in the Bastogne Salient.

A column of tanks from Combat Command R of the 4th Armored, consisting initially of seven tanks and other vehicles, had moved ahead to Bastogne on December 26. The linkup occurred in the late afternoon at a Belgian fortification on the outskirts of town. Lieutenant Charles Boggess led three tanks toward the linkup and symbolically ended the siege by shaking hands with Lt. Duane Webster of the 326th Engineers, 101st Airborne.[39] A lot more fighting remained before Bastogne could truly be considered liberated, however. The supply line into town was not secure, and Bastogne's ability to stand was still in doubt.[40]

Early on December 27, shortly after Boggess linked up with the Bastogne outpost, a four-man patrol from the 318th's 2nd Battalion, including 1st Lt. Walter Carr and three enlisted men, went into enemy-held territory to establish contact with the command elements of the 101st Airborne at Bastogne. The patrol made it through 4,000 yards of enemy-held terrain, contacted an outpost of the 26th Engineer Combat Battalion on the defensive perimeter, and was escorted to the 101st Airborne's command post.[41] The patrol returned to the 318th's headquarters with vital intelligence, including an exceptionally useful overlay map of positions within the circle.[42]

On December 27, the 2nd Battalion of the 318th continued to slog forward with the 10th Armored Infantry, finished taking the village of Hompre, and by nightfall reached the outskirts of Bastogne at the small village of Assenois, where German soldiers still blocked the supply route into Bastogne.[43] During the night,

---

39 Green and Brown, *Patton's Third Army*, 205-8; Christer Bergstrom, *The Ardennes, 1944-1945: Hitler's Winter Offensive* (Havertown, PA: Casemate, 2014), 298-99; Cole, *Ardennes*, 554-55.

40 Barron, *Patton at the Battle of the Bulge*, 317. Most historians take the view that the linkup of Boggess and his tanks with the Bastogne forces represents the symbolic end of the siege, although most point out that much more fighting was needed to make the supply line secure and assure American control on the town. The 318th Regiment, which had its own first-into-Bastogne claim (Lt. Walter Carr's patrol), took a different view: the unit history for December somewhat dismissively stated, "Early in the evening of 26 Dec tank elements of the 4th Armored Division were able to get into the beleaguered city but unable to return" (318th history, December 1944, 6).

41 Carr was something of a patrol specialist. An undated *New York Daily News* article titled "Claims 'First' into Bastogne" described Carr as "an experienced night prowler" who had earned a Silver Star for bringing back valuable information on previous patrols (and a second for his Bastogne mission).

42 History for December 1944, 318th Infantry Regiment, 6; Action of the 2nd Battalion, 318th Regiment, 80th Division, in the Bastogne Salient.

43 Action of the 2nd Battalion, 318th Regiment, 80th Division, in the Bastogne Salient; Interview with Lt. Col. Glenn Gardner et al.

the battalion's commanding officer received intelligence that as many as 4,000 enemy troops and 25 to 40 tanks occupied the nearby woods. The men in the depleted battalion nervously waited until daybreak, not certain when an attack might occur. It fortunately turned out to be a false alarm; the Germans had evacuated the woods.[44]

The 1st Battalion of the 318th, now commanded by a captain, fought off opposition and seized Liverchamps on December 27. The Germans counterattacked with automatic weapons and nebelwerfers.[45] American tanks blasted the woods around Liverchamps, and air strikes were called in. The tanks stayed with the infantry when permitted by the steep and wooded terrain and fired into the woods to keep the opposition in check. The infantry later took the town. Shortly afterward, the 1st Battalion was relieved of its attachment to the 80th's task force and did not enter Bastogne.

Sergeant Lembo took a few moments to write on December 27: "We've been away from our company and . . . today we are having a late meal. We're up here (?) with some infantry and armor, or in other words we're organic again." He told Betty, "The battle that was going on Christmas day is still going on in increasing fury. I guess something has got to give soon, and I doubt it will be us. I guess this damn war will never end and no doubt you people back home got a severe jolt." During the bitter fighting Frank must have missed his buddy Scotty, who had left the outfit for a hernia surgery months earlier. In the midst of the battle, he wrote, "From the look of things I don't think Scotty will be back with us. He should have been here by now but he hasn't arrived so he's with another outfit I guess. It's just as well he's left because there's only a few men left of his original squad."

On December 28, the 4th Armored led off when the 318th's 2nd Battalion attacked through the woods toward the Bastogne perimeter. At 8:00 a.m. the first company from the battalion reached the engineers' outpost line around Bastogne, and two other companies moved off and occupied buildings on the town's

---

44 History for December 1944, 318th Infantry Regiment, 6; Action of the 2nd Battalion, 318th Regiment, 80th Division, in the Bastogne Salient.

45 Staff Sergeant Bob Burrows requested a transfer from a position as a driver at corps headquarters to the infantry at the beginning of the Battle of the Bulge, joining the 2nd Battalion of the 317th. He commented about being under fire: "We were always under fire, but you didn't take it personal: they're not shooting at me." Regarding machine guns, he fatalistically observed, "you get the fire, you don't know where it's coming from, you just hear the bullets zipping by, like bees. There's not much you can do about it unless you get a mortar on it." Regarding *nebelwerfers* ("screaming meemies"), he said, "They sent chills down my spine." (Interview with Rishi Sharma, September 14, 2017.)

southeast corner. The proud author of a summary report on the 2nd Battalion's actions at Bastogne wrote: "At exactly 1000 the company commander of G company reported to Col. Gardner that the mission was complete, the company had reached the outpost line around Bastogne."[46]

By afternoon the action had slowed enough to allow troops from the 2nd Battalion to warm up and put on dry clothes. They even joined in on a belated Christmas dinner in the ruins of the buildings in Bastogne—turkey with all the trimmings.[47] For once, the depleted status of the battalion (187 total members at the start of the day's attacks) was an advantage. A soldier noted, "Since rations had been drawn for 350 men, there was ample food for all."[48] By December 28, after days of bitter fighting, the enemy was cleared out of the area south and west of Bastogne, and the task force from the 80th Division consolidated its position. On December 29, the 2nd Battalion and its supporting troops were relieved from attachment to the task force; the men from the 80th left Bastogne and worked their way through a barrage of nebelwerfer fire, in blinding snow and bitter cold, to rejoin the rest of the division at Ettelbruck.[49]

Five days after taking off to join in the relief of Bastogne, Frank Lembo and the rest of the 305th's 1st Platoon rejoined the rest of B Company. The task force elements went back into combat around Ettelbruck, and Lembo and the remainder of the 1st Platoon resumed its engineering work.

On December 29, Patton praised the troops who had fought through the German ring and relieved Bastogne: "The relief of Bastogne is the most brilliant operation we have thus far performed and is in my mind the outstanding achievement of the war."[50]

In the aftermath of what became known as the Battle of the Bulge, the 2nd Battalion of the 318th Infantry Regiment received a Presidential Unit Citation for its actions to relieve Bastogne. The citation was also extended to units attached to the 318th, including the 1st Platoon of B Company, 305th Engineer Combat Battalion. Forty-four engineers (including Sgt. Frank T. Lembo) were duly "authorized to wear the Presidential Unit Citation Badge." This was one of only six

---

46 Annex 1 to 318th Infantry Regiment After-Action Report for December 1944; Action of the 2nd Battalion, 318th Regiment, 80th Division, in the Bastogne Salient, 7.

47 History of the Second Battalion, 318th Infantry Regiment, 28.

48 Action of the 2nd Battalion, 318th Regiment, 80th Division, in the Bastogne Salient, 7.

49 After-Action Report, 318th Infantry Regiment, December 1944.

50 Blumenson, *Patton Papers*, 608.

Presidential Unit Citations issued to 80th Infantry Division units throughout the war.

The citation reads:

> The 2nd Battalion, 318th Inf. [and all attached units] is cited for outstanding performance of duty during the period 25-28 December 1944. The battalion was heavily engaged with the enemy in the vicinity of Ettelbruck, Luxembourg, when it was withdrawn from the front lines for the movement to the Bastogne, Belgium area. Its effective rifle fighting strength had been reduced to 200 men. Attacking on Christmas Day after several days without rest, the Battalion began its assault of the enemy position encircling Bastogne. Throughout the next four days and three nights the depleted Battalion battled its way in freezing temperatures through the strongly held woods and villages separating our troops from the besieged forces in Bastogne. The stubborn resistance of the enemy, and well dug in positions required constant use of the bayonet and hand grenade in their destruction. Suffering heavy casualties, constantly exposed to raking enemy machine gun fire and small arms fire from flanking positions, the battalion fought on with an unrelenting determination that overcame all obstacles, routed the enemy, and established contact with the forces within Bastogne. The aggressiveness of the heroic infantrymen of the 2nd Battalion, 318th Infantry reflects the finest traditions of the Army of the United States.

While the 318th's 1st and 2nd battalions were engaged with the Bastogne task force, the 80th's other regiments continued to struggle with the Germans around Ettelbruck. On December 25, the 3rd Battalion of the 318th fought for control of the city, supported by B Company's 2nd and 3rd platoons, while the 317th attempted to seize Kehmen and Bourscheid against heavy resistance and the 319th fought off an afternoon counterattack and seized Ringel.[51] On December 26, a patrol from the 318th's 3rd Battalion found that resistance had ceased in Ettelbruck, and the battalion occupied the town.[52] Nevertheless, Ettelbruck remained the focus of operations by the infantry and B Company through the end of December.

On December 28, Field Order 24 put the entire XII Corps, including the 80th Division, in defensive positions.[53] The 305th maintained its defensive posture

---

51 After-Action Report, 80th Infantry Division, December 1944; Reducing the Bulge, interview with Capt. George Harmon, 319th Infantry Regiment.

52 History, 318th Infantry, December 1944, 7; After-Action Report, 80th Division, December 1944.

53 80th Infantry Regiment Operational History, December 1944, 24.

between December 27 and 29, but the engineers' work continued. They laid minefields, blew five bridges, installed abatis and roadblocks, cut log foxhole covers, cleared enemy mines, buried dead animals, destroyed enemy ammunition and explosives, and sanded and maintained the roads. At the end of the month, the company's after-action report noted the engineers set up and maintained roadblocks on bridges northeast of Ettelbruck and on roads northward.[54]

Frank's final letter of 1944 was datelined "Somewhere in Europe, December 30." It was a newsy communication: "It sure is funny, one day you're living in a two-room shack in one country and the next you're in a huge mansion in another. I've been in four countries [England, France, Luxembourg, Belgium] since I've come overseas, and the one I'm in now [Luxembourg] seems most like the states."

He told her he had "returned back to the company yesterday and there was quite a lot of mail for me. I received your sweater and thanks a lot. It will come in handy with this cold weather we are having. I had a field day with three other packages from mom. We ought to get some letters one of these days. Mom sent me a little bottle of rye whiskey, so we killed it. It was in a hair tonic bottle so it's the first time I've ever drunk out of a spoon. There was only about two glasses full." He mentioned, "Someone was telling me Scotty is in a General Services Engr Regiment so I guess he won't be around us any more. He's just as well off because they are quite a way back and not in any danger. I had hoped that he would return to us. Well Toots I'm going to go get some fresh air so until the next letter I remain your G.I. Joe overseas and with it all the love in the world."

He included a small card with Patton's Christmas message to Third Army troops: "To each officer and soldier in the Third United States Army I wish a Merry Christmas. I have full confidence in your courage, devotion to duty and skill in battle. We march in our might to complete victory. May God's blessing rest upon each of you on this Christmas Day."

On the reverse side of the card was Patton's weather prayer, written for the general by his chaplain amid the drenching downpours of the Lorraine Campaign and distributed during the Bastogne Campaign:[55]

54 After-Action Report, 305th Engineer Combat Battalion, December 1944.

55 The movie "*Patton*" shows Patton requesting this prayer during the relief of Bastogne, and this is a popular myth, but he actually had it written several weeks earlier. The author of the prayer, Msgr. James H. O'Neill, described the story of the prayer in "The True Story of the Patton Prayer," *Review of the News*, October 6, 1971 (www.pattonhq.com/prayer.html).

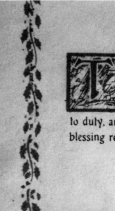

HEADQUARTERS
THIRD UNITED STATES ARMY

To each officer and soldier in the Third United States Army, I wish a Merry Christmas. I have full confidence in your courage, devotion to duty, and skill in battle. We march in our might to complete victory. May God's blessing rest upon each of you on this Christmas Day.

G. S. PATTON, JR.,
Lieutenant General,
Commanding, Third United States Army.

General Patton's Christmas greeting to the soldiers of Third Army. *Third Army artist*

Almighty and most merciful Father, we humbly beseech Thee of Thy great goodness, to restrain these immoderate rains with which we have to contend. Grant us fair weather for Battle. Graciously hearken to us as soldiers who call upon Thee that armed with Thy power, we may advance from victory to victory, and crush the oppression and wickedness of our enemies and establish Thy justice among men and nations. Amen.

PRAYER

ALMIGHTY and most merciful Father, we humbly beseech Thee, of Thy great goodness, to restrain these immoderate rains with which we have had to contend. Grant us fair weather for Battle. Graciously hearken to us as soldiers who call upon Thee that armed with Thy power, we may advance from victory to victory, and crush the oppression and wickedness of our enemies, and establish Thy justice among men and nations. Amen.

Patton's weather prayer, distributed with Patton's Christmas greeting to Third Army.

Third Army artist

American GIs dig in near Bastogne. *US Army*

The December 1944 after-action report of the 305th Engineers concluded with these rare words of wisdom: "We are now a battle-wise outfit, know our jobs well, and look forward to an early victorious end."[56] Their most challenging river crossing (the Sauer), difficult fighting, and many miles still lay ahead of them before that victorious end would be achieved more than four months later.

56 After-Action Report, 305th Engineer Combat Battalion, December 1944, 3.

CHAPTER 11

CLOSING UP THE BULGE: JAN. 1-31, 1945

THE relief of Bastogne did not end the Germans' Ardennes offensive or eliminate the danger. A month of hard winter fighting remained before the Germans could be pushed back to the positions they had held on December 16, 1944, prior to the campaign.

New Year's Day 1945 found the 305th Engineer Combat Battalion operating chiefly west and northwest of Ettelbruck in support of the 80th's infantry regiments, which were fighting to gain control of the surrounding towns and woods. The B Company command post was a few miles from Luxembourg City, at a site not far from an imposing castle at Chau de Birtrange. The company remained in this position through January 20.

Although the Allies had effectively blunted the Nazi counteroffensive into northern Luxembourg and southern Belgium, German troops continued to fight ferociously around Ettelbruck and other towns near the German homeland. Ironically, many of the defenders were youths and older men—less adept than typical German soldiers but just as fanatical and no less deadly.

Despite January's heavy fighting to close the bulge, hectic days were interspersed with boredom, and Frank found some quiet time to renew his correspondence with Betty. He began the New Year on January 1, 1945, with a letter from "Somewhere in Luxembourg" (the military censor's designation for Frank's location). "New Year's evening and now all the holidays are gone, and my fondest hope now in this coming year is we will be able to get back together again. Today was a simple G.I. day for us here, we finished a bridge we started yesterday and late in the afternoon we had a turkey dinner."

US Armor fighting Germans on January 1, 1945, in Ardennes campaign. *Army Signal Corps*

Perhaps it was the New Year that led Frank to reflect on his experiences since leaving the States six months earlier. The fact that so many positive memories were fresh on his mind, in a year that was so horrific, testifies to his hopeful nature. As if to remind Betty that the Frank she knew as her Hawthorne sweetheart had changed and grown as a result of his experience in Europe, he wrote,

> I was just thinking about that last day together that we had, and how perfect it was, and how long a way I've come since then. I can remember that boat ride to England, our trip across the Channel, going into action and suffering a thousand deaths when we heard our first artillery shell, the mad dash across France—a ride with its wine, flowers, ripe tomatoes and eggs—the storming of our first river and the fighting beyond, Christmas in Belgium, New Year in Luxembourg. . . . Yes we've come a long way. We're a little tired, a little older, and a little bitter. We fight hoping each battle is the last one with thoughts of going home and enjoying a peaceful life. Our thoughts run to our sweethearts who we long for, each letter being a five-minute furlough with the one you love—yes darling just thinking—

As usual, Frank was able to see beyond the destruction that disfigured the villages to reflect on the beauty of the landscape surrounding him. He never stopped feeling awe at the sights of Europe. "Luxembourg would be an ideal place to spend the holidays if it were peaceful. Christmas trees line the roads in the thousands and all were bedecked with snow. I rather like the country. We were recently on a mission in Belgium and spent Christmas day there."

He added, "Things have quieted down a little since we first got here, every now and then a shell plunks in, and a few German planes come over, but that's about all now. That's the way this war goes, for a few days all heck pops loose and you wonder if you'll come out in one piece and then it quiets down to a lull again. I'm waiting patiently for that last lull."

Frank shared several of his grumblings. A recurring theme was his perception that American civilians led a cushy lifestyle with little regard for the war. He confessed, "Last night we all had a good time and we all felt pretty good. I guess if the people back home can do it we could too for a night, so we 'dood' it." On a more personal level, he admonished Betty in a way that was almost unheard of from a man of Frank's civility. He told her in no uncertain terms that he was "sorry to hear my swearing offends you. I guess I just forget myself, but honey if it was when I said Heine is a bastard, I still will say the same. I'll try to remember, though if I forget bear with me. I must say it's going to be hard to get used to civilian life without some embarrassment."

Frank felt no pity for the Nazis, having observed firsthand the cruelties they inflicted on civilians. And like the brass and many people on the homefront, Frank was rattled by his recent experience in the Ardennes offensive. He angrily wrote,

> From the looks of things we'll have to fight our way right to Berlin, and I hope we burn that path soon. We all thought this war was over, and I guess the only way to get it over with is to destroy Germany, her soldiers, her civilians, and the ground they live on. We are just too damn soft. Instead of killing their prisoners we take them. I can't complain, I've done it myself, but I do hope we all learned a lesson. If our own eyes can't teach us, then nothing else will.

A day or so later he wrote, "I'm pretty darn disgusted with everything over here. We fight like heck and then someone screws up and Heine sets us for a loop, but at home no one seems to care, and here we beat our heads for nothing. I don't know, it's a screwy world."

As if to remind the engineers that the Battle of the Bulge was not yet over, the men were awakened at 4:00 a.m. on January 2 by a two-hour enemy artillery barrage, combined with an air raid, that pounded their Chau de Birtrange billeting area. Twenty-four shells were counted after the morning light. Later that morning, Frank told Betty:

Things are normal around here, and I'm a little tired. We had a little excitement last night. Heine bombers were over and dropped some bombs in the vicinity. I thought the house was going to fall. The house started shaking us in the middle of the night and every five minutes they threw another shell in uncomfortably close. You would just about get to sleep and another one was singing on its way, and the glass would fly and you'd wait for the next one, so I lost some sleep. War is a crazy thing—believe me.

In these early days of January, B Company supported the infantry regiments as they struggled to advance through the difficult terrain around Ettelbruck toward their next objective, Wiltz. At the same time the infantry needed to protect itself against possible enemy counterattacks from the north and east. The 305th maintained the 80th Division's defenses, laying minefields, constructing abatis, digging in command posts for the infantry, and providing GIs with log foxhole covers and dug-in machine gun emplacements.

Heavy combat persisted day after day, but the infantry's progress toward Wiltz was impeded by the unrelenting subzero temperatures, snow, and ice. The incidence of frostbite increased.

Sergeant Gerald Virgil Myers of Company G, 317th Infantry, commented on the weather:

By the end of December, winter had set in with a vengeance. There were fifteen to eighteen inches of snow on the ground, with the winds blowing at ten to forty miles per hour. We were finally issued long overcoats. After plodding around in the snow, ice formed on the bottoms of our coats from being dragged in the snow. I seen as much as twenty to twenty five pounds of ice collected on our coats. The GI's would take either their bayonets or daggers to knock off the ice.[1]

Staff Sergeant Bob Burrows of the 317th also spoke of the conditions during the Battle of the Bulge Campaign: "There were no living conditions. It was survival conditions. The clothes I had on the whole month were the clothes I had on when I left Corps headquarters. I had no overcoat, no blanket."[2]

The weather also impacted engineer operations. According to a 305th after-action report: "During the entire month the weather was bitter cold and below freezing. Our men were out day and night. In addition, they were subjected

---

1   Quoted in Douglas Rice, *Through Our Eyes: Eyewitness Accounts of World War II* (New York: iUniverse, 2008), 135.

2   Interview with Rishi Sharma, September 14, 2017.

to more artillery, mortar and nebelwerfer fire than ever before." It further notes that bulldozer blades could not penetrate the frozen soil, so "the initial hole had to be blasted before the men could go to work digging emplacements or burying dead animals."[3] The 305th Engineers supply section added that artillery units "began to draw demolitions in order to make gun emplacements."[4] The after-action report did have one positive observation, however: "bridging operations were not on an extensive scale" because the rivers were not that wide and simple bridges sufficed.[5]

Road-clearing operations continued to consume much of the engineers' time. Snowdrifts made roads nearly impassable, particularly along the narrow, winding roads that surrounded the small towns. Every day's fresh snowfall complicated the work even more. Where engineer patrols identified hazardous areas of snow and ice, the men hauled in sand from the only sandpit in the sector, spread sand and cinders, and used their equipment to scrape off the accumulations of ice. Snow fences had to be improvised. The army found the engineers a handful of plows to attach to their two-and-a-half-ton trucks, but these makeshift plows were ineffective and unreliable. They were soon abandoned in favor of more traditional methods of snow clearing: picks and shovels.[6]

On January 6, the 80th Division was ordered to resume a limited offensive. The 166th Engineer Combat Battalion put in a bridge across the Sure River, and the 319th conducted an attack across the bridge to seize the towns of Goesdorf (1st Battalion), Dahl (3rd Battalion), and Heiderscheid (2nd Battalion). The 1st Battalion of the 317th fought its way into Niederfeulen.[7] The attack was supported by engineers from the 305th's C Company, who were called in to act as infantrymen in the attacks on Goesdorf, Dahl, and Nocher.[8] After taking these towns, the infantry fought off several counterattacks over the next few days, and for the moment the 80th did not attempt to continue the advance.[9]

Frank couldn't help but dwell on the foul weather and incessant artillery barrages in his letters to Betty. On January 7, he wrote, "Today was a rather busy

---

3 After-Action Report, 305th Engineer Combat Battalion, January 1945, 3.

4 Historical Journal of Supply, 305th Engineer Combat Battalion, January 1945, 3.

5 After-Action Report, 305th Engineer Combat Battalion, January 1945, 3.

6 Historical Journal of Supply, 305th Engineer Combat Battalion, 3.

7 Reducing the Bulge, interview with Capt. George W. Harmon, 319th Infantry Regiment, 10; 80th Division Operational History, January 1945, 5.

8 80th Division Operational History, January 1945, 5.

9 80th Division Operational History, January 1945, 6.

Soldiers of 317th march across temporarily repaired bridge near
Goesdorf, Luxembourg. *Army Signal Corps*

day and it was unusual for a change. We've been sanding roads down because of the
slippery conditions and this evening we blew a bridge sky high." He continued,
"We're in the midst of a snow storm now, so when we wake up in the morning we'll
probably have a nice layer of snow. There's a pair of ski's in the house here and a
nice hill in back so maybe we'll have some fun."

Being mindful of fun, he continued, "This is certainly a 'Pin Up' world, almost
everything we get there's a so-called pin-up picture, 'Yank,' 'Stars & Stripes,'
'Newsweek,' 'Time' and almost everything else. I guess they want to boost our
morale, only we don't want pictures we want the real thing—our girlfriends and
wives."

Frank's resumption of letter-writing increased his concern about mail delivery
to the front: "We haven't had mail delivery since my last letter. I guess one of these
days all heck will pop loose, but for now it's just sitting and waiting for Heine to
bump his head against a stone wall." He added, "I believe that most of the mail is
going by boat, and will so until summer comes, but we're satisfied with mail
whether it's late or early. I guess it's because we have to be." Mail never came often
enough for the GIs. Without mail the evenings went by slowly and the dark seemed
deeper. Frank let her know that a lot of the mail coming through was from early
November, "so you can see it's a screwed up affair. Every once in awhile we'll get a
letter that took about nine days to get here, but they are really few and far between."

305th Engineers work on roads. *US Army*

On January 11, the 319th Infantry sent a patrol toward Bockholz. When it encountered no opposition, the patrol took the town almost without firing a shot. E Company entered the area without being discovered and "entered the enemy CP, capturing the entire CP group taking 25 PWs in the building." Other German soldiers were also taken by surprise. The company cleared the town in only two hours, took 78 prisoners, and fired only five shots.[10]

10 Reducing the Bulge, 2nd Battalion, 319th Infantry Division; Interview with Capt. George W. Harmon, 11; see also 80th Division Operational History, January 1945, 9; Reducing the Bulge, 319th Infantry Regiment, interviews with Maj. Ralph Wevers and Capt. Harold Memmer, 8.

The tasks of the 305th Engineers were modified to fit the evolving tactical situation as the line advanced. They blocked the eastern approaches to the flanks and cleared roads along the division's path of advance. The latter involved removing wrecked vehicles and other obstacles, clearing mines, and checking towns for mines and booby traps. The engineers also constructed a bypass, filled a bomb crater, retrieved American tanks that had slid off the road, and installed trip flares to prevent infantrymen at the front of the line from being surprised.[11]

B Company's demolition men were also kept busy. The company's 2nd Platoon went into enemy territory to destroy a stone bridge, and a patrol demolished another bridge east of Ettelbruck, across the Sure River. On January 9, in preparation for the bridge demolition, the 3rd Platoon put in a crater to use as a roadblock.

The engineers were surprised by some unexpected free time; the army was clearly aware the fighting at the bulge had taken its toll on the troops. Frank wrote to Betty "from Luxembourg" on January 10 and happily reported: "Today there wasn't any work for us and about five miles back there was a U.S.O. show so we jumped on the trucks and took off. It was fairly good and there were four girls and

305th Engineers prepare abates. *US Army*

11 After-Action Report, 305th Engineer Combat Battalion, January 1945, 1-3.

two men in it. The humor was of the raw type and the singing and dancing fair, but it did give us a laugh and was worth going to."

Betty seemed to have a casual attitude toward the details of the war, which Frank found frustrating and even negligent, especially now, after the Ardennes offensive. He told her, "I'm sending tonight's 'Stars & Stripes' home and you can put the whole issue away for me in the scrap book. A lot of it has to do with our Christmas and it will be a good remembrance. What amazes me is the lack of interest in the news you show. This counterattack affects us all so vitally over here and yet you never mentioned it in your letters, but I guess you're too busy to read the newspapers, or people just get accustomed to a war being on."[12] Despite his irritation, he proudly added: "I imagine you have your troubles keeping track where we are at, but usually where it's roughest or someone is needed in a hurry you'll find our division."

He wrote bitterly the next day on the same theme:

Some of our boys who were wounded in our earlier days returned today and the stories of civilian life and the attitudes in England seem to show the same end as the last war, to hell with the guy fighting the war. Oh well we'll have to get it over with first, and then we find our place in civilian life. It's not a problem, after fighting a war civilian life should be easy but we all wonder what the future will bring.

Frank filled the rest of his January 11 letter with some small details of soldier life: "I was debating whether to buy a watch, but it's a cheap price. The one I got from you keeps such good time, and besides I was given a Bulova when I took over as Platoon sergeant." He let her know about friends in the squad: "Bill is a good kid, and he's loads of fun. His first wife died, and he got married again while in Dix—as for corresponding it's up to you honey. His wife seems to be a nice person." He added: "I was just singing and Whitey came in to see what the disturbance was. Every night we usually discuss the situation of the war, and it gets to be a pretty good argument sometimes."

---

12 Given the obvious attention Betty gave to the news and the care she took in clipping newspapers and keeping a scrapbook about the Third Army and the keepsakes Frank sent back home, this criticism of Betty seems harsh. It is certainly true soldiers felt civilians back home (as well as uniformed people in the rear echelons) had it soft and didn't appreciate the sacrifices of the soldiers at the front. And the month-long slugfest to clear the bulge had to be a particularly frustrating time for Frank and other 80th Division soldiers. But it is clear that Betty *was* paying careful attention to the war's progress and to what Frank was doing. Clearly, she was as anxious as Frank for the war to be over so her man could come home.

Clearing roads didn't only involve snow and ice; the engineers also needed to build drains and bypasses, put in sidetracks, remove abatis and bombed-out vehicles, and fill craters. They also installed improvised trip flares in front of the advancing infantry. The corps-level 166th Engineers often joined the 305th's B Company to build, maintain, and guard obstacles to shore up the 80th's defenses.

Snowdrifts mined by the Germans added to the hazards of the front line, and the rate of casualties from mines surged in January. Engineers were forced to risk using bulldozers to scoop the mines off the roads, "which was very effective with AP mines but entailed the risk of the dozer being hit by an AT [anti-tank] mine."[13] S-2 of the 305th reported a prisoner revealed a new type of the dreaded Schuh mine[14] that were housed in wooden boxes so mine detectors couldn't find them. According to an officer of the 313th Field Artillery (FA) Battalion: "All over town we could hear mines exploding. No one wanted to leave the main road or even jump into the snow from a truck . . . even to answer a call of nature."[15]

These ongoing tasks persisted through January, but there was not enough mental and physical activity to keep the engineers engaged and boredom set in. Frank told Betty: "Today I didn't do very much, went on a reconnaissance and then this afternoon I got a haircut and washed and shaved. Our days and life over here are boring, you do the same things, wear the same clothes, write the same things and millions of other things the same, day in and day out."

Frank's boredom was partially alleviated by quirky emergencies at his billet. On January 12, he wrote,

> After experiences of the past four hours you'll probably think we're crazy. Just now as I started this letter to you we smelled smoke and found out our generator in the next room was on fire. We finally got it out. Earlier in the afternoon the squad next to us saw smoke coming through the floor and walls and after chopping up the floor they found the beams underneath on fire. I think tonight I'll sleep with a bucket of water next to me. It was a bit of fun though.

Writing on January 15, Frank told Betty: "I haven't been doing very much for the past four days. We went to a civilian church yesterday in town to the rear and then in the afternoon we had to repair a bridge. I'm sending you a picture of the

---

13 After-Action Report, S-3, 305th Engineer Combat Battalion, January 1945.

14 Summary of Events, S-2 Section, 305th Engineer Combat Battalion, January 1945, 1.

15 Lieutenant John Ingles, quoted in Craig, *The 80th Infantry Division*, 46.

Photograph of bridge built on January 1, 1945, by Frank Lembo's platoon.

Battalion photographer

bridge we built New Year's Day here in Luxembourg. You can put it in your scrapbook. I've also got a scarf made out of parachutes that were used to drop supplies to Bastogne that I'll send to you."[16] On the rear of the photo of a jeep driving over the bridge, Frank wrote: "January 1, 1945. Luxembourg. Built by 1st Platoon B Company 305th Combat Engr. Btn."

Frank began his January 20 letter by remarking he hadn't written in a few days because there just wasn't any news.

> Things around here are normal as usual and outside of a little work now and then, we haven't very much to do. Almost our only work has been sanding roads and we got as far as the front lines so there isn't much of that left either. I've been spending a lot of my time reading, and then again our bull sessions take up half a day. We argue about the war, civilian life, army life, liquor, women and everything else. We also play a few practical jokes on each other. It's just the fortunes of war, one day you are busy as heck, and then the next you don't have anything to do.

The monotony was coming to an end, however. Patton launched a drive to trap the retreating German troops before they could escape to Germany, and the 80th Division had a big role to play. On January 18, a new field order took effect, and

---

16 The scarves were souvenirs from the defenders of Bastogne to members of the relief columns from the Third Army. Unfortunately, the scarf wasn't included in Betty's collection.

within three days the 80th's three regiments were on the attack. In fairly short order, the 319th seized the towns of Mocher and Masselar while the 317th attacked and occupied Hocher.[17] On January 20, the 318th sent a patrol to Burden. The town was unoccupied so the patrol moved in and occupied the town.[18] For the remainder of January, the infantry regiments slugged it out on a slow advance toward the Sauer River and the German border.[19]

The 305th Engineers operated in support of the infantry advance. One company of engineers built wooden covers for machine gun emplacements and brought them to the front lines under cover of darkness because of heavy mortar fire. The 305th prepared defensive positions in anticipation of enemy counterattacks.

Frank told Betty:

> We are now back in the wars again, and personally I like it. For a while we laid around and it gave me too much time to think and such. We haven't been too busy and our efforts have been in removing mines so our infantry could move. I was out this morning to put signs on a minefield and when I got back I found that Scotty was back with the company. He's looking good and not suffering any ill effects of his operation. I'm glad he's back.

B Company had spent almost a month at Chau de Birtrange, supporting the 80th's infantry operations in the slow advance toward Wiltz and Germany. The company left Chau de Birtrange on the morning of January 21 by motor convoy and moved five miles away to Niederfeulen, Luxembourg.

Shortly after arriving in Niederfeulen, the company was put on alert for a move to Wiltz, and a party went out to reconnoiter a billeting area. But B Company was still in Niederfeulen on January 24 when Frank wrote to Betty: "Before going to bed I better drop you a few lines because I have a feeling we'll be busy for a few days. Things are normal and the only work we've had was being called out last night to check some mines. We had to ride about fifteen miles through rather heavy snowfall, but it was fine. It was in an open jeep but not too cold."

The 317th and 318th were ordered to take Wiltz on January 23, and the regiments moved forward early that day and met strong resistance. John Ingles, an

17 Reducing the Bulge, 319th Infantry, 11; After-Action Report, 318th Infantry Regiment, January 1945.

18 Craig, *The 80th Infantry Division*, 46.

19 After-Action Report, 80th Infantry Division, January 1945.

officer with the 313th Field Artillery Battalion, observed the scene in Wiltz during the attacks "would have been right in place in Dante's Inferno'" The town was burning and soldiers added to the flames by starting bonfires for warmth.[20] The regiments occupied Wiltz on January 24 and moved on to clear the Clerf River and mop up the surrounding villages. The division was finally at the shores of the Sure/Sauer River.[21]

On January 25, B Company traveled 20 miles to reach a billet at its long-sought objective, Wiltz. Frank wrote on January 26:

> The weather has been pretty cold and I really felt it for the first time. Yesterday it was down to four below zero. The only thing that really gets me is my feet, and I guess it just can't be helped. We've moved around a little since my last letter. I like to ride through these forests. It's very rugged country with deep valleys and thick pine forests. I imagine the spring is beautiful in these parts. The towns have all been pulverized, and the house we're staying in had a bomb drop in the front yard so doors and windows are out.

B Company's motor convoy left Wiltz after two days, and on January 27 it drove another 20 miles to Christnacht, Luxembourg, where it stayed overnight. The next day it pushed on another mile to Waldbillig, near the banks of the Sauer River. Frank was apparently pleased with the billeting at Waldbillig. Once he settled in, he wrote: "We're living in a rather comfortable house now. The whole platoon (46 men) is in one house and they keep things pretty clean and in order. Most of the men will make damn-good house-husbands after the war."

January 28 is generally fixed as the last day of the Battle of the Bulge. Looking back, Patton noted with pride: "During this operation the Third Army moved farther and faster and engaged more divisions in less time than any other army in the history of the United States—possibly in the history of the world. The results attained were made possible only by the superlative quality of American officers, American men, and American equipment."[22]

On the same day, the 80th was relieved by the 17th Airborne Division and went into reserve.[23] During the month of January, the 80th Division captured 1,005

---

20 Described in Craig, *The 80th Infantry Division*, 46.

21 80th Division Operational History, January 1945, 17-19.

22 Patton, *War as I Knew It*, 217.

23 Craig, *The 80th Infantry Division*, 46.

Soldiers from 317th line up for chow in Bockholz, Luxembourg, January 27, 1945.

Army Signal Corps

prisoners, for a total of 12,545 prisoners taken in the six months since the activation of the Third Army.[24]

During their two-week rest period in Waldbillig, the men relaxed and cleaned their equipment. B Company's engineers were given the luxury of passes to the rear, far enough from the front that they could think of something besides the war. Frank wrote: "Passes are starting to Luxembourg and I think after payday I'll take a trip. It should be a rather nice city and will break the monotony." By the time payday rolled around the next day, he mused:

> We were paid this morning and I think after my pass to Luxembourg I'll send the rest to the bank. I earned about $70 this month and it's a little too much to carry around. It's going to be strange getting used to the value of money again. For the past seven months money has had no value for us. Here it buys nothing and serves no purpose to us, but I guess it won't take me many days to learn. Our first date darling will be a wild spree.

24 After-Action Report, 80th Infantry Division, January 1945.

General Eddy and an aide run for shelter in Echternach, Luxembourg. *Army Signal Corps*

He concluded: "P.S. I'm enclosing an editorial in 'Stars & Stripes.' I thought it hit the point." The editorial was titled "Everything for the Front." It noted the lack of sacrifice Americans were willing to make for the war effort, especially when compared to that of the Russians:

> They don't understand the Saar, the Ruhr, the Rhine, out there where feet freeze. Where hands are numb. Where noses, cheeks and ears turn white with frost. Where fires burn low and there's no warmth indoors to which a man can go. The home folks have given all they've been asked for. It's just that they haven't been asked for enough. It's just that 'everything for the front' still doesn't have quite the same meaning in the U.S.A. as the U.S.S.R.[25]

This editorial represented a fairly widespread view within the army at this point, from the high command to the GI. A few months earlier, during the Normandy breakout and the chase across France, the high command, the news media, and most people on the home front believed the Germans were finished and the war was almost over. This conviction held even as German resistance

25 "Everything for the Front," *Stars and Stripes,* January 26, 1945.

stiffened and logistics brought the Allied advance to a crawl. The Ardennes Offensive, however, came as a shock and made many at home and in the army realize the war would be going on for a long time. Many of the GIs felt that "after all, we're short of everything and what have the folks on the home front done for us?"

In a January 31 letter, Frank observed, "Everyone here seems to be waiting for the Russians to end the war and now can't figure a thing out by the news. It seems to me as if the same optimism that prevailed before the counter attack is coming up again. When I'm on a boat and heading home, then and then alone will I believe this is over with."

The company diary for January 31, 1945, reported another significant development: Capt. Robert C. Marshall returned to command of Company B of the 305th Engineers. The men were happy to see their trusted captain return.

B Company's command post stayed at Waldbillig through February 14. While the company remained there, the engineers prepared for the next push, which would take them over the Sauer River and into Germany. It had been a long time coming. The 80th Division had been at this point in mid-December (during the Saar offensive about 100 miles to the south) before being diverted to the Ardennes. The 80th now remained in its northern position and was ordered to break through the Siegfried Line and capture Bitburg, another communications center important to the Nazis. As January closed, the 80th Division joined with other elements of the U.S. Army in what would become an awesome show of force at the German border, preparatory to the final push into Germany.

CHAPTER 12

THE SAUER CROSSING: FEB. 1-17, 1945

IT may not have been apparent to the GIs, but the December and January campaigns had depleted much of the strength of the German Army. Casualties in the Ardennes Campaign had been brutal for the Nazis, and Hitler had further weakened his forces by redeploying nine of his best divisions from the Western front to the East after the Ardennes counteroffensive came to an end. On paper, the German divisions outnumbered those of the Allies, but the German units tended to be understrength and made up of replacements and recruits.[1] Despite these shortcomings, the remnants of the German Army still had some fight left in them, and the defenses at the German border and the Siegfried Line were formidable.

The 80th Division opened the month of February with the 318th Infantry holding the line in the eastern sector near Heller, the 319th holding the west near Diekirch, and the 317th in reserve.[2] For the first six days of the month, the infantry regiments patrolled, searched for crossing sites, and trained replacement troops.

The last formidable natural obstacle in the 80th's path to the Rhine was the Sauer River. The weather had finally warmed, but there was no letup in the troops' misery—they could not escape the constant drenching downpours. The runoff

---

1 Bradley, *A Soldier's Story*, 494.

2 After-Action Report, 80th Infantry Division, February 1945.

sometimes froze, leaving the countryside covered in a layer of ice. Moreover, the snowmelt and steady rain swelled the rivers to many times their normal size.[3]

The Sauer River crossing would prove to be the most challenging and treacherous of the war for the engineers. In addition to the hazards presented by rushing waters, competing demands for resources within the Allied command had slowed the Third Army's advance, allowing the Germans to further strengthen their defenses. Once again the soldiers would cross the river in the face of intense artillery, mortar, and small arms fire.

Patton, however, did not consider the deplorable conditions at the river to be a sufficient reason to delay the crossing. His sense of urgency was based on more persuasive considerations than his usual "there is only *attack* and *attack* and *attack* some more" philosophy. Allied high command politics was in the background, as it was so often in the ETO.

On February 1, Eisenhower had informed 12th Army Group commander Omar Bradley that, once again, priority would go to Montgomery's 21st Army Group. According to Bradley, Patton's Third Army would shortly be forced onto the defensive.

Eisenhower's decision was a reasonable one, since Bradley owed Montgomery the return of divisions that had been loaned southward to help stop the Ardennes offensive. Nonetheless, Eisenhower told Bradley and Patton they could keep the troops until Montgomery had time to regroup before resuming his own offensive.[4] Eisenhower authorized the American generals to conduct "probing attacks"—not an all-out offensive—until February 10 and possibly later if casualties and resource expenditures were not extreme. Patton thought these limitations on offensive action were the "height of folly." He envisioned the possibility of a major breakthrough (what turned out to be the Palatinate Campaign), if only he could keep the pressure on.

Eisenhower's decision, in fact, was not as restrictive as Patton believed. Both Bradley and the army's official chronicler of the final campaign of the European war said that Eisenhower was fully aware of Patton's aggressive plans and was willing to accept them. But the pressure flowing down from Patton to his Third

---

3 Charles B. MacDonald, *Victory in Europe, 1945: The Last Offensive of World War II. Dover Books on History, Political and Social Science* (1973, reprint, Mineola, NY: Dover Publications, 2007), 100.

4 Ibid., 56-57.

Army divisions to regain the offensive while there was still time was more intense than usual.[5]

At the beginning of February, B Company's engineers were going out nonstop to reconnoiter the Sauer and the towns along the riverbank. As early as February 2, Sgt. Frank Lembo, Lt. Arthur Henke, and other men from the 1st Platoon were examining potential crossing sites at the Sauer and scouting roads and approaches.[6] Captain Marshall, B Company commander, and engineers from the 2nd Platoon performed reconnaissance on other parts of the river. The company diary reported the battalion photographer went along to take pictures of the engineers at work.

As the crossing date approached, B Company intensified its reconnaissance of the Sauer on February 3. A 1st Platoon patrol came under small arms fire as it surveyed the road network around Reisdorf; a night patrol went to the edge of the Sauer to reconnoiter an area southeast of Dillingen; and a third patrol investigated an old bridge site south of the town. The company diary reported all of these patrols met their objectives. An enlisted man from a patrol led by Captain Marshall was slightly wounded when he stepped on a booby trap

Road and bridge work intensified in the days before the crossing. The Germans had blown up bridges, laid mines, and put up obstacles as they moved out. The engineers found friendly and enemy minefields, bridge demolitions, and craters on both sides of the river. B Company patrols went out to check and clear the minefields that had been reported by other friendly units. A field in Reisdorf had an abundance of Schuh mines, and Teller mines were cleared from a nearby field. Engineers had more mundane work to do as well; they still had to remove snow from the steep, twisted roads, bring in sand from the nearby sandpits, and bury dead animals after bombings and barrages.

In a series of last-minute preparations for a night crossing that would involve multiple 80th Division units, the men from B Company gave the final instructions

---

5 Blumenson, *Patton Papers*, 636; Bradley, *A Soldier's Story*, 501; MacDonald, *Victory in Europe*, 1945, 68.

6 The B Company diary became significantly more informative at the start of February. Previous entries were minimal, but the February entries were comprehensive. For example, a typical entry for January might be "19 January: Company sanded and maintained roads in 318th Infantry Regiment sector" or "25 January: Company left Niederfeulen 0730 by motor convoy and arrived new area Wiltz 1030. Distance traveled 20 miles." But many entries for February are two paragraphs long and provide details on the activities of each squad. The diary entries for the month of January took less than a full page; the reports for February took eight pages.

305th Engineers check out river shore. *Battalion photographer*

to infantry battalions in procedures for crossing streams with assault crossing equipment.[7]

On February 4, after a five-day hiatus from writing, Frank wrote to Betty. He didn't give her any details about the operations at the Sauer other than to say, "We've been busy on and off the past few days, in fact you never know when you are going to have to go out, you can't plan to do anything the following day and so on. I guess we'll never be satisfied until we are civilians again." He continued on a more personal note: "I'm glad you received the pictures we took over here, and I'm sorry there weren't more of me, and from the looks of things there won't be any more until this war is over with." He added that even with all preparations to cross the Sauer, the men managed to have a little fun back at their billet. "Tonight for supper we had ice cream. We have been making it from the snow, but this tasted like the real stuff. Yesterday for the first time in months we got a real orange, believe me I don't know what this world is coming to."

On February 5, the company's 3rd Platoon ferried a combat patrol from the 318th Infantry across the Sauer south of Dillingen, but the patrol encountered heavy machine-gun fire. One engineer was killed and four were seriously wounded, three by machine gun and the fourth by a Schuh mine. The patrol was pinned down by heavy fire, and casualties could not be evacuated until after nightfall. The patrol

7   After-Action Report, 305th Engineer Combat Battalion, February 1945.

Engineers load engineer boat. *Battalion photographer*

was also hampered by swift water and chunks of ice, which dammed up behind the boat and forced it downstream. The current in the Sauer, easily crossed during normal conditions, was estimated at 15 mph.[8] A 318th Infantry unit history noted, "Very few patrols returned in the same strength as they departed. . . . Our patrols fought the elements and the enemy, both seemingly insurmountable."[9]

Also on February 5, two squads from B Company's 1st Platoon searched for mines in an area designated for an artillery company. Another patrol surveilled the road leading in and out of Bigelbach for mines and roadblocks but was turned back by machine-gun fire. Later, after dark, the company was able to open the road. But B Company's bulldozers were prevented from digging in positions for an antiaircraft platoon due to direct observation by the enemy.

On February 4, amid all this engineering work, a sudden change of orders for the 305th arrived. Without notice, the corps-level engineers—the 1135th Engineer Group, consisting of the 150th, 166th, and 179th Engineer Combat Battalions—was designated the lead engineering element in support of the Sauer crossing.[10] In some ways the decision to put the 1135th in charge of the crossing

8 Craig, *The 80th Infantry Division*, 48.

9 318th Infantry Regiment Unit History, February 1945, 4.

10 Bridging Sauer and Our Rivers, Interview with Lt. Col. H. B. Hines, 1135th Engineering Group, February 13, 1945; Crossing of the Sauer River at Dillingen, Interview with Capt. Dale

was understandable, since the Siegfried Line was directly beyond the landing and the 305th would be heavily engaged clearing the way for infantry on the far bank; however, in other ways the decision was questionable. As the work progressed, it became apparent the corps engineers were not prepared to support the assault crossings. Traditionally, the expertise of the corps-level units was in the rear areas, building heavier vehicular bridges once the infantry had crossed, not in moving the initial assault waves.

Some 1135th engineers stated during the crossings that they didn't know how to operate the assault boats.[11] Additionally, several of the newly assigned battalions of corps engineers expressed concern they were unfamiliar with the river and their areas of responsibility and didn't have time to plan or reconnoiter the site.[12] The little reconnaissance they accomplished didn't generate much useful information. For example, the 150th went out on the night of February 5-6 "with an infantry patrol from the 319th. It was so dark, however, that little definite information about the river could be obtained.... Lt. Villadson brought back data relative to the rate of flow of the stream and its width (this data was later found to be inaccurate)."[13]

The 166th Engineer Combat Battalion joined with the 305th in the final run-up to the crossing. The 166th was assigned to take the lead for the crossing of the 318th Infantry, a role the 305th usually played.[14] Officers from B Company and the 318th oriented the 166th officers to the river and the situation on the ground in the 318th's sector. Three trucks of Brockway Treadway (a bridge-building version of the Army's 6x6 6-ton cargo truck which contained a twin-armed hydraulic boom to self-unload bridge components), one tank bulldozer, and one tank retriever were attached to B Company for the operation.

On February 6, B Company readied for the difficult days ahead. Since the engineers wouldn't be able to get their vehicles and equipment across in the first

Wallace et al., 166th Engineers, February 14, 1945; Our and Sauer River Crossings, Interview with Lt. Col. Bruce W. Reagan, 150th Engineers, February 13, 1945.

11 Crossing of the Sauer, 318th Infantry, 2nd Battalion, 5.

12 Bridging Sauer and Our Rivers, Interview with Lt. Col. H. B. Hines, 1135th Engineer Group, 1.

13 Our and Sauer River Crossings, Interview with Lt. Col. Bruce W. Reagan, 150th Engineers, 1-2.

14 Crossing of the Sauer, Interview with Capt. Dale Wallace, 166th Engineers, 1.

wave, they were preparing to move to the opposite bank equipped as infantry but also laden with engineering tools and demolitions.

The 80th Division would cross in the area between the towns of Bollendorf and Wallendorf. At 5:00 p.m. on February 6, the 318th was alerted that the assault crossing would jump off at the Sauer riverbank on February 7.[15] The 318th and 319th were ordered to launch their attacks at 3:00 a.m.

In many ways this crossing was the most challenging of the major contested crossings conducted by the 80th Division, including the Moselle, Seille, Nied *francaise*, Nied *allemande*, Rhine, and Inn.[16] Both the river and the enemy opposition presented significant obstacles. Although the Germans were not as numerous or, in some cases, as motivated as those who had defended the Moselle a short five months earlier, many were prepared to fight hard, and they had the additional protection of West Wall defenses. Because of the swift flow of the current, most infantrymen would have to cross in assault boats. Heavy vehicular bridges could not be built for nearly a week after the assault started, so the infantry would be required to fight without armored support.

According to a history of the 166th Engineers, the plan called for engineer guides to meet the infantry, who would carry the assault boats to the riverbank. The 166th was also assigned to put in a footbridge almost immediately and an infantry support bridge and a class-40 treadway bridge shortly afterward.[17]

The infantrymen made their way to the river, and their problems began before they reached the bank. Rain, mud, and enemy fire prevented the engineers from getting the equipment to the shore. A unit history described the challenge faced by the 318th and the engineers as they got underway that day: "The 2d Bn moved out at 0300 . . . under a dense smoke screen which rendered the river almost invisible. The men of the 1st Battalion trudged slowly down the perilous slippery slope to the bank, which then had a sheer drop of several feet to the water's edge."[18] A history of the 2nd Battalion added, "To reach the banks of the Sauer River the battalion had to carry assault boats a distance of some 500 yards over treacherous, hilly

15 Action Northern Luxembourg; Crossing Sauer River, Interview with Capt. Charles D. Cookfield et al., 318th Infantry Regiment, February 25, 1945.

16 The attack was perilous enough. When the 80th Division staff published the divisional history, *Ever Forward*, they selected the Sauer crossing as the dramatic introduction to the story of the division.

17 Crossing of the Sauer River at Dillingen, 166th Engineer Combat Battalion, Interviews with Capt. Dale S. Wallace et al., February 14, 1945, 1-2.

18 318th Regiment Unit History, February 1945, 5.

terrain, through snow, ice and mud. The enemy added to the hazardous task with constant barrages of 'screaming meemies,' heavy and light artillery, mortar and small arms fire"[19]

The situation deteriorated further when the infantry and engineers reached the river, struggled to get into their boats, and made their way into the rushing water. A 318th soldier recalled, "With difficulty, wooden assault boats were launched into the swift, muddy, debris-filled, icy water."[20] The troops were under heavy fire as they fought their way across the flooded river and as they climbed up the bank on the far shore. The assault boats were riddled by machine gun fire and many were lost. An 80th Division history concluded: "All efforts by Engineers to span the raging torrent of now more than 200 feet with bridges was unsuccessful as heavy enemy artillery barrages consistently knocked out half completed bridges."[21]

Companies E and G of the 318th's 2nd Battalion didn't get their boats to the bank until daylight, and by then the Germans were aware of the crossings and the two companies were subjected to intense mortar, artillery, and machine gun fire. A 318th soldier later recalled several boats overturning during a night crossing. "It was brutal. I remember a couple of the platoons in E Company never made it; they came across in daylight and got blasted out of the water. This was one of the worst experiences of the war with the cold, the snow, the mud, and the very swift, very high, river."[22] The 318th's F Company was more fortunate; it crossed on schedule at 3:00 a.m. on February 7 with no opposition and reported it had reached the other side by 3:07 a.m.[23] The entire 2nd Battalion of the 318th had crossed and established a firm bridgehead on the opposite side by the end of the day.[24]

Although the 1135th Engineer Group and component units had taken the lead on the crossing, all B Company platoons were detailed to assist the 318th Infantry.[25] Lieutenant Henke and two squads from the 1st Platoon went out in

19 "Baptism of Fire," Summary of Actions of Company F, 2nd Battalion, 318th Infantry Regiment, August 44 to May 45, 12.

20 Fred Witzgell, 318th Regiment History, February 1945, 5.

21 "Baptism of Fire," Summary of Actions of Company F, 2nd Battalion, 318th Infantry Regiment, August 44 to May 45, 12.

22 Clayton Warman, quoted in Elvin, *The Box from Branau*, 114.

23 80th Division Operational History, February 1945, 5.

24 Ibid.; Witzgell, "318th Regiment History," chap. 6.

25 Morning Reports, Companies B and C, 305th Engineer Combat Battalion, February 7, 1945; Unit history, 319th Infantry Regiment, February 1945.

close support of one battalion of the 318th, and two squads from Lieutenant Smith's 2nd Platoon operated in close support of another battalion. The company was issued SCR-300 backpack radios (the first walkie-talkies) for communication between engineer units and regiments. By February 8, the impatience of the 305th Engineers—and the brass—was boiling over. At 3:30 am, a 305th staff officer reported, "Col. Curtis [166th Engineer Combat Battalion] requests our help in getting the footbridge in for the 318th. 318th is not getting any more men over." By 4:30 reports indicated the 318th had not crossed any more troops and the crossing area was still under fire. At 7:45 a.m., a message advised, "Gen. McBride wants to see Col. Hines [1135th Engineer Group], he has advised Gen. Eddy that Engr support is inadequate." And at 9:26 am, a battalion officer reported to the executive officer, "B Co. will build footbridge in Hamper [318th regiment] area."[26] A 318th soldier described the problem: "The engineers on hand at the original crossing claimed to have no knowledge of assault boats and as a result the infantry had to maneuver the boats themselves." Later that day, "more engineers [presumably the more experienced platoon from B Company of the 305th] arrived and took over the ferrying operation."[27]

Meanwhile, assisted by two platoons of the 305th's C Company, the other assault regiment, the 319th, crossed on February 7. The 319th faced difficulties in getting across "due to the high flood level of the Our River [a tributary of the Sauer] and the swiftness of the current and heavy enemy artillery and nebelwerfer concentrations."[28]

The 319th's 1st Battalion had a quick start on February 7 from a crossing site north of Wallendorf. Companies B and C were across by daybreak, though many boats were lost. After that, the crossings came to a halt, due to heavy resistance from defenders hiding in Siegfried Line communication trenches. The two companies, alone on the enemy shore, recognized they could not survive pinned down. Their only option was to attack the pillbox that was tormenting them, so they charged up the hill and captured several emplacements along the Siegried Line. Later that day, the 1st Battalion's A Company arrived and captured Wallendorf.[29]

26 305th Engineer Combat Battalion Journal, Serial 3, 12, 13, and 17, November 8, 1944.

27 Sauer Crossing, 2nd Battalion, 318th Infantry, 4; 80th Division Operational History, February 1945, 2.

28 After-Action Report, 80th Infantry Division, February 1945.

29 Crossing the Sauer River, Interview with Maj. Arthur H. Clark, 2-3; Reports After-Action Against Enemy, 319th Infantry Regiment, February 1945.

Two companies of the 319th's 2nd Battalion made it across by 6:25 a.m., and a third reached the far side within the next half hour.[30] On the day of the attack, the 150th Engineers had been unable to complete the footbridge they were supposed to construct. The 2nd Battalion's commanding officer stated, "The smoothness of the operation as planned was non-existent," and he noted the crossing was further impeded by the fact that 25 percent of the participating troops were replacements who were seeing their first combat.[31] The 150th again failed to get a footbridge in on the evening of February 7-8, and only a few more troops from the 319th's 2nd Battalion were able to cross the second night. Because of artillery fire and the current, the battalion commanding officer and significant reinforcements did not get across the river until February 11.

The 317th Infantry, which was earlier in reserve, did not enter the battle until February 10, three days after the initial attacks. Despite the intensive work by the engineers to build bridges across the river, the 317th faced the same problems as the 80th's other infantry regiments. A member of the 317th Infantry recounted his harrowing experience at the river:

> The current was so strong it tore the engineer raft to pieces, and several of his men drowned. . . . [The engineers] had a cable stretched across the river and had a system rigged up where the current would pull across the assault boats and rafts. . . . I sat down on the banks of the river with my hand on the cable. That way I could tell when a boat was coming across. The cable tightened. A boat was coming over. The cable grew tighter and tighter—and then it snapped. . . . It was an awful thing to witness. The night was so black we couldn't see our hands in front of our faces, and yet we could hear people yelling for help only a little way out in the river. We were helpless. . . . Even an excellent swimmer couldn't have gotten out of that death trap.[32]

After it had crossed the Sauer, the 317th continued the attack up the steep hills that stood only a few hundred yards east. The troops were hit by machine gun fire from the top of the hills as they struggled up the steep, muddy slopes. Communications went out and there were shortages of critical supplies.

Efforts to cross the 80th Division's men, equipment, and vehicles over the Sauer continued for several more days, during which the current and opposition

30 Reports After-Action Against Enemy, 319th Infantry Regiment, February 1945.

31 Attack Across the Our River into the Siegfried Line, Interview with Lt. Col. Paul Bandy et al., 2nd Battalion, 319th Infantry Regiment, March 1945, 3.

32 Adkins and Adkins, *You Can't Get Closer than This*, 151-52.

did not diminish. Part of the delay in crossing follow-up units came from a shortage of assault boats and oars. In typical crossings, the first footbridges were put in shortly after the first assault boat crossings, but this time the boats were needed for several days to get the troops across. Already by 9:20 a.m. on February 7, Col. Olen Curtis of the 166th Engineer Combat Battalion reported to the 305th commander that he was trying to put in a footbridge, but that a machine gun on the opposite shore made it impossible. At 2:30 p.m., Curtis reported to 305th engineers commander Lieutenant Colonel McCollam that no part of the footbridge was in the water. Ominously, he also reported that "infantry are throwing away paddles on far shore." The 305th's adjutant noted, "He is getting more boats and paddles and fresh crews." At 3:20 p.m., the 318th reported they needed new paddles, and by 9:15 p.m., the 166th was "down to [the] last nine boats with paddles. Has plenty of boats but no paddles. Boats on return trip are going out of zone of assault so that boat and paddles are a loss."[33]

Two days after the crossings began, the corps engineers' lack of experience continued to hinder the operation, and B Company stepped in to assist. The B Company diary for February 9 reported, "The Company C.P. was the busiest spot in the whole sector, I do believe. There were officers from 166th Engineers trying to get information on river and river bank." Three of the company's sergeants worked as guides all night, taking men from other units down to the river.

Diary entries, morning reports, and after-action reports enumerated a long list of missions performed by the engineers in the early days after the initial crossings. On February 8, Sergeant Lembo and other men from the 1st Platoon prepared to put a footbridge over the Sauer for infantrymen from the 318th's 1st Battalion. The plan called for the 2nd Platoon to set up machine guns to protect the engineers while they worked. Engineers were struck with heavy fire as they labored on the footbridges and retrieved bridging equipment that had washed downstream. In addition to helping to man the assault boats, C Company assisted with bridge building on February 9.

Attacks on the Siegfried Line commenced even as the infantry was struggling across the river. In the 318th's sector, the 2nd Battalion was able to take the crest above the river by February 8. It found the enemy "had developed forts with overlapping fields of fire. Camouflaged pillboxes resembled houses, barns, haystacks; the dense foliage covered numerous foxholes, minefields, and

---

33 305th Engineer Combat Battalion Journal, Serial 13, 32, 36, and 48, November 7, 1944.

Engineers prepare to remove a felled tree from the road. *Army Signal Corps*

booby-traps. Literally into the gaping jaws of Hell moved the 2nd Battalion."[34] Companies from the 319th's 2nd Battalion identified the sites of fortifications in their sector, and through combined artillery, mortar, and armored vehicle fire from the Luxembourg side of the river, they were able to isolate individual strongpoints and pave the way for ground assaults. Many of the German defenders quickly surrendered. When the commanding officer of the 319ths 2nd battalion crossed and linked up with his small detachment on February 11, he said he had never seen troops so weary.[35]

Much of B Company's work was on the opposite side of the river, clearing mines and repairing roads. On February 8, a squad went on a night mission to clear the roads of mines from Beaufort to Dillingen, and they removed four Riegel mines and a roadblock of five felled trees. American artillery began shelling Dillingen just as the squad reached the town, but the men got out without casualties. On February

34 Witzgell, "318th Regiment History," February 1945, 7.

35 Attack Across the Our River into the Siegfried Line, Interview with Lt. Col. Paul Bandy et al., 2nd Battalion, 319th Infantry Regiment, March 1945, 7.

10, a squad from Lieutenant Smith's 2nd Platoon crossed the Sauer and swept the roads on the far side. The squad also reconnoitered all roads and roadblocks on the far shore across from Dillingen. They were shelled by deafening enemy artillery and nebelwerfers the whole time. Other missions included recovering equipment lost in the assault and bringing engineering equipment and supplies down to the riverbank.

On February 9, Frank was able to compose a letter to Betty in which he provided a brief update on the latest happenings in his usual understated way: "I'm finally getting a chance to write my honey a few lines and I'm sorry I haven't been able to write you sooner. The past few days have been rather hectic and about the roughest we've had over here, but I'm okay and in good health, a little tired but that's all."

The next day Frank added, "Today we got a little rest, and I'm glad of that. I was a little worn out, and I guess all our spirits were pretty low, but they have risen somewhat." In a digression, Frank again vented at folks on the home front who were unable or unwilling to comprehend what was really happening in the war. He saw it as an affront to the men with whom he served. "I see where the papers back home have this damn war over with again, the only thing I can say is the past few days I've seen more hell and the fiercest fighting since we've been in action, and the past hasn't been a picnic, but I guess people are just that way."

But Frank preferred to go on his "five-minute furlough" rather than dwell on his weariness or the events at the Sauer. He told Betty:

No you don't have to worry about my changing a bit. I'm the same 'ole Lem who left you back in the States, and with you the same ideas as I had then, nothing ever will change me. If there was anything to change me it would have happened long ago when I was back in the States. Someday honey I'll be again holding you tight and telling you how much I love you. Until then you'll just have to bear with some of the misery this war brings. God only knows how bad I want you but three thousand miles is just a little too much for me to overcome.

On February 11, Sergeant Lembo was promoted from sergeant of the 1st Platoon to staff sergeant and given temporary command of B Company's 3rd Platoon. His promotion to a slot generally reserved for an officer was an honor for an enlisted man of Frank's rank and background. Reassignments were made within the company to fill vacated platoon sergeant and squad leader positions. The departing commander of the platoon, Lieutenant La Prade, went on furlough back to the States, and according to the company diary, "He is afraid that he will not return to this Company."

Immediately after his promotion, Staff Sergeant Lembo and two squads from 3rd Platoon crossed the Sauer in the vicinity of Dillingen and started clearing the roads on the far shore, which were heavily mined. That same day, B Company commander Capt. Robert Marshall made a reconnaissance of the riverbank where company engineers had come under fire while attempting a night mission to cross a combat infantry patrol. The body of one of the company's enlisted men was recovered.

Also on February 11, the engineers bridged craters and removed obstacles to prepare the ground for infantry trains, and by the end of the day, the roads had been opened for the infantry as far forward as Biesdorf, a few kilometers to the north. Men from B Company put treadway bridges over two craters, 36 feet and 25 feet long. Other men reconnoitered a 60-foot crater in Biesdorf. They were pinned down by sniper fire and forced to crawl 150 yards on their way back.

The company diary for February 11 also noted that one of the former company members who had been transferred to the infantry in January, a Native American named Harold Deer, was killed in action. Deer had been known within the company as "Chief" or "Light Horse Harry." On a lighter note, the diary reported that a Tec "promoted" a spring for a jeep and a shock absorber for two-and-a-half-ton truck. That day the company had chicken with trimmings for dinner and ice cream for dessert.

Attempts had been made to bridge the Sauer since February 7, but the first bridge (a 204-foot treadway) was only completed on the morning of February 12. The second bridge, a 312-foot treadway, was completed the following afternoon. By then, construction was underway on numerous Bailey bridges so the armor could begin to cross.[36]

February 12 marked the day the 318th and 319th regiments linked their bridgeheads over the Sauer, and that evening the 80th also linked up with the 5th Infantry Division.[37] Thanks to the U.S. infantry, German artillery had been pushed back far enough from the river to allow full-scale crossings. The Sauer bridgehead was fairly secure. A history of the Blue Ridge Division noted: "Now the 80th Division was on enemy soil. The infamy of Nazism had just three months left."[38]

---

36 Bridging Sauer and Our Rivers, Interview with Lt. Col. H. B. Hines, 1135th Engineer Group, February 13, 1945, 3.

37 MacDonald, *Victory in Europe*, 106.

38 Craig, *The 80th Infantry Division*, 48.

Patton visited the Sauer crossing operation on February 12. He was reportedly appalled at the condition of the roads when he first reached the site but confident the crossings were no longer in danger.[39] He wrote in his diary that night, "They are making fine progress." He also revealed a bit of management psychology: "I have given the XII Corps permission to stop the attack if they want to, but any such permission always works in reverse on Eddy, so he continued the attack." Two days later, he wrote to his wife, Beatrice, "I got up closer than I intended to but nothing happened, and the soldiers were all glad to see me." Characteristically, he added that he could break through if he had only one more division, "but the brains are all set on another fool move."[40] A memoir from a 317th soldier recounted a story in *Stars and Stripes* that claimed Patton swam the Sauer with his assault troops during his visit. A soldier asked, "If you tell me it's humanly possible for a living soul to swim those rushing cold waters I'll call you the biggest liar in this man's army." It turned out that "Patton crossed the Sauer on a partially submerged footbridge under a smokescreen, almost giving the impression of walking on water."[41]

Despite the problems encountered at the river and the subsequent delays they caused, Patton was satisfied. Two days after his visit, he wrote to his wife about his troops' achievements: "The forcing of the crossing of the Sauer and Our Rivers … was a Homeric feat. …" He noted the proximity of the Siegfried Line, the flooded river conditions, and other adverse conditions. "One day we lost 136 boats but not all the men. We built bridges under enemy fire, and even when I crossed they still had to keep them covered with smoke."[42]

B Company was still occupied with reconnaissance and engineering work at the Sauer on the day of Patton's visit. Lieutenant Henke and some men reconnoitered the 318th Infantry sector for possible sites for additional bridges. Another squad cleared the roads and the ground on the far shore south of Dillingen and removed and destroyed 127 Schuh mines, 51 Riegel mines, and 2 Teller mines. Another squad from B Company worked the area across the river southwest of Dillingen and found and destroyed 72 Schuh mines and 7 Riegel mines. As a

---

39 MacDonald, *Victory in Europe*, 106.

40 Blumenson, *Patton Papers*, 639.

41 Adkins and Adkins, *You Can't Get Closer than This*, 156.

42 Blumenson, *Patton Papers*, 638-39.

testament to the 305th's effectiveness in mine clearing, by the end of February the battalion removed its 10,000th mine since arriving in France in August 1944.[43]

In his February 12 letter, Frank returned to personal matters after warning Betty "you might go quite awhile without letters," anticipating an aggressive offensive pace. He and Betty seemed to enjoy jerking each other's chain when they could. He would have known Betty would have been delighted to hear about his promotion to staff sergeant and temporary command of the 3rd Platoon, but he remained silent about it, if only for now. The ribbing went both ways. Betty got Frank's goat when she told him she planned to go on a Florida vacation with friends—always a sore subject with him. Betty valued her independence, but Frank sometimes wanted different things for his fiancé. He sternly responded, "I'm just wondering if you were serious about a trip to Florida. I personally think you were kidding. I hope so." Frank had reacted similarly a few months earlier when Betty raised the possibility of joining the WAVES. He obviously rethought his reply, and a few days later he wrote, "Received your letter giving me holy hell and I took it in good humor. I'm sorry I stirred you up a little."

Frank's appreciation for his combat buddies deepened as distance from home and his loneliness grew. He had a special place in his heart for the men he'd met during the stateside training and who had remained with him in B Company—Scotty, Eddy, and Whitey. A few days earlier he'd written, "Scotty is getting along fine and I'm glad he is back with us. After the war we'll have to get together again. Lately we haven't talked about our girls much, things are too serious out here, but one of these nights we'll have a bull session." He reported, "Eddy came back from Paris and he enjoyed it as much as I did. I hope everyone has a chance to get there before we come home again. I wish eventually you and I have enough money so that we can take some time and see some of the sights." About Whitey he wrote, "Whitey is still the same person and he's a corporal now."

He also enjoyed the camaraderie of newer friends in the company. "Helen's husband is about 32 years old and is about half bald, but he's a lot of fun. . . . Harrison is a regular Texan and another good fellow. They are all a good bunch of boys." He even had good words for Betty's brother: "Damn—Leslie must have a nice time with his job. Teaching school shouldn't be bad, even if you are away from home." As always, Frank had no difficulty making the best of things and caring for the people around him.

---

43 After-Action Report, 305th Engineer Combat Battalion, February 1945.

Now that Patton's offensive was back on, the 305th Battalion and other engineers were under enormous pressure to complete their bridgework and open the roads so troops and vehicles could flow. B Company's diary for February 13 recorded: "The Sauer River is an obstacle, but the first two days ice flows and debris made it impossible to cross over bridges, then rising water continued to hamper bridging operations." In fact, the water in the river didn't subside until long after fixed bridges were constructed. On February 13, engineers installed a treadway bridge at Dillingen, and Bailey bridges were under construction at both Dillingen and Wallendorf.[44]

Interest in the details of the Sauer crossing was intense in the assault's aftermath. Patton's praise notwithstanding, it was generally agreed that the mechanics of the Third Army's crossing hadn't gone well, even if the mission itself was a success. The 305th's after-action report and interviews with officers of the 1135th Engineers conceded that losses of men and equipment had been significant.

In particular, the engineering group was slow to get the bridges built and the boats ferried across the swollen river. The executive officer of the 1135th said, "This bridging operation was the most difficult the group has had," citing lack of advance knowledge, limited time for reconnaissance, the physical challenges, and military resistance. He stated that although some of the criticism of the engineers' failure to put in bridges might be justified, "he felt the units had done a good job and had tried their best."[45] In retrospect it's clear the 80th Division's own integral engineering battalion—rather than XII Corps engineers new to the site—should have taken first place in the assault. The 305th's after-action report dryly noted "invaluable assistance was provided" by the corps' engineer group, which did most of the assault crossings and "built all the larger bridges." Overall, the 305th seemed happy the combined operation was over: "Once the bridgehead was secure and all bridges in, we again agreed on an engineer rear work boundary."[46]

On February 13, Lieutenant Henke's 1st Platoon opened the roads for the regimental trains into Biesdorf. The platoon left the company area in Waldbillig at the break of dawn and crossed the Sauer with three truckloads of Brockway treadway bridging equipment. A few men with a bulldozer removed a large portion of German bridge equipment that had been knocked out by Allied air power. Men

44 After-Action Report, 80th Infantry Division, February 1945.

45 Bridging Sauer and Our Rivers," Interview with Lt. Col. H. B. Hines, 1135th Engineer Group, February 13, 1945.

46 After-Action Report, 305th Engineer Combat Battalion, February 1945, 2.

from B Company went forward to reconnoiter a 60-foot crater. The diary reported that B Company took time to "set up housekeeping in the pillboxes" and watched while antiaircraft fire blew up an ME 109 that had flown over the company area. The diary reported that the company had no billeting area and was bivouacked in the woods, but happily reported that the men "seemed to enjoy roughing it once."

Biesdorf was a main line of defense in the Siegfried Line and became the scene of intense fighting in the days after the Sauer crossing. An 80th Division history reported that Biesdorf was defended in part by a chain of pillboxes. On February 13, the 2nd Battalion of the 318th bypassed the enemy strongpoints and achieved an element of surprise. Nevertheless, the 318th had to fight house-to-house until the town was cleared."[47]

In the meantime, the bridgehead at Dillingen was enlarged, opening the route for heavy vehicle traffic, including infantry trains and the 4th Armored Division. The company diary for February 14 was again marked by intensive engineering activity in the 318th's sector. The 2nd Platoon of B Company removed an enemy minefield consisting of 19 Teller mines and 27 Riegel mines, while another platoon guarded previously installed bridges and dug in the 318th Infantry's command post. Engineers cleared and repaired roads that were now breaking down beneath the tracked vehicles in an unseasonable thaw.

On February 14, B Company left its billet at Waldbillig, Luxembourg, and motored five miles across the Sauer to a new area near Biesdorf, where the company stayed until February 19. Frank told Betty that Biesdorf was "a battered German village." The February rains were unceasing, and since the company arrived in Biesdorf without an identified billeting area, the men slept the first night in dugouts and shelters.

Frank wrote, "The weather is the same as usual and I guess the rain will stop when the war is over. So I think we'll be spending our time sleeping outdoors. There isn't much left of the towns already, but maybe we can find some boxes or shelters until spring." But by the next day, the company diary was able to report that the men "are preparing their new homes, improving their sleeping quarters and cleaning their tools and equipment."

The next day, Frank explained: "We moved in from the woods into houses again, although it isn't very much it's a little better than living in a pup tent." He expressed the by-now common GI view of Germany and Germans: "From all indications we'll be wrecking a lot of German towns from here on in. As long as

47 Craig, *The 80th Infantry Division*, 50; History of the 2nd Battalion, 318th Infantry, 32.

American soldiers look down on Siegfried Line. *US Army*

Heine persists in fighting, the only thing left is to pulverize him until he has [had] enough. It's just as well though to give them a taste of what happened to the other countries in Europe." Frank added, "There are about four or five German civilians in town here. We don't bother with them, there's a fine for talking to them, but most of the boys don't want anything to do with them, and neither do we have any pity on them."

He apologized to Betty that he hadn't had a chance to mail the scarf made from the parachute used at Bastogne: "I haven't mailed that scarf yet, but I will do so as soon as I find a suitable box for it. I was all ready to send it in an envelope, but it was too frail so I've been looking for something since."

The Sauer River was the boundary between Luxembourg and Germany, and the company diary observed, "It might be interesting to note that Company B was the first company in our battalion to set up a CP on German soil." It had become a long, hard push since the heady days after Normandy.

Although the Sauer River crossing had been successful, the 80th Division still had to deal with the Siegfried Line's dragon's teeth—five rows of pyramid-shaped concrete pillars designed to slow or stop tanks. On February 14, B Company

Tank crosses Saar River, February 1945. *Army Signal Corps*

engineers went up to the Siegfried Line to remove the antitank obstacles. The engineers also demolished five pillboxes while they were there. There would be many more in front of them.

On February 17, the consolidated 80th Division attacked the Siegfried Line along a wide front. The 318th's attack was met by machine guns, mortars, and artillery, but the Germans resisted with less ferocity than expected. The Americans learned the Germans had pulled back from many of the Siegfried Line fortifications. Morale within the German ranks was low, and troops had begun to surrender en masse. Engineers from B Company moved out with the infantry as it went on the attack. Squads of engineers removed dragon's teeth, demolished fortifications, and destroyed doors and embrasures. Earlier, papers found on a German engineer prisoner allowed the 305th to pinpoint almost every pillbox and bunker and minefield as well as demolitions in the vicinity.[48]

Sergeant Gerald Virgil Myers in the 317th Infantry described the way men worked together to take out a bunker: "There were four engineers who crossed the river with us, and they were carrying explosives just in case of situations like this. . . . The engineers made their way to the bunker where they placed satchel charges (10 to 12 pounds of nitro-starch in a canvas bag) at the base of the bunker door. . . . Ten pounds of nitro-starch makes one hell of a noise. . . ." After that they threw in phosphorus grenades. "Phosphorus creates a tremendous amount of acrid smoke

48 After Action Report, S-2, 305th Engineer Combat Battalion, February 1945, 1.

and fire in an enclosed building. When the grenades exploded, we could hear the German soldiers hollering 'comrade, comrade,' and trying to open the door. . . . Twelve German soldiers came rushing out with their hands in the air. We captured the bunker without a casualty."[49]

The 80th Division quickly breached the West Wall, and the groundwork was laid for the 4th Armored's rush to the Rhine.

Captured German troops were impressed with the Americans' superiority of arms and equipment, especially the accuracy of their artillery and coordination of armor, infantry, and artillery. They reported the 80th Division "packed more firepower than other units they had seen in the war." At this point, the German Army was running out of fuel, as well as men and equipment, and the cards were stacked against it. The Luftwaffe by now had all but disappeared, and Allied planes now ruled the skies.[50]

Frank must have dashed out his February 17 letter to Betty in a brief free moment. His handwriting is rushed and the ink on the page is splotched.

> A few short lines to let you know that all is well and tell you a little bit about the way we are living now. We moved out of buildings and now I'm in a pup tent again somewhere in this damned Heine land. Things have returned to normal and I guess will stay this way for awhile. It isn't very warm yet, and your day is done as soon as it gets dark. We've been pretty busy on roads and they are a mess around here, but we do our part by working and trying to keep things moving. Needless to say, I'll be glad when this war is over with.

He obliquely referred to his experience during the Sauer crossing, careful to avoid the eyes of the censor. "Coming into Germany my passage was by boat the first time, and after this war I'll tell you all about it. The country in this part is rugged and maybe later it will get a little better. We have had about three days of sunshine and I hope it keeps up."

The 80th Division's after-action report considered February 17 to be the end of the campaign to cross the Sauer/Our River and consolidate its bridgeheads. Starting the next day, the engineers took on their next mission—the Prüm River and beyond.[51]

---

49 Quoted in Rice, *Through Our Eyes*, 139-40.

50 Craig, *The 80th Infantry Division*, 51.

51 After-Action Report, 80th Division, February 1945.

CHAPTER 13

ENTRY INTO GERMANY: FEB. 18-28, 1945

THERE was no pause for the 80th Infantry Division after it established its bridgehead across the Sauer River. On February 17, Maj. Gen. Horace McBride issued Field Message 1, which ordered the division to launch an attack east toward the Prüm River the next morning.[1]

The Allied attacks along the Siegfried Line may have taken a serious toll on the German Army, but the enemy still created havoc with mines, booby traps, artillery strikes, and demolitions. B Company, operating in close support of the 318th Regiment, went ahead of the infantry on February 18 to clear mines, mark roads, remove obstacles, and fill craters. The company also maintained the roads by hauling rocks and sand, filling ruts, and improving shoulders.

The consolidated Allied force gained momentum as it surged into the German interior against light opposition. The 2nd and 3rd battalions of the 318th attacked northward and seized Cruchten, encountering "stronger resistance and AT defenses" as it left the city.[2] Engineers from B Company's 2nd Platoon moved into Cruchten with the infantry under a heavy mortar and artillery barrage. The 2nd Platoon captured 36 prisoners, one of whom was a sniper who had fired a few rounds at Captain Marshall and then came out with his hands up. Lt. Gilbert

---

1 80th Division Operational History, February 1945, 17; After-Action Report, S-2, 305th Engineer Combat Battalion, February 1945, 1.

2 After-Action Report, S-3, 80th Division, February 1945; 80th Division Operational History, February 1945, 17-18.

Soldiers from the 305th pose with "Recon" the bird dog. *Battalion photographer*

Smith's dog, "Recon" chased four of the prisoners out of the hayloft of a barn where members of the company happened to be eating supper.[3]

On the night of February 18, the men from B Company's 1st and 2nd platoons moved from Biesdorf into billets in Cruchten, where they were pounded by enemy artillery at intervals during the night. The next morning, Staff Sergeant Lembo's 3rd Platoon and company headquarters joined the others at the Cruchten billet. Enemy artillery shelled the town for an hour after the convoy's arrival, wounding several B Company enlisted men and damaging vehicles.

3   After-Action Report G-3, 80th Infantry Division, February 1945.

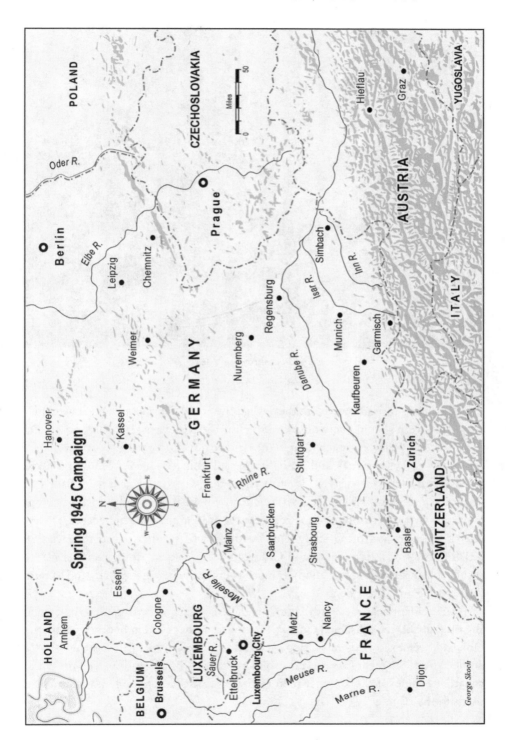

Engineers build corduroy road. *Army Signal Corps*

Mine clearing continued into the daylight hours of February 19. Squads from B Company were sent in every direction to clear the roadways so the infantry could pass. The 2nd Platoon, which cleared the roads from Cruchten to Hommerdingen, removed 20 Teller mines and 22 light antitank mines. The 1st Platoon cleared mines from the roads east and west of Cruchten, where they also demolished an abandoned 88mm artillery piece. American infantry turned back a squad of engineers that was reconnoitering roads north of Hommerdingen because a heavy enemy weapon was firing straight down the road. Another squad removed 28 Teller mines from the road west of Cruchten, while a squad doing reconnaissance on another road leading to Hommerdingen found a 60-yard-long abatis and a crater 22 feet long and 7 feet deep.

An accident near the 305th's command post on February 19 rattled the men in B Company. After a disabled tank was removed, mines hidden beneath where the tank had been exploded, destroying a jeep and killing four men from the 244th field artillery. Staff Sergeant Lembo and a soldier from one of his squads filled the crater caused by the explosion. Other men in Frank's platoon repaired and maintained roads in the regimental sector.

The actions of Lembo's 3rd Platoon featured prominently in the company diary as crews reconnoitered and kept the roads open in the vicinity of Cruchten. On one occasion, men from the platoon built a 100-foot-long corduroy (log) road for the infantry. On February 20, Lembo's platoon and a tank bulldozer removed two tanks and an enemy assault gun from a roadway and cleared rubble and debris from the roads around Frieligen.

B Company's 1st and 2nd platoons were also engaged in mine clearing around Cruchten and other nearby towns. Lieutenant Henke's 1st Platoon cleared 30 Teller mines from the roadway between Hommerdingen and Freilingen and 52 Teller mines at a nearby road junction. The platoon's work was interrupted by enemy fire. Lieutenant Smith's 2nd Platoon also drew fire when it cleared the roads from Hommerdingen to Kewenig to Huttingen.

The company lost count of the number of mines demolished by its three platoons; however, the crews found some unusual items during their reconnaissance and mine-clearing operations. The 1st Platoon found a knocked out friendly tank as well as four scuttled Tiger tanks that had run out of fuel. A night detail went out to remove booby traps from an enemy 88mm gun. They disabled a charge they found in the muzzle and turned the piece over to the 318th to use against the enemy.

The men found ways to add some interest to their mine-clearing activities. The company diary for February 20 reports that Staff Sergeant Lembo's platoon blew up 500 Teller mines in piles of 50 to 200 in a field. "All the windows in buildings in our billeting area were broken. Everybody in town thought a new 'V' weapon was coming in and started for the cellars. It was really comical."

Frank told Betty about this humorous episode in a February 20 letter as he was "sitting here before the fire with a candle going and writing to my honey. What could be better in Germany?" He mentioned the mine demolition: "There hasn't been much doing since my last letter. We took out a rather large minefield today and the only fun in it was when we blew them up and shook hell out of everything around. There were 500 of them, and they didn't cause us any trouble so I didn't mind taking them out. I'd just as soon leave them in so that after the war the Heine would have to put up with them but there is always a chance that our own men might run into them."

The image of Betty and memories of the time they spent together before he left were clearly etched into his mind. In his letters, he often expressed the hope they could recapture these treasured moments when it came time to take up where they'd left off. Frank never doubted their time would come. In his February 20 letter he observed that she looked thin in the photo she'd sent, "but I guess by the time I get home you'll be just like when I left you." He added, "Honey I wish I could be with you even if for just a few minutes. I've missed you so much in the past seven months and miss you more as each day passes."

On February 21, he reported, "The artillery is laying down a barrage and this house shakes and shudders, the table jumps, the lights flicker, and the damn windows nearly blow in. All is quiet again." He continued, "Our electric lights won't work, so we have to resort to the use of candles again. We need a good battery I guess. There is a Heine tank knocked out about ½ mile away, so tomorrow I think we'll get a battery from there. I'll be glad when we are back in civilian life and then all we'll have to do is press a switch and presto."

In a blasé way Frank told Betty, "We had a little work today up at the front but we didn't get very much. There were some Germans around and it's a nuisance trying to work with someone annoying you. They knocked one of our trucks out so we left." The company diary recorded the action: "First platoon and one squad of the third platoon were sweeping roads of mines in the vicinity of Freilingen, Germany. They were fired on by the enemy. Pfc Isaac Stumbo set up a Cal. 30 machine gun and with Capt. Robert Marshall directing fire engaged the enemy in a fire fight. They inflicted unknown casualties on the enemy; later withdrew without a casualty."

On February 20, the 317th met surprisingly strong resistance when it attacked toward Mettendorf, "the largest town and key road center in the area." The next evening the 318th made a surprise night attack and seized the high ground south of the town, bringing the town under direct fire. Fighting in Mettendorf continued until February 25, when the 317th entered the town in the early morning hours. The 318th completed mopping up Mettendorf later that day.[4]

By this point the mine-clearing work had become so extreme the engineers received some sorely needed assistance. On February 22, the 318th Infantry's mine platoon, consisting of one officer and 19 enlisted men, was attached to B Company to aid in mine-clearing operations. Unsurprisingly, according to the diary, "they are glad to be with us." In a month when the 318th suffered 311 killed and seriously wounded, attachment to the engineers seemed like a good option.

Also on February 22, B Company prepared for its next move, sending two men from each platoon to Hutteringen on a quartering party, but they found nothing but ruins. A squad subsequently discovered several mines in and around the town, including 68 Teller mines and an unknown quantity of igniters for Schuh mines.

4 Ibid.

Frank Lembo and one of his squads went to clear an S-minefield in the town that had caused five casualties, but they were unable to clear it by nightfall. The squad marked the field with tape, and the next morning they removed 27 S-mines. They also found more igniters at a dump.

The 305th's B Company platoons kept busy repairing, maintaining, and sweeping the roads in the 318th's sector as the days of February wore on. The number of Teller mines the company located and destroyed continued to rise. The company diary reported that two officers and a sergeant visited the prisoner of war cage while intelligence officers were interrogating some German engineers, presumably to gain information about patterns used in their minefields and obstacles.

In the midst of this intense engineering activity, Frank's life took a sudden turn. On February 23, twelve days after being named temporary commander of the 3rd Platoon, he spent the morning getting a physical prior to his being commissioned a 2nd lieutenant. Later that day he wrote to Betty: "I had a physical examination today and my blood pressure and pulse was a little high so I have to go back again tomorrow. It will probably be normal." Hopefully, she took Frank's hint and guessed he had been promoted.

Frank's letter was filled with optimism despite the external conditions. "Today there was a little break in our work. I went back and got a shower and needless to say it hit the spot. Then I had to go back to the rear areas on business. It's funny, a month ago we were near a city and it was a ghost town, rather ruined and the stink of dead around.[5] Today I went through it and it's amazing how fast a city can rebuild, we darn near got lost in it."

Frank's thoughts were drawn to old friends and acquaintances. "Sup must be out of school now and on a new assignment. I don't hear too much from him, and usually the only news I get is from Jo. Her boyfriend is back in action again so he must not have been wounded seriously. Glad to hear Lou Bay and Flo are getting along okay. They are lucky to be able to be together in the States. Some people have all the luck, but honey our time will come sometime, and you can be sure when it comes we'll be happy and have our share of fun."

Army buddies were also on his mind. He gave Betty an update on his friend Scotty. "I was talking to Scotty today and he said he owed you a letter, and it reminded me that I never answered Terry's letter. We discussed your worries and

---

5 The business he refers to could have been related to his pending promotion (which he still apparently hadn't told Betty about) and the city quite possibly was Ettelbruck.

our views were in common. Scotty by the way is looking good. I believe his operation did him good, or maybe it was the rest he got." About another friend, he wrote, "Bill Wiediman right now is working Heine prisoners on the road in the rear areas. I passed him today and got a heck of a good laugh. They are getting wise and not handling prisoners with kid gloves anymore."

On February 24, one of Lembo's squads cleared a field of 217 Teller mines west of Hommerdingen and then they took advantage of another opportunity to have fun with their cache. In a field about 75 yards from town, the platoon piled them up in stacks of 60 and placed a charge against them. The concussion from the explosion shattered all the plaster from the kitchen ceilings around town and "destroyed the best supper 'Pappy' Lynch had prepared for some time." Later that day, Lembo's 3rd Platoon was back to work, clearing the minefields near Cruchten.

He wrote to Betty the next day and casually referred to Teller mine demolition. "Yesterday was a hectic day. They were blowing mines about a hundred yards from our house, and all the windows blew out and it knocked us for a big loop. About every ten minutes you were jumping out of your seat for one thing or another." Despite the damage his boys had done to Pappy Smith's kitchen, Frank added, "Lately we've been eating very good, and it's amazing. Yesterday it was eggs and toast for breakfast, hamburgers for dinner, pork chops, and French fries for supper. I hope it continues."

February 25 was a Sunday, and Frank took the opportunity to go to church for the first time in quite a while. His religious upbringing was deeply ingrained, and religious observances brought to mind other memories as well. "Easter isn't too far off, and I wish I could be where I was last year, but it doesn't look that way. Gee, I remember last year you got so mad because I didn't send you flowers."

He again voiced the hope that things would be the same when he returned home. "I've been thinking of you lately and hoping that soon we [will] have our own little home and get settled down. We've been waiting so damn long and I think we were fools not to get married before I came over here, but it's too late to think about it now. We'll just have to make up for it all, and I think we can." He added, "Outside of getting married honey I haven't thought too much of the future. I think I'd like to get into radio, it's one of the best fields, I think, and if I could get into a good television school I'd like it."

The company departed Cruchten on February 26 and motored to a new billeting area, where the infantry and engineers had been operating. The company diary noted, "Lt. Gilbert Smith and two squads from the second platoon left Cruchten at 1530 for Mettendorf to hold onto a billeting area for the company."

On the same day, Frank sent Betty another letter on U.S. Army stationery. He opened up in an uncharacteristic way, articulating discouragement about his life as a GI and platoon leader. He seldom expressed such thoughts in his letters. He told Betty, "For the past three days it's been raining continuously and besides having our blankets wet, we've been wet to the skin. It was so darn miserable that we just stayed up at night trying to keep warm. All I can say is damn the desert and damn California."

He continued, "Tomorrow I hope to be able to shave and clean up. If you were to see me now I don't think you'd recognize me but that's that. My feet from this rain are a heck of a mess. They are split open at the toes, and everything is no fun. I can't imagine what caused it, but it really came on me fast. I hate the thought of going to bed tonight. My blankets are wet and it's still raining so there isn't much chance of their drying, but I guess I'll be able to manage." Clearly, if Lieutenant Smith had been able to get a billeting area for the company, it was far from a desirable one.

Problems with the cold and rain were exacerbated by pressures from the senior officers, who expected the men to work even harder, despite the miseries they encountered every day.

> We Sergeants have been catching hell on every turn of the road and it seems we can't please our officers. They're working our men to death and want us to keep pushing them. This past week was a tough one and the boys did a good job, but still they weren't satisfied. Around eight at night they go to bed and expect us to take the men out and keep them working all night. In this rain they put tents up and kept dry and the boys had to stay in foxholes with water up to their knees. It was hard for me.

He then voiced concerns about the future: "Yes dear I've been thinking a lot about getting married and the sooner we get together the better. OCS would have helped so darn much, but now I don't know when I'll go. I'm supposed to be next, but the same thing that happened this time could happen again."[6]

The infantry needed to pass through Mettendorf and clear the way for the armor, but mines still presented obstacles. The Germans had destroyed all the bridges over a cobweb of rivers surrounding the town and had planted mines on every roadway and waterway before withdrawing. One of the engineer squads was

6   Frank was discouraged that fellow platoon commander Gilbert Smith had been promoted to 1st lieutenant while he was still a sergeant and an acting platoon commander. In reality, his promotion to 2nd lieutenant was less than two weeks away at the time he wrote this letter.

Engineers ferry a tank destroyer. *Army Signal Corps*

checking possible fords when it found 13 Teller mines in a ford downstream from one of the blown bridges. Another 21 Teller mines were destroyed at a nearby road junction.

Once the infantry had seized Mettendorf, German resistance became much lighter, and the 80th Division moved out quickly, coming up behind the 4th Armored. The 80th advanced to the Prüm River by February 28, and shortly afterward it would cross the Prüm, Nims, and Kyll Rivers with the help of the 305th Engineers. A history of the Third Army summarized the month's actions: "By the end of February, Third Army had opened a path up the Prüm Valley toward the Rhine River, cleared the Moselle-Saar Triangle, and passed through most of the West Wall defenses in its sector to within three miles of the city of Trier."[7]

Despite Frank's complaints, in truth, B Company's hard work and accomplishments in support of the 318th Infantry did not go unnoticed. After the February campaign, the company received a commendation for its "magnificent work" with the 318th between February 10 and 25, 1945.

The prisoner count swelled as the Germans made a hasty and disorganized retreat across the Rhineland. Between February 18 and 28, the division captured more than 2,700 prisoners. German soldiers increasingly were deciding their fight

7   Green and Brown, *Patton's Third Army in World War II*, 248.

was over.[8] Nevertheless, American casualties ran high during February, and the 80th Division suffered 448 killed and 247 severely wounded in action. The 318th Infantry suffered the largest number of casualties in the division.[9]

Frank and the men in the 3rd Platoon finally got a break on February 28, when, according to the company diary, "18 EM [enlisted men] received passes to Luxembourg City, Luxembourg. S/Sgt. Frank T. Lembo was in charge of the party."

On February 27, the eve of his departure, Frank happily wrote to Betty: "We've moved up since my last letter and our new location is a lot nicer. Plenty of chickens running around, running water and fairly nice surroundings. It seems honey as if this damn thing may end in the next four months. I guess no one could really say

German POWs held by 8oth Division. *Army Signal Corps*

8   After-Action Report G-3, 80th Infantry Division, February 1945.

9   Murrell, "80th Losses in Action," February 1945.

and the only way we would know for sure is if we knew the true state of the German nation. They sure can't last forever."

Frank's thoughts again drifted toward home. "I imagine you're quite busy at your job. By the way, how is Wrights [Frank's former and Betty's current employer] doing, still going full blast. I guess they'll be busy for quite awhile yet. The Jap war will keep them going."

He enclosed with his letter "something about the division. It should give you a little more information about us." The title of the document, issued by Maj. Gen. Horace McBride, was "Our Motto—The 80th Only Moves Forward." The document gave a synopsis of the Blue Ridge Division's illustrious history, training regimen, and exemplary service during both world wars. It highlighted some of the epic battles Frank had been a part of while in Europe. He wanted to let Betty into his world, and this was the best way he knew how.

He concluded, "Honey when we have children I think we better concentrate on girls. I believe you'd like that and I would too. I hope though that we can soon start our home and get around to raising a family. I believe we were fools to wait, but then we all make mistakes. I love you dearly darling and hope to be able to hold you in my arms again. Good night. For now, Love always, Frank."

That February 27, 1945, letter is the final installment in Frank Lembo's correspondence with Betty Craig from Europe. Betty saved all of Frank's letters as he fought his way across Europe and into Germany (and hundreds more during training). Frank sent her dozens more letters before returning home in January 1946, but none of them have survived.

There were still momentous events to come, however. The war in Europe would continue until May 8, 1945, when the Nazi regime finally capitulated, and the 305th Engineers continued to play an important role in the Third Army's victorious advance.

CHAPTER 14

ACROSS THE RHINE: MARCH 1-31, 1945

A_T the end of February, Third Army was once again under threat of a removal of resources to meet other SHAEF priorities. February 27 was Patton's deadline to halt operations and transfer several Third Army divisions to other commands. The deadline had been set by Eisenhower on February 1 when he delayed the order to halt. But on the evening of February 27, Patton called Bradley to ask about the halt order. He recorded that Bradley authorized Patton to keep attacking "until higher authority steps in. He also said he would not listen for the telephone."[1] Increasingly, as the war continued, Bradley seemed to side more frequently with Patton in SHAEF's political wars.

On March 1, acting quickly before Eisenhower could make good on his threat to cut off supplies and manpower, the Third Army captured the ancient city of Trier on the east bank of the Moselle in the Rhineland.[2] The 1st Battalion of the 318th Infantry was the only 80th unit involved in the assault on Trier.[3] The rest of the 80th Division spent the first nine days of March in defensive positions 30 miles north of the city, mopping up and training, resting, and rehabilitating.[4]

---

1 Blumenson, *Patton Papers*, 648.

2 Ibid., 648-49; Green and Brown, *Patton's Third Army*, 248-49; Patton, *War as I Knew It*, 236-37.

3 After-Action Report, 318th Infantry Regiment, March 1945, 3.

4 After-Action Report, G-3, 80th Infantry Division, March 1945; After-Action Report, S-3, 317th Infantry Regiment, March 1945.

On March 1, Bradley ordered a new Third Army offensive, this time to the Kyll River, 12 miles farther into Germany, and then an advance to the area on the Rhine between Mainz and Koblenz.[5]

In the early morning hours of March 1, while Staff Sergeant Lembo was on leave in Luxembourg City, B Company left its billeting area in Mettendorf and drove 35 miles under blackout conditions to Idesheim. The 3rd Platoon repaired the roads from Idesheim to Welsbillig to pave the way for the next stage of the advance.

The company was placed on alert to move to a rest camp in Arlen, Luxembourg, but the alert was canceled and the convoy instead motored 30 miles in the darkness from Idesheim to Seffern, arriving on March 3 and staying for a week. The company set up a command post—evicting nine German families in the process—and found time to wash its vehicles and inventory its equipment and supplies. A contingent from the medical unit came to the billeting area to give the men shots and monthly physicals and, according to the company diary, "also inspect clothes for cooties."

The rest period did not mean B Company stopped its engineering work. While in Seffern, on March 3, the three platoons of B Company cleared mines and maintained roads in the 318th's regimental sector. On March 5, Lembo's 3rd Platoon removed roadblocks with a bulldozer, repaired culverts, and filled craters. On the same day, engineers found a booby-trapped abatis and 24 improvised antitank mines composed of one-kilogram charges. On another mission, the company's demolition men removed 57 S-mines attached to trip wires.

On March 8, Frank Lembo reached a goal he'd been hoping to achieve since entering the army in November 1942. He had held the rank of staff sergeant and been temporary commander of B Company's 3rd Platoon for only a few weeks when he was commissioned a second lieutenant. His appointment as commander of the 3rd Platoon was made permanent. From the start of his training more than two years earlier, Frank had a passionate desire to become an officer, but his efforts to gain admission to OCS during training were repeatedly frustrated, to his and Betty's dismay. He gave up hope when he went overseas, but his persistence now paid off and his dream was realized.

The company's motor convoy left Seffern on March 11 and traveled 35 miles to a billet in Erpeldange, Luxembourg. Two enlisted men were wounded on the

---

5 Green and Brown, *Patton's Third Army*, 249.

Newly promoted 2nd Lieutenant Frank Lembo. *Battalion photographer*

first night when the billeting area was shelled by German artillery and nebelwerfers. The company didn't stay in Luxembourg for long as a new mission awaited them. B Company turned back into Germany, where they did river and bridge reconnaissance preparatory to the crossing of the Saar River.

Meanwhile, the Third Army was again on the move. On March 8, Eisenhower approved a plan for an offensive through the Palatine region of Germany. Originally the Third Army was assigned a supporting role to "make diversionary attacks . . . to protect the Sixth Army Group's left flank." But on the same day, Bradley approved Patton's plan for an attack in the Palatine, which Eisenhower ultimately approved as well.[6]

German forces were well entrenched, but by this time many German troops seemed eager to surrender[7] and the Third Army units advanced rapidly. By the end of the campaign, for the first time since the race across France the previous summer, Patton's armored columns were rampaging in the German rear. Advances of 15 miles or more in a single day weren't uncommon.[8]

The 80th Division was ordered to take Zerf, a town on the banks of the Saar, where the Germans were holding firm. The 317th's advance toward Zerf was slowed by heavy nebelwerfer and artillery fire aimed at the town. The 2nd Battalion of the 318th moved into Zerf on March 11, despite heavy artillery fire.[9] Meanwhile, the 318th was aiming at its next objective: Oberzerf.

---

6 MacDonald, *Victory in Europe*, 239; Bradley, *A Soldier's Story*, 516.

7 Craig, *80th Division*, 51; After Action Report, 80th Infantry Division G-3, March 1945.

8 MacDonald, *Victory in Europe*, 248.

9 Baptism of Fire, 318th Infantry Regiment, 14.

On March 13, Captain Marshall's B Company and Lieutenant Smith's 2nd Platoon entered Zerf for road reconnaissance and were forced to remain there overnight because of enemy shelling. The Germans threw over another 600 shells in the early morning hours. The company diary reported: "Capt. Marshall and Lt. Smith barricaded the windows with sandbags. Lt. Smith's famous dog 'Recon' was along with the platoon and he seemed to hear the nebelwerfers before anyone else heard them. He would start for the cellar. It got to the point where the men would watch the dog and the moment he took off, so would the boys." At a time like this, there was nothing like a recon dog (and GI humor) to ease the tension.

On March 14, the company moved to a billet in Zerf. The heavy shelling of the town continued unabated. Second Lieutenant Lembo's 3rd Platoon encountered such intense shelling along the approaches to the town that it had to interrupt a road-clearing mission and temporarily abandon its bulldozers. The next day, Lembo's men continued to remove sperries (log cribs) from the roads leading to Zerf while the 2nd Platoon removed antitank traps made up of boards laid across 150mm shells. A patrol of eight Germans fired on a reconnaissance detail led by Captain Marshall, wounding an enlisted man. The men were forced to abandon their jeep and crawl 400 yards to safety. Marshall later went back to get the abandoned jeep. The company diary reported, "The humorous part of this deal was instead of coming back with one jeep they came back with two. It seems that the Germans captured another jeep at one time or another and it took B Company to get it back."

One of B Company's platoons operated in close support of the 318th Infantry and a company of Sherman tanks. A squad improved the Zerf road for two-lane traffic. At the outskirts of Zerf, the 80th Division came under heavy artillery fire and 150mm and 300mm rockets. Lembo's 3rd Platoon removed demolitions from trees and cleared roads in the sector, marking off mines with barbed wire. Persistent firefights along the Zerf road resulted in several engineer casualties.

On March 14, the 318th began the assault on Weiskirchen, and the resistance was strong.[10] On the night of March 15, the enemy established a roadblock that cut the battalion's supply line into Weiskirchen. The 318th's 1st and 2nd battalions continued advancing through the town while Lembo's 3rd Platoon worked to reestablish the supply line. The 2nd Battalion reached the center of Weiskirchen by

---

10 History of 2nd Battalion, 318th Infantry, 35-37; After-Action Report, G-3, 80th Infantry Division, March 1945; Witzgell, "318th Infantry Regiment Unit History," 11-12.

early morning on March 16 but still faced heavy resistance.[11] The town was finally occupied by the 318th Infantry Regiment on March 17 after several days of house-to-house fighting. The defeat of the enemy forces in the town smashed the last line of resistance west of the Rhine and left the road open to the river.[12]

On March 17, the 318th combat team, which included B Company, was assigned to XX Corps and attached to the 10th Armored Division.[13] That day B Company left its billet in Zerf for one in Weiskirchen, clearing roads for the oncoming infantry and armor.

As these events with the 318th transpired, the 317th Infantry, closely following armor, seized a crossing over the Prims River. In the early evening of March 17, the 319th forced another crossing of the Prims and worked all night to expand the bridgehead.

In the five-day campaign to the Prims River (March 13-17), the 80th took 2,505 German prisoners. The division's after-action report revealed a celebratory tone: "The 80th Inf Div shattered the enemy's defensive lines, opening the way for the armor to break through to the east. . . . This being accomplished, the 80th Div went over to the pursuit."[14]

Unlike so many times in the past, when the 80th faced a temporary pause before it could complete a campaign, there was no talk now of stopping the Third Army or adopting a defensive posture.

The Rhine Valley was next in the 80th Division's sights. At the start of the campaign, Patton told his corps commanders they would aim to cross the Rhine at sites near Mainz. On March 7, General Hodges's First Army had found a bridge intact at Remagen and had crossed, but Patton intended to get across the Rhine before his rival, Montgomery.[15] The 80th Division set out to do this on March 18. During the next four days, the division advanced 115 miles, seized the key cities of

11 Witzgell, "318th Infantry Regiment Unit History," March 1945, 10-11; History of 2nd Battalion, 318th Infantry, 36.

12 Baptism of Fire, 318th Infantry Regiment, 15; After-Action Report, G-3, 80th Infantry Division, March 1945.

13 Witzgell, "318th Infantry Regiment Unit History," March 1945, 11.

14 After-Action Report, G-3, 80th Infantry Division, March 1945.

15 MacDonald, *Victory in Europe*, 241.

Third Army tanks pass by abandoned German vehicles and dead horses. *Army Signal Corps*

Kaiserlautern and St. Wendel, and took more than 5,000 German prisoners.[16] The 318th remained attached to the 10th Armored Division during this period.

On March 17, engineer units from the 305th were working ahead of the infantry, preparing roads for the Rhine advance. Enemy activity north of the main supply route forced men from B Company's 2nd Platoon to dismount their trucks and advance on foot. They removed 30 Teller mines and two abatis of 60 logs each. Lembo's 3rd Platoon removed roadblocks, and the 1st Platoon constructed a treadway bridge across a stream near Lenheim.

The 80th Infantry Division advanced quickly now that it was undeterred by major resistance from the bulk of the retreating German forces, but it nevertheless confronted persistent opposition from enemy rear guards as well as mines and booby traps. On March 19, B Company left Weiskirchen, covered 17 miles, and reached St. Wendel. Roadwork and reconnaissance in the 80th's sector continued over the next few days. Lembo's platoon repaired a ford near St. Wendel and checked the division command post for mines and booby traps.

On March 20, the company advanced 20 miles to Niederbahr and another 25 miles to Bad Durkheim. It didn't spend any time at these locations; in fact, it hadn't spent more than a day in one place since Zerf.

---

16 After-Action Report, G-3, 80th Infantry Division, March 1945; Witzgell, "318th Infantry Regiment Unit History," March 1945, 14.

The road was relatively free of German troops but contained many obstacles. Dogged by air attacks, the Germans had left huge amounts of vehicles and equipment and dead horses in their wake, and it was the engineers' responsibility to clear them out of the way. On the road from Kaiserslautern to Bad Durkheim, six of the engineers' bulldozers cleared an estimated 500 vehicles in one afternoon. The division also took in an ever-increasing number of prisoners and, according to the diary, "practically 2/3 of the company found themselves a pistol or some other souvenir."

The 318th Infantry reported the regiment had sustained moderate casualties during the past four days and made an observation that presaged the experience of 80th Division soldiers during the remaining campaigns: "After the breakthrough at Weiskirchen enemy resistance had virtually collapsed as the enemy withdrew NE across the Rhine River, leaving only moderate pockets of resistance along the withdrawal route."[17] The 317th had a similar experience, noting the regiment had captured 26 towns on March 19-20 and took 275 prisoners of war on March 20

Division soldiers march past destroyed half track. *Army Signal Corps*

17 Witzgell, "318th Infantry Regiment Unit history," March 1945, 14.

318th infantry enters Warden, Germany, March 21, 1945. *Army Signal Corps*

---

alone.[18] Nevertheless, what remained could still be deadly as American forces approached the Rhine.

On March 22, the 80th Division was replaced in the front lines and ordered to an assembly area to prepare for the Rhine crossing. The division moved into this area over the next two days.[19] On March 22, B Company's convoy traveled 25 miles and arrived at Grundheim, where the company's officers reconnoitered the 318th combat team area. Over the next two days, the men were able to take a short break and clean and repair their equipment.

The motor convoy was on the move again on March 24 and covered 25 miles to Gundersweiler. The company pushed another 30 miles closer to the Rhine on March 26 and arrived at a billet in Partenheim. The company diary reported a reconnaissance mission to Mainz on the river that night, which resulted in a noteworthy occasion. Captain Marshall, Lieutenant Smith, and an enlisted man found an abandoned enemy machine gun and celebrated their arrival at the Rhine by firing it at the Germans on the distant bank.

On March 26, the 80th Division received orders to cross the Rhine. Patton had brought one Third Army division across a few days earlier at Oppenheim, south of

18 After-Action Report, S-3, 317th Infantry Regiment, March 1945, 2.

19 After-Action Report, G-3, 80th Infantry Division, March 1945.

Mainz. But on March 28, the Third Army descended on the Rhine in force. In this sector all the bridges over the Rhine had been destroyed, so supporting engineers and naval boat operators took the lead role in the crossings. For the most part, the 305th was not directly involved in the assault crossings or combat bridge building; these chores were handled by the 1139th Engineer Group.[20] B Company's platoons worked clearing mines and preparing landing zones during the March 28 crossing.

Elements of the 80th Division met varying amounts of resistance in their crossings. The first two companies of the 317th Infantry crossed under moderate fire in assault boats and experienced some casualties, but resistance quickly faded once the first few troops were on the east bank. G Company was one of the first companies to cross, and Sgt. Gerald Virgil Myers reported: "Each boat held twelve men and one engineer. We were given orders to put our weapons across our neck and shoulders so we would be able to use the oars. . . . A boat about fifty feet from ours was hit by a Quad 20mm, causing it to fill with water and sink in the middle of the river. Right after that incident, the boat I was riding in caught four bullets from the sweep of a German machine gun. The second man from the front and the one sitting in the rear were killed outright. . . . Within an hour or so, enough men from the 317th had made it ashore, which caused those firing from the warehouses to fall back."[21]

The rest of the 317th crossed the Rhine in navy LCVPs (Landing Craft, Vehicle, Personnel), the famed Higgins boats used in the D-day landings and other amphibious operations.[22]

The 318th and 319th Regiments met only light resistance during their Rhine crossings. The 319th crossed on a XII Corps bridge near Oppenheim, while the 318th, which started the day in division reserve, crossed in LCVPs into the 317th's zone.[23] Both the 317th and 319th continued their attacks beyond the Rhine on the day they crossed.[24]

B Company's motor convoy traveled 35 miles and finally arrived in Mainz, on the banks of the Rhine, on March 28. Two squads from each of B Company's

---

20 After-Action Report, 305th Engineer Combat Battalion, March 1945, 2.

21 Quoted in Rice, *Through Our Eyes*, 145.

22 After-Action Report, S-3, 305th Engineer Combat Battalion, March 1945.

23 After-Action Report, 305th Engineer Combat Battalion, March 1945, 2; After-Action Report, G-3, 80th Division, March 1945.

24 After-Action Report, G-3, 80th Division, March 1945.

Navy LCVP transports Sherman tank across Rhine River. *US Army*

platoons went across the Rhine on navy landing craft. The men cleared mines and worked to secure the bridgehead.[25]

The remaining squads from the company cleared mines in Mainz and crossed the river two days later on an 1,851-foot-long treadway bridge, the longest built by Americans across the "mighty river" and one of the longest of the war. The company had been attached to the 6th Armored Division while coming across the Rhine, but now reverted to its support role for the 318th.

The 305th's two other companies, A and C companies, guided infantry to their boats, constructed landing sites and approaches for the 318th on both sides of the river, and cleared roads.[26] The next day, March 30, any men and vehicles still remaining at the Mainz billet crossed over the 1,851-foot-long bridge.

By the end of March 1945, most elements of the 80th Division were on the eastern side of the Rhine and quickly charging northeast through central Germany,

25 Morning Report, B Company, 305th Engineer Combat Group, March 28-29, 1945.

26 Morning Reports, A and C Companies, 305th Engineer Combat Battalion, March 28-29, 1945.

toward the city of Kassel.[27] Reports were filed citing even longer distances of travel than before; for example, a typical unit reported that it "moved 51 miles . . . along the Autobahn."[28]

In the last few days of March, B Company continued to operate in support of the 318th Infantry. On March 29, it removed roadblocks and cleared roads from Kassel to Erbenheim to Bierstadt to Aleppenheim and did general engineering work in the 318th's sector.

On March 31, B Company left the Rhine behind and motored 59 miles to a new billeting area in Lendorf, Germany, stopping to do bridge repair in the town of Zinnern.

There had been a distinct change in the character of the fight once the Third Army's tanks were unleashed earlier in the month. The 317th Infantry reported, "German resistance during this period was sporadic and of not too determined a character." The regiment was now able to take calculated risks "which would not have proven feasible under conditions of combat prior to this period."[29]

The breakthrough also affected the lives and work of the men of the 305th. For one thing, the division was now advancing on good roads with fewer obstacles, so comparatively less roadwork and mine-clearing efforts were required. A report noted, "Once we broke through, as expected, the enemy did not have sufficient time, or organization, to plan and lay minefields. We found, as in the past, that in a fast-moving situation, few mines are laid." Similarly, once they had passed St. Wendel in midmonth, the 80th Division was moving so quickly that "most bridges were captured intact." Still, the road wasn't entirely clear; friendly bombers created many road craters that the engineers had to fill in.[30]

In sum, success made its own success: the collapse of enemy resistance allowed the 80th Division to advance rapidly, which in turn meant less damage to the road network and fewer obstacles, which allowed the rapid advance to continue unabated.

---

27 After-Action Report, 80th Division, March 1945.

28 After-Action Report, 318th Infantry Regiment, March 1945, 18.

29 After-Action Report, 317th Infantry Regiment, March 1945, 3.

30 After-Action Report, 305th Engineer Combat Battalion, March 1945, 3.

CHAPTER 15

INTO THE HEART OF GERMANY: APRIL 1-20, 1945

THE next major operation assigned to the 80th Division's three infantry regiments was to seize and secure the city of Kassel, a major rail, industrial, and communication center. It was also a critical supplier of war materiel, including tanks, locomotives, aircraft engines, heavy-duty trucks, and antitank guns. Allied bombers had hit Kassel hard beginning in 1942, destroying a large segment of its infrastructure and causing civilians to flee. The population had been reduced by 80 percent by the time the 80th Division arrived.[1]

General McBride ordered the 318th Infantry to advance into Kassel, and the 317th and 319th were ordered to seize the outlying towns and attack the Germans as they withdrew from the city.

There was plenty of engineering work to do as the 80th Division passed through town after town, from Lendorf and Zinnern to Guderberg and Brasselburg. On April 1, B Company left its billet in Lendorf and arrived at Zinnern, six miles distant. While the company was temporarily attached to the 6th Armored during its earlier movements, it now reverted to supporting the 318th Infantry Regiment. The Germans had left mines and obstacles behind them, closing off essential roads and bridges. The engineers removed sperries from the entrances and exits of almost every town between the Rhine and Kassel. Engineers

---

1 "Ten Most Devastating Bombing Campaigns of World War II," www.onlinemilitary education.org/posts/10-most-devastating-bombing-campaigns-of-wwii/ (Accessed January 25, 2017.)

also needed to establish a series of bridgeheads over the Edder and Ems rivers along the route from the Rhine.

On April 2, as the 80th Division neared Kassel, squads from B Company did reconnaissance, removed roadblocks, filled craters, and hauled off burning and abandoned vehicles of all kinds, including five Tiger tanks.

A motor march of seven miles on April 3 brought the company to Brasselburg. Along the way there was also a considerable amount of demolition work to do. In the vicinity of Kassel, a detail from Lieutenant Lembo's 3rd Platoon destroyed eight 88mm artillery pieces, six 20mm antiaircraft cannons, and a large amount of explosives and ammunition. The 2nd Platoon destroyed three 88mm guns. The engineers came under fire and some of their number provided security while others did the engineering work. A number of enemy aircraft flew over the area.

By now American tanks were rampaging freely in the German countryside. The army's official history noted, "For both the 4th and 6th Armored, the attacks on . . . 29 and 30 March were little more than road marches."[2] But the initially weak German resistance strengthened as the 80th closed in on Kassel.[3] The 305th Engineer Combat Battalion's companies moved with the three infantry regiments as they closed around the city; B Company supported the 318th, as before. The three combat teams from the 80th met stubborn resistance in and around the city.

The 80th found the German forces had been reinforced. According to one story, the Americans were frustrated because as soon as they took out one tank another would appear. It was later learned the tanks were being made at a nearby underground factory and pushed into battle, manned by recruits from a nearby training school.[4] The Germans put up everything they could find to defend one of their last remaining strongholds.

The fighting was often house-to-house.[5] The Germans held fast, and the 318th engaged them for two days. There were constant demands on the engineers during the engagement in Kassel, and they had to stand up in unexpected ways. In close fighting, men from Lieutenant Smith's 2nd Platoon captured 13 German soldiers who were guarding a roadblock.

2 MacDonald, *Victory in Europe*, 374.

3 Patton, *War as I Knew It*, 266.

4 Craig, *The 80th Infantry Division*, 53.

5 Baptism of Fire, 318th Infantry Regiment, 16-17.

The 318th finally secured Kassel on April 4, supported by attached tanks and tank destroyer units.[6] Inside the city, the 318th's combat team took a record number of prisoners, a considerable amount of equipment, and numerous key installations, including rail yards, factories, and power plants, as well as bridges over the Fulda River.

In addition to withstanding fire on the battlefield, the 80th encountered opposition from the skies over Kassel when enemy aircraft strafed the division's positions. B Company's column was strafed on April 5 and again by eight enemy aircraft two days later.

By April 5 the 80th was in control of Kassel and the outlying towns, earning hard-won praise from Patton: "Whenever we turned to the 80th Division on anything, we always knew the objective would be attained."[7]

Amid the fighting at Kassel, the company diary reported the unexpected news that Lt. Arthur Henke, longtime commander of the 1st Platoon and Lembo's former commanding officer, left the company to become assistant division engineer. Henke had been one of B Company's officers since its arrival in Normandy and was one of Lembo's best friends in the war. Lembo had gone on many difficult missions with Henke across France, Luxembourg, and Belgium before being promoted and taking over his own platoon. Lembo must have been sorry to see the trusted Henke go. On the same day as his promotion, the company diary reported that Henke discovered an enemy arsenal in Kassel.

The days in and around Kassel had a few light moments. On April 4, one of the company's squads found a German PX truck amid the abandoned vehicles. Despite enemy small arms fire, the squad brought back chocolates, champagne, milk, and salmon for B Company. The next day, Capt. Robert C. Marshall added to the company's largesse when he brought the men "300 rolls of film, shaving lotion, and cigarette lighters." The company also took possession of an enemy Buick and, as the diary described it, "a six-by-six truck, and what a six-by-six."

Once Kassel was captured, B Company aided the 80th's efforts to patrol the city, maintain law and order, and establish roadblocks. The company performed these duties in the city until April 6.

With the disintegration of the German defenses and the fall of Kassel, Eisenhower ordered Patton to shift the army's axis and get into position to attack east toward Chemnitz rather than continuing to attack to the north. But he also

---

6 Ibid., 16; After-Action Report, 80th Infantry Division, April 1945.

7 Patton, *War as I Knew It*, 266; Craig, *The 80th Infantry Division*, 53.

ordered Patton to halt his forces temporarily to allow the U.S. First and Ninth armies to come on line with him. Although Bradley considered holding up Patton's advance long enough to allow the First Army to catch up, opportunity overwhelmed his caution, and despite Ike's wishes, he ordered Patton to advance.

The Allied command received intelligence that a German command and communication center was situated underground near the village of Ohrdruf, 100 miles beyond the Third Army's current position. Patton's troops were dispatched to seize the facility and potentially isolate senior-level members of the German command structure.[8] The 80th was ordered to push toward Gotha, about 25 road miles from Ohrdruf, following and mopping up behind the 4th Armored. As the Third Army's vanguard, the 4th Armored was rolling toward Gotha, Erfurt, Weimar, and Chemnitz.

Third Army forces discovered there was indeed a Nazi communication center in Ohrdruf, but it wasn't in operation. It had been built in 1939 during the crisis over the annexation of Czechoslovakia, but it had never been activated.

American troops, however, found something more disturbing when they arrived at Ohrdruf: a concentration camp.[9] Soldiers from the 4th Armored Division, which had moved ahead of the 80th to search for the rumored command and control center, discovered the concentration camp on April 4. The finding confirmed what the Allies had only feared until then—the Nazis' atrocities against Jews. Ohrdruf was the first of many camps liberated by the soldiers of the Third Army.

When the 4th Armored entered the camp, they found corpses piled in barracks like logs and scattered on the ground. The few prisoners who were alive were near death, emaciated, and diseased. One of the first soldiers to enter the camp said, "I still have vivid memories of what I saw, but I try not to dwell on it. We had been warned about what we might find, but actually seeing it was horrible. There were so many dead, and some so starved all they could do was gape open their mouths, feebly move their arms and murmur."[10]

Ohrdruf, a subcamp of the notorious slave-labor camp at Buchenwald, had once housed 10,000 prisoners, but nearly all of the inmates had been evacuated on April 2 in a forced march to Buchenwald, only a few days before the 4th Armored

---

8 MacDonald, *Victory in Europe*, 376-77.

9 Ibid., 378.

10 A. C. Boyd, 89th Infantry Division, quoted in Jimmy Smothers, "World War II Veteran Recalls Scenes at Death Camp," *Gadsden Times*, May 4, 2009.

arrived. Many prisoners had originally been brought to Ohrdruf to construct the vast underground communication center Patton was searching for.

Patton's soldiers made a discovery of a different nature near Gotha. On April 7, the 90th Division entered the Kaiseroda salt mine near Merkers and found the entire gold and currency reserves of the Reichsbank and art treasures from Berlin museums. The Germans had moved the art to the mine to protect it from Allied bombing, and the surprising speed of Third Army's advance prevented them from moving the treasures out of the Americans' path.[11]

Within a week, the Allied high command—including Eisenhower, Bradley, and Patton—visited the prison camp and the mine to see the discoveries for themselves. In the meantime, the troops were ordered to secure the Ohrdruf camp and leave it intact until the generals arrived. Elements of the 80th moved in to provide guard duty.

Angered by what he saw at the camp, Col. Hayden Sears, the commander of 4th Armored's Combat Command A, ordered the citizens of Ohrdruf to come to the camp to witness what had happened under their noses. For perhaps the first (but not last) time, a citizen shouted out that only a small fraction of German soldiers committed these atrocities and the rest should not be blamed. Sears replied, "Tell them that they have been brought here to see with their own eyes what is reprehensible from any human standard and that we hold the entire German nation responsible by their support and toleration of the Nazi government." Reportedly, the mayor and his wife hanged themselves that night.[12]

News of the Ohrdruf camp spread by the time B Company arrived at Gotha. The company's motor convoy went 72 miles southeast from Kassel, traveling all night, and reached a billeting area in Hania, not far from Gotha, on April 7. Enemy aircraft strafed the column as it motored to its new location, and the American troops encountered uneven opposition on the ground, meeting "resistance that could now be considered normal—roadblocks manned by motley contingents of infantrymen, antiaircraft artillerymen, Volkssturm, whatever; an occasional tank or

---

11 Greg Bradsher, "Nazi Gold: The Merkers Mine Treasure," *Prologue: Quarterly Magazine of the National Archives and Records Administration* 31, no. 1 (Spring 1999), . https://www.archives.gov/publications/prologue/1999/spring/nazi-gold-merkers-mine-treasure.html. Accessed April 2, 2017.)

12 Saul Levitt, "Ohrdruf Camp," *Yank Magazine*, May 18, 1945, 4.

self-propelled gun; sometimes a quick strafing run by one or two Me 109s; blown bridges."[13]

As the 80th advanced through central Germany, American GIs encountered refugees who were fleeing any of the hundreds of concentration camps, slave-labor camps, and prisoner-of-war camps that dotted Germany's towns and countryside. Thousands of refugees clogged the roads in the path of the men and vehicles making their way to Gotha, and Lembo's jeep was no doubt among them. Most of the men, women, and children wandering the roadsides were dazed, sick, or near death while others fell beside the road. The need to share roads with the homeless added to the other stresses of combat for the men of the 80th Division.

The refugees added to the Third Army's challenge of providing food and water. Much of the local infrastructure was wrecked, and the presence of Third Army overwhelmed the area's support structure. Since Normandy, one of the functions of the engineers was to establish water points to distribute water to the troops—and also sometimes the local populace.

The 317th and 318th Infantry moved into Gotha on April 7, while the 319th, in divisional reserve, moved from Kassel and took over the duties of maintaining law and order in the city.[14] B Company assembled with the rest of the 80th when it reached Gotha and began to operate toward Erfurt, about 14 miles to the east. The 305th reconnoitered the Reich autobahn southeast of Gotha in preparation for the division's movement to Erfurt and Weimar. The retreating Germans had blown many of the autobahn bridges, and the road was heavily mined. The 206th Engineer Combat Battalion, in support of the 305th, constructed Bailey and treadway bridges to span gaps in the autobahn. This road would become the backbone of the Third Army's drive east.

On April 8, B Company traveled another 20 miles to Seebergen and immediately began to reconnoiter the roads in the 318th's sector. The 318th met sporadic opposition as it moved through the towns between Gotha and Erfurt, leading the 80th's advance. One of the company's patrols stopped Germans who were moving a railroad engine out of a railyard. Demolition men were called in to destroy the tracks. The company continued to operate under fire, and enemy air activity intensified. That day the men watched in astonishment when enemy planes

13 MacDonald, *Victory in Europe*, 376.

14 After-Action Report, 80th Infantry Division, April 1945.

were engaged in a dogfight with P-47s. They watched for 20 minutes until a Thunderbolt shot down a Messerschmitt.

Patton described a new method of taking a town that had been devised by the 80th Division. On approaching a town, artillery would fire several projectiles containing messages to warn the townsfolk they must surrender or face destruction. The bürgermeister (mayor) was required to personally surrender and affirm that no resisting German troops remained in town. Then a few flights of fighter-bombers passed over the town, flying lower on each pass. If no surrender was forthcoming at the end of a set period of time, the aircraft bombed the town and the artillery opened fire on the town. Patton was pleased to observe that many towns surrendered "without difficulty."[15] During this final attack to the east, Weimar surrendered after the ultimatum was delivered, but the division encountered "determined resistance" or "a fanatical group" or "stubborn resistance" in Allach, Erfurt, and Gera.[16] An April 13, an AP story reported that the German commander at Jena refused the ultimatum, but the 80th Division captured the town after a short "honor battle," during which the Germans only fired a few shots.[17]

On April 10, while Lieutenant Lembo was on a quartering party, the company moved six miles from Seebergen to Kleinrettbach and pursued a wide range of missions. A detail was fired upon while on road reconnaissance toward Erfurt, and another detail found a crater while doing road reconnaissance in Nad-Dietendorf, but they were unable to fill it because American artillery was shelling the town. A detail led by Capt. Robert Marshall and Lt. Gilbert Smith reconnoitered into Volleberr to determine the strength of the enemy defenses.

On April 10, the 2nd Battalion of the 318th was attacking toward the southeast section of Erfurt. The battalion met "stiff resistance all day" but captured Schmira and Bischleben.[18] The attack toward Erfurt continued the next day as the 318th seized the high ground and prepared to assault the city. One squad from Lembo's 3rd Platoon went on patrol with the 318th's 2nd Battalion and removed roadblocks south of Erfurt, and another squad of company engineers removed destroyed

---

15 Patton, *War as I Knew It*, 278. Examples of the use of ultimatums can be found in After-Action Report, 80th Infantry Division, April 1945 (Weimar); 80th Division Operational History, April 1945, 23 (Erfurt); and "Town of Jena Taken After 'Honor Battle,'" Associated Press, April 13, 1945.

16 After-Action Report, 80th Infantry Division, April 1945.

17 "Town of Jena Taken After 'Honor Battle,'" Associated Press, April 13, 1945.

18 After-Action Report, 80th Infantry Division, April 1945.

enemy vehicles that were blocking the main supply route. Seven enemy aircraft flew overhead, and four were shot down by antiaircraft fire.

During one action, B Company's 1st and 2nd platoons were removing roadblocks while under fire near Erfurt, and Captain Marshall was slightly wounded. The company diary reported, "He was hit in the upper abdomen. The bullet went through his binoculars and a 'D' ration bar, which probably saved him from serious injury."

A movement of eight miles brought the company to Newerhauser the next day, April 11. Lembo's platoon continued to operate in support of the 318th's 2nd Battalion and removed roadblocks in Erfurt. Other squads did reconnaissance. By dark on that day, the 2nd Battalion of the 318th reached "the SE outskirts of Erfurt and occupied positions to launch the final assault on the city" in concert with the other two battalions as well as the 317th. The 319th, accompanying the 4th Armored, bypassed Erfurt.[19] That night, the 318th Infantry delivered the division's "surrender or be destroyed" ultimatum, but the German garrison ignored the message.[20]

The 80th had to fight its way into Erfurt. On April 12, the 318th broke through the enemy lines in town and the resistance crumbled. By 7:00 p.m. all resistance had been overcome. The 4th Armored was out ahead of the 80th, accompanied by elements of the 319th, traveling on the autobahn that B Company's engineers had cleared and repaired only days before.[21]

On April 12, Eisenhower, Bradley, and Patton visited the Merkers salt mine, shortly after follow-ups confirmed the mine was indeed holding extensive deposits of gold, currency, and artwork. After lunch, the party continued on to the Ohrdruf concentration camp.[22]

According to one account, when they arrived at Ohrdruf, "the generals, though used to carnage in many forms, were shocked."[23] Bradley recalled, "The smell of death overwhelmed us, even before we passed through the stockade. More than 3,200 naked emaciated bodies had been flung into shallow graves. Others lay

---

19 Ibid.

20 Operational History, 80th Infantry Division, April 1945, 23.

21 After-Action Report, 80th Infantry Division, April 1945.

22 Patton, *War as I Knew It*, 274-76.

23 Robert H. Abzug, *Inside the Vicious Heart: Americans and the Liberation of Nazi Concentration Camps* (New York: Oxford University Press, 1985), 27.

Generals Patton, Eisenhower, and Bradley view Ohrdruf concentration camp. *US Army*

in the streets where they had fallen. Lice crawled over the yellowed skin on the sharp, bony frames."[24]

Visibly shaken, Eisenhower insisted on seeing everything, including the sheds with ceiling-high piles of bodies, mass graves, torture devices, and a pyre with half-burned corpses. In a letter to army chief of staff George Marshall, Ike wrote: "The things I saw beggar description. . . . The visual evidence and the verbal testimony of starvation, cruelty, and bestiality were so overpowering as to leave me a bit sick. In one room, where there were piled up twenty or thirty naked men, killed by starvation. . . . I made the visit deliberately, in order to be in position to give first-hand evidence of these things if ever, in the future, there develops a tendency to charge these allegations merely to 'propaganda'."[25] The Nazi masters of the camp had tried desperately to eliminate the evidence of their acts before the Allies closed in.

24 Bradley, *A General's Life*, 539.

25 Dwight Eisenhower, letter to George Marshall, April 15, 1945. . www.lettersofnote.com/search/label/dwighteisenhower(Accessed November 17, 2016.)

In his memoirs, Eisenhower wrote, "I have never felt able to describe my emotional reaction when I first came face to face with indisputable evidence of Nazi brutality and ruthless disregard of every shred of decency.[26] Patton called Ohrdruf "the most appalling sight imaginable"[27]; he reportedly vomited behind the barracks.

Eisenhower ordered as many American troops as possible to visit the camp. He also wanted to confront as many Germans with the barbaric acts done by their society, and he wanted as many witnesses as possible to forestall any future claims that such accounts of the death camps were exaggerated.[28]

Three enlisted men from B Company were among the servicemen who toured the camp at Ohrdruf at the direction of Patton. The company diary reported the three men "made a trip to Ohrdruf Germany to see a former German concentration camp and saw the methods of torture used by the Germans. Approximately one hundred and fifty slave laborers from occupied countries were murdered and piled in one room of a building." The diary does not say how the information brought back about the camp affected the men. As an officer and platoon commander, Lembo would have known what was going on, but he never spoke of his experiences at the camps once he came home from the war.

A flood of German soldiers surrendered to the 80th as city after city fell and the Wehrmacht's outlook turned increasingly bleak. A soldier from the 80th Division recalled the German soldiers' attitude "was one of complete abandonment to his fate. He found his fate lay only in two directions, death or the P.W. camp. P.W. figures grew astronomically, and interrogation degenerated into a simple counting of those who passed through the tills of the IPW cage."[29] Ultimately, the division had to contend with processing, housing, and guarding tens of thousands of prisoners in its sector. By the end of the war, over 200,000 German soldiers had surrendered to the 80th.[30]

---

26 Eisenhower, *Crusade in Europe*, 409.

27 Patton, *War as I Knew It*, 276.

28 Leo Hirsh, *The Liberators: American Witnesses to the Holocaust* (New York: Bantam Books, 2010), 100.

29 "The Heart of Germany," G-2, 80th Division, www.thetroubleshooters.com/ww2/ptger02.html. (Accessed January 3, 2017.)

30 80th Division History, www.thetroubleshooters.com/ww2/ptger02.html (Accessed February 15, 2017.)

American GIs who entered Germany were often disgusted by the brutality they saw, and their anger sometimes came out in their dealings with German civilians and prisoners. Tempers ran high and the men didn't always follow the rules. The company diary tells an "amusing" story about a staff sergeant who was overseeing a detail of prisoners working on a roadblock near Erfurt. When one prisoner wasn't working hard enough, the sergeant "hit him over his head with his carbine, breaking his stock." This certainly wasn't the only extreme reaction to minor provocations.

On April 12, the company received the shocking news that President Franklin D. Roosevelt had died. Harry S. Truman, who succeeded Roosevelt as president, was not well known to most GIs, especially those serving overseas. Frank had earlier reported to Betty that most of the soldiers had supported Roosevelt's opponent in the 1944 election, but even so, the loss of a man who for the younger troops (including Frank) had been president for most of their lives was a shock. The men in the company were uncertain what lay ahead.

The engineers were now in frequent contact with surrendering German soldiers and civilians, many of whom were openly hostile. Details of B Company's soldiers stumbled into towns that were still occupied. The outcomes were surprising. The company diary reported on April 14 that 3 enlisted men returned from an occupied town with 47 prisoners in tow, including 2 officers. In another instance, a vehicle with 4 of the company's enlisted men and a bulldozer missed a convoy and mistakenly entered an occupied town. The noise startled the German soldiers who were sleeping in their foxholes. The men managed to bring back 2 German officers and 31 enlisted men, along with a weapons carrier.

On April 12, the division, spearheaded by the 319th Infantry, pushed on to Weimar, 20 miles east of Gotha. The town had been totally destroyed by the time it surrendered to the 80th Division, with almost all its buildings in ruins and the bodies of civilians littering the streets and buried in rubble.[31]

The 80th confronted additional evidence of Nazi atrocities at a slave-labor camp at Buchenwald, five miles northeast of Weimar. Soldiers from the 6th Armored Division initially stumbled into the camp two days earlier, and they "discovered the horrible evidence of unbelievable terror and brutality which the Nazis inflicted upon their helpless victims." Buchenwald was the largest concentration camp in Germany, and there were approximately 21,000 prisoners in

31 After-Action Report, 80th Infantry Division, April 1945.

the camp on the day it was liberated. Men from the 80th entered the camp to relieve the 6th Armored shortly after arriving in Weimar.

Journalist Edward R. Murrow accompanied the American soldiers into the camp, and he famously told the American public: "Men and boys reached out to touch me. Death already had marked many of them. . . . I looked out over the mass of men to the green fields beyond, where well-fed Germans were ploughing. . . . I report what I saw and heard, but only part of it. For most of it, I have no words."[32] The American command ordered 2,000 Weimar citizens to go to the camp and see the brutality of the Nazi regime and the evil consequences of their ignorance.

The 305th Engineers were confronted with the smells from the camp and the sight of liberated prisoners as it operated in the vicinity of Weimar. A soldier from the 120th Evacuation Unit recalled, "The smell of death was not unfamiliar to me and I thought we had probably run by some bodies that had been left by the side of the road. But the smell got stronger as we got to . . . our destination, which was Buchenwald."[33] A combat engineer from a different battalion simply recalled the scene was "worse than seeing their own comrades blown to pieces by land mines and left strewn in frozen fields."[34]

On April 14, B Company stopped only briefly near Weimar before driving 30 miles farther east to Lebensten. The 80th was making rapid progress toward the long-anticipated attack on Chemnitz. The next day the company traveled another 70 miles to Oberwein. The convoy passed through more occupied towns without resistance and took more prisoners. The Germans were retreating so quickly they hadn't had time to do significant damage to the roadways, which must have been a relief to the engineers.

Also on April 14, 1945, Lt. Gen. George S. Patton Jr., commander of the Third Army, was promoted to four-star general along with a group of others. Although he was pleased, he noted in his diary, "I would have appreciated it more had I been in the initial group [with Bradley, Devers, etc.] as I have never had an ambition to

---

32 "Edward R. Murrow Reports from Buchenwald, April 15, 1945," . www.lib.berkeley.edu/MRC/murrowbuchenwaldtranscript.html (Accessed March 23, 2017.)

33 Milton Silva, quoted in Hirsh, *The Liberators*, 108.

34 Lia Russell, "World War II Vets Recall Horrors of Buchenwald," *Virginian Pilot*, November 8, 2009, pilotonline.com/news/local/world-war-ii-vets-recall-horrors-of-buchenwald/article_5bbe7d6-3805-5cef-bd6f-4b8e7f0759b6.html. (Accessed March 3, 2017.)

be an also-ran." He noted that his aide, Lt. Col. Charles R. Codman, "secured for me the last two 4-star pins in existence in Paris and also a 4-star flag."[35]

On April 15 and 16, B Company halted with the rest of the 80th Division while preparations were made for the infantry to relieve the 4th Armored and get into position to assault Chemnitz, whose commander had chosen to refuse the 80th Division ultimatum.[36] The men took advantage of this rare delay and were soon playing fast-pitch softball and going on passes to Paris and the French Riviera. They also took time to repair and maintain their equipment. It was a sign of the times that the men in B Company were now instructed to familiarize themselves with Russian aircraft.

As the assault on Chemnitz was in final preparation, the division received a change of orders.[37] Eisenhower had halted Patton's eastward rush just short of Chemnitz. Soviet troops were closing in on Berlin, and Eisenhower redirected Patton away from the capital so the Russians could take it without interference. By an agreement of the major powers, Berlin would be in the Russian occupation zone (though the city would have small enclaves occupied by the Americans, British, and French), and Eisenhower reasoned that any blood spent conquering territory the Americans would have to withdraw from would be wasted.

In the same letter in which he described the horrors of Ohrdruf to General Marshall, Eisenhower laid out his plans for the rest of the war. Much of the forces in the center would come to a halt, and the remaining heavy work would be done on the flanks. "Bradley's main offensive effort will be the thrust along the line Wurzburg-Nuremberg-Linz, carried out by the Third Army with about 12 divisions. Devers, with another 12 U.S. divisions and 6 French divisions, will capture Munich and all of the German territory lying within his zone of advance."[38]

---

35 Blumenson, *Patton Papers*, 690. Colonel Codman gave an insight into the demands of staff work for a high-maintenance general officer. After seeing the announcement, Codman said he had "a busy morning. The PX, Ordnance, Chief Quartermaster. The last set of Four-Star collar insignia in the ETO. Orly. By the time the General got there we had the plane really fixed up. Four-Star pennants outside, huge Four-Star flag inside, on a table-shelf by his seat Four-Star auto plates, and a bottle of Four-Star Hennessey. Upon his arrival, we formed squads of four, and stood at rigid attention. He got quite a laugh out of it. As a matter of fact, he was very much pleased. So are we all" (Codman, *Drive*, 291).

36 After-Action Report, 80th Infantry Division, April 1945.

37 Ibid.

38 Dwight Eisenhower, letter to George Marshall, April 15, 1945.

Eisenhower sent Patton's Third Army southeast into Austria to hook up with the Russians at the Enns River.[39] Patton's troop movements also provided insurance against any possible enemy deployment to a much-rumored last stand in a "National Redoubt" in the Alps. If rumors about the National Redoubt proved true, Patton would be in position to seize the eastern part of the redoubt in Bavaria.[40] Patton was skeptical of the existence of the redoubt, but he followed orders and turned his army to the south.[41]

The battalion's after-action report follows the 305th as it cleared roads and performed general engineering work to support the 80th Division's advance through Gera to Arnstadt, near Bamberg. Arnstadt held a slave-labor camp where Polish and Russian refugees worked in an aircraft engine factory. According to one account, a contingent of men from the 305th spent four days performing tasks at the camp between April 18 and 22.[42]

B Company completed a 181-mile trip from Hortmann to Kettensdorf on April 18, and enemy planes strafed the convoy during the long all-night trip. On April 20, B Company turned in all captured German vehicles and joined the rest of the 80th Division in corps reserve.

Despite the daily movement of the company's motor convoy, the soldiers found time for pranks, which interrupted their stressful days with a welcome dose of humor. The company diary recorded a story about one of Frank Lembo's pranks gone awry:

> The enemy abandoned a 75mm gun. It was parked in company area. Lt. Frank T. Lembo and Tec 5 John Orleski were looking it over when the gun was accidentally fired. The recoil knocked them both to the ground. The A.P. projectile hit our supply truck damaging it slightly. S/Sgt. Richard A. Cleary standing about ten feet from the truck was injured slightly. He ate his meals off the mantle for the next couple of days. Lt. Frank T. Lembo, TEC 5 John Orleski and S/Sgt. Richard A. Cleary received first aid at the dispensary and returned to duty. The biggest tragedy of all was that Lt. Lembo had two bottles of Scotch on the trail legs of the gun. Upon a hasty reconnaissance of the area it was discovered that the scotch was smashed to smithereens.

---

39 MacDonald, *Victory in Europe*, 421.

40 Blumenson, *Patton Papers*, 690.

41 Patton, *War as I Knew It*, 286-91.

42 After-Action Report, S-3, 305th Engineer Combat Battalion, April 1945, 2.

305th Engineers convoy. *Sgt Erwin Knauper*

This story earns a special place in this chronicle because it's the one story that Frank Lembo never tired of telling, always with a gleam in his eye. The conclusion of the story was that "the truck was dragged down by a creek a ways down from camp and shelled so that it could be reported 'destroyed' by enemy fire." When telling the story, Frank said that this incident was the main reason he made sure to "promote" the company diary (take it home) and for years afterward he looked over his shoulder to make sure the army wasn't coming to court-martial him or at least demand payment for the truck. When all was said and done, Lembo loved the army.

CHAPTER 16

NUREMBERG TO THE DANUBE VALLEY: APRIL 21-MAY 3, 1945

O N April 21, the 80th Infantry Division was ordered to rush southeast, with every available vehicle, to Nuremberg to secure the city and oversee the thousands of refugees that were thronging the streets. Nuremberg was a tinderbox, and military guard duty was essential to keep the peace and ensure the roads remained open for military traffic.

At the same time, B Company of the 305th Engineers was alerted to leave the corps reserve at Kettensdorf, and it immediately left for Nuremberg, a trip of 45 miles. The 318th Infantry led the division's advance.

Nuremberg—the shrine of Nazism—was the site of Hitler's Nazi Party conventions and rallies and retained great significance for the Nazi regime. It had once been one of the country's most beautiful, historic, and quintessentially German cities, with a castle crowning the medieval city center. It was also the headquarters of a military district and the site of considerable defense materiel production, including aircraft, submarine components, and tanks. The defense industry was propped up by slave labor, housed in a subcamp of the Flossenberg concentration camp. At the end of the war, it was estimated that 400,000 slave laborers—100,000 of them foreigners—had passed through Nuremberg and the nearby districts.

Allied strategic bombing over the preceding years had turned much of Nuremberg into rubble by the time American ground forces arrived. Reportedly, about 90 percent of Nuremberg's medieval city center was destroyed in only one hour of aerial bombardment on January 2, 1945, with 1,800 residents killed and roughly 100,000 displaced. Upon entering Nuremberg, the B Company diarist noted: "The City of Nurnberg is 'Kaput.' Bombers have done a good job of it."

Engineer bulldozers clear the streets of Nuremberg. *US Army*

The company reached its Nuremberg billet on April 21, only a day after the city capitulated. The company diary noted, "Lt. Gilbert Smith found good quarters for the company," despite the city's wholesale destruction. A crew from B Company also found shower facilities, and it stayed in Nuremberg for a week.

The 80th Division's mission here was to relieve the 3rd Infantry Division, which was maintaining law and order after battling through to the city center the day before. As soon as the 80th arrived, its three infantry regiments—and the 305th Engineers along with them—took over security operations and opened the rubble-clogged roads.[1] The 318th led the way into the city and relieved the 3rd Infantry Division on April 21 while the 317th and 319th moved in on April 22 and relieved the remaining elements of the 3rd Division.[2]

Upon entering the city, the 305th stepped into the work begun by the engineers who had arrived on the scene in the immediate aftermath of the fighting. The company removed roadblocks and widened Nuremberg's roads to make way for two-way military traffic. Frank Lembo's 3rd Platoon filled craters and shell holes, and the battalion helped with traffic circulation.

---

1 Craig, *The 80th Infantry Division*, 54.

2 After-Action Report, 80th Infantry Division, April 1945.

Many thousands of refugees had gravitated to Nuremberg when German territory began falling into Allied hands. These displaced persons (also known as DPs) had gained their freedom from Nazi captivity—victims of the newly liberated slave-labor and concentration camps—or were former political prisoners and foreign prisoners of war. Their numbers were constantly swelling as the German military abandoned its installations and retreated.

The refugees who filled Nuremberg's streets became an important part of the 305th's security duties. Most of the refugees needed shelter, food, and water, and many required medical care. The men of B Company patrolled the streets and rounded up refugees for transportation to Allied installations set up for that purpose. Ironically, the Nuremberg SS barracks was converted into a displaced persons center for freed foreign workers and former prisoners of war. DPs were also housed temporarily in a former Nazi camp, where they received food and medical care.

The Nuremburg streets also teemed with German civilians who had lost their homes and livelihoods, and they now wandered without food and shelter. B Company also had to deal with these civilians as the dust settled. The company diary noted the Americans also had to attend to civilians seeking safe-conduct passes through the city to contact family and friends.

Tensions were high and the volatile environment complicated the security challenge for the 305th. Most of the DPs were hungry and desperate, so warehouses, supply depots, and fresh water points had to be guarded to preserve essential supplies and keep the city calm. There was always a threat of violence when grievances bubbled to the surface, and the 305th was necessarily concerned with the safety of German citizens in the city. Some of the former camp inmates were enraged by German soldiers and civilians alike and felt they had nothing to lose.

German troops—officers and enlisted men—surrendered to the 80th in droves, and they brought with them weapons, ammunition, explosives, vehicles, equipment, and supplies of all kinds as well as an expectation of protection. Hoping to be taken prisoner by the Americans rather than the Soviets, entire companies had tried to surrender to the 80th as it motored toward the city. With so many prisoners, some men from B Company were diverted from engineering work to guard duty. One of the company's platoons repaired five miles of barbed-wire fencing that stretched around a prisoner-of-war enclosure.

Demolition crews were in high demand. The 305th had garnered a considerable amount of explosives and ammunition, as well as artillery pieces and *panzerfaust* antitank weapons. Lembo's platoon demolished two 88mm guns, the

Soldiers from 305th hold a souvenir Nazi flag. *Sgt. Erwin Knauper*

2nd Platoon hauled four truckloads of enemy small arms and ammunition to ordnance, and demolition teams searched the division's Nuremberg headquarters for booby traps and time bombs. On April 24, Captain Marshall inspected railroad cars loaded with ammunition and munitions for booby traps. The 1st Platoon then lined up the cars and distributed them to various other rail yards.

The 305th had some time for recreation while stationed in Nuremberg. According to the company diary, some men attended a GI show at the Nuremberg stadium—the place where Hitler delivered some of his most fiery speeches. The men organized softball games and engaged in serious competition with teams from other 80th units. They reportedly took advantage of opportunities to get souvenirs, especially Lugers and Nazi flags. The end of the war was clearly in sight. A sergeant brought in four cases of wine found in a Nuremberg warehouse, and "the Company had its usual distribution."

The company stayed in Nuremberg from April 21 to 27, when the 80th Division received orders to move south through Regensburg into Austria.[3] The immediate objective was to move across the Danube River and attack southeast to the Isar River.[4]

The company engineers drank the last of their cognac and left Nuremburg with the rest of the division on April 28. After a long 70-mile motor march, the men bivouacked in the open air at Ober-Isling. The next day the convoy motored another 35 miles to Wechshown.

Meanwhile, the 65th Infantry Division had moved ahead of the 80th, and the day before the 80th arrived, they established a Danube River bridgehead and took the city of Regensburg. The 80th passed through the bridgehead, assembled south

3   Craig, *The 80th Infantry Division*, 54.

4   Drive from Regensburg to Vocklabruck, Interview with 1st Lt. Rex L. Pruitt, division liaison officer, June 19, 1945, 1.

of the city, and then turned toward the Danube Valley.[5] The roads were in poor condition and the engineers had to do roadwork to relieve the backed-up troop train. B Company's 1st Platoon operated in direct support of the 318th's 1st Battalion on April 29 and removed enemy vehicles from the roads while the remainder of the company repaired a bridge and moved five roadblocks, all the while keeping a nonstop forward pace.

The 179th Engineer Combat Battalion and 1154th Engineer Combat Group worked alongside the 305th, constructing Bailey and treadway bridges to open the routes for supply traffic. The battalion's after-action report noted that efforts to coordinate the several engineering elements sometimes hindered rather than helped the 80th make rapid progress. The 305th's report indicated the supporting engineers had failed to make continuous aggressive reconnaissance and had not carried their own bridging equipment; the need to ship such equipment forward caused unnecessary delays.[6]

The 80th Division had to contend with the three tributaries of the Danube—the Isar, Inn, and Enns rivers—as it moved southward down the Danube Valley toward Austria. It first faced the Isar River. An officer and 22 enlisted men from the 528th Engineers were attached to the 305th, bringing with them assault boats and footbridges for the crossing.

On April 29, Captain Marshall and two of his platoon leaders, 2nd Lt. Frank Lembo and Lt. Gilbert Smith, reconnoitered the Isar to identify any bridges that were still intact and find potential sites for the forthcoming assault crossing. On April 30, B Company moved by motor march to a new area in Sessau and continued the reconnaissance of the river.

It was a historic and momentous day when, on April 30, American troops received the news that Adolf Hitler had died by his own hand in his bunker in Berlin. It was good news, but it didn't have an immediate impact on the troops in the field. They still had a job to do.

The Isar crossing by the three 80th infantry regiments commenced on the day of Hitler's death. According to the company diary,[7] Lembo's platoon and the 179th

---

5   Ibid.

6   After-Action Report, S-3, 305th Engineer Combat Battalion, April 1945, 2-3.

7   This account comes from entries in the 305th's B Company diary. There are significant discrepancies in the accounts of the crossing of the Isar from the diary and other contemporary accounts, including the 305th and 80th Infantry Regiment after-action reports. The B Company diary stated the company crossed two battalions of the 318th in assault boats on April 30. The April after-action report of the 305th Engineers stated the engineers crossed the

Engineers built a ferry to get the light vehicles across the Isar, but the motorboats provided by the 528th Engineers for this purpose weren't strong enough to push against the river's swift current, and the ferry had to be abandoned. The ferry site was also shelled by heavy mortar fire. An enlisted man was wounded at the site and needed to be evacuated, and another fell in the river but was able to return to the riverbank.

The diary recorded the 305th's 1st and 3rd Platoons subsequently took the 1st and 2nd Battalions of the 318th Infantry across in assault boats under enemy mortar fire. Then, in an operation that took only 80 minutes, the 3rd Platoon, with the mine platoon as guides, took the 305th medics across. One of B Company's noncommissioned officers and other enlisted men had to be rescued "by their buddies" after falling into the rushing river.

An unseasonable snow fell on May 1, and at the river the company engaged in cleanup activities as the crossing neared completion. The 1st Platoon disassembled the ferry they had attempted to use to cross the river and loaded the equipment onto trucks. With that, the men from the 528th Engineers, who had been attached to the 305th, returned to their unit. Lieutenant Gilbert Smith led a detail across the Isar in an assault boat and made a foot reconnaissance of the roads in the town of Digelfen to identify craters and sites for roadblocks. The 2nd Platoon crossed the Isar on a ferry to support the 318th on the far shore. Finally, the company completed the bridge over the Isar at 10:00 p.m. Shortly thereafter the remainder of B Company departed, eventually arriving in a new area in Mamming at 2:00 p.m. the next day, May 2.

The 80th Division moved with a sense of urgency that day; it had an appointment to meet a vanguard of the Soviet Army, and nobody wanted to be late. The 305th after-action report noted, "With only scattered resistance hindering the forward push . . . all units went steadily ahead. Bridges were de-mined, roadblocks were removed, enemy ammunition was captured and destroyed by engineers of the Division, and preparation for continued engineer support of the swift infantry advance maintained."[8] By May 2, the 317th reported it was not meeting even

---

318th, 319th, and one battalion of the 317th in assault boats on April 30, but the May engineers' report indicated the infantry crossed on May 1. The April 80th Division after-action report noted two battalions of the 318th crossed on April 30 via a railroad bridge while the other regiments remained on the north side of the river. The May division report indicated the 319th crossed on May 1 and the 317th on May 2.

8   After-Action Report, S-3, 305th Engineer Combat Battalion, May 1945, 1.

scattered resistance. Over the next few days, the 317th reported, "All enemy troops encountered surrendered without resistance."[9]

Second Lieutenant Frank T. Lembo was soon able to put the river crossings behind him, at least temporarily. He went on a three-day pass to Paris, his second to the city, on May 2. The remainder of the company moved 35 miles to Rimbach. The engineers maintained the roads and repaired the bridges along their route. That day the company was joined by a Brockway treadway bridge truck from the 997th Engineers.

While Lembo was away, B Company's 2nd Platoon went to Simbach to repair a railroad bridge over the Inn River, the next tributary of the Danube, and then into Austria at Branau. The 1st Platoon repaired a bridge in the vicinity of Reisbach, and the 3rd Platoon repaired and maintained roads along the route of march.

B Company and the remainder of the 305th Engineers joined up in Simbach in anticipation of the next crossing, the Inn River. It would mark the engineers' second assault crossing in three days. This time they were supported by extensive air reconnaissance, which pinpointed roads and bridges.

On May 3, B Company's 1st and 3rd Platoons moved the 3rd Battalion of the 318th and other infantry elements across the swiftly moving Inn in assault boats. Later, the 1st Platoon returned to its assault boats and crossed the 1st Battalion of the 318th. They struggled against the fast current, which was reported as 10 feet per second. The company diverted civilian barges and powerboats to assist in crossing the men and supplies.

B Company's 2nd Platoon had a more difficult challenge. It assisted the 1st Battalion of the 318th across by putting a scaffold and ladder over a damaged railroad bridge, which it had repaired earlier. The crossing over the makeshift bridge wasn't easy; a member of the 318th remembered it as "a narrow, rickety, partially destroyed railroad bridge, awash in the swift Inn River" that could "only be negotiated with the greatest difficulty, due to the slipperiness of the bank and the swift current."[10]

The company was relieved when they finished crossing the infantry over the Inn into Austria. B Company remained at the river for a day, bringing across the remaining men and supplies, before loading the assault boats onto trailers on May 4

---

9 Unit history, 317th Infantry Regiment, May 1945, 3.

10 Robert T. Murrell, "The Blue Ridge Division Answers the Call in World War II" (N.p., 2015).

Engineers begin construction of Treadway Bridge over Inn River. *US Army*

and moving out across the Inn to Ranshefen, Austria, five miles from their previous billet in Simbach and four miles from Branau.

Bridge repairs continued, and demolition men removed 2,100 pounds of bombs from a bridge in Simbach. Meanwhile, the 318th moved into Branau to maintain law and order.[11]

The engineering activity had been exceptionally intense at the start of May, as the 80th Division moved into Austria. The 305th's after-action report enumerated the engineering support provided on both sides of the Inn over the course of an active three days: the battalion performed an infantry assault crossing, cleared roadblocks, erected two 24-foot treadway bridges, performed a second assault crossing, constructed two timber bridges, de-mined bridges, and captured and destroyed enemy ammunition.[12]

As it happened, 2nd Lieutenant Lembo was in Paris and missed most of the action at the Inn before returning to the company and his platoon.

11 After-Action Report, 80th Infantry Division, May 1945.

12 After-Action Report, S-3, 305th Engineer Combat Battalion, May 1945.

CHAPTER 17

AUSTRIA TO WAR'S END:
MAY 4-9, 1945

B Company completed its last major assault crossing of the war on May 4, 1945, when it moved the elements of the 80th Division across the Inn River into Braunau, Austria. A constant flow of American soldiers coming across the river flooded the town's streets. Ironically, the 80th's divisional command post was set up in the house in which Hitler was born.[1] Aside from American soldiers, the town was also teeming with thousands of recently freed displaced persons, homeless Germans and Austrians, and freed prisoners of war. Frank Lembo's platoon and the rest of B Company provided aid to the refugees and would continue to do so through the end of the war and beyond.

Among the 12,000 former POWs in the town were 4,000 Americans, including a group of airmen who had just arrived at a small camp on the outskirts of Braunau after an 18-day forced march. The airmen had been imprisoned at the Stalag XVII-B POW camp (scene of the 1950s stage play and movie of the same name) and were freed by the 13th Armored Division just before the arrival of the 80th in Braunau. The B Company diary entry for May 5 noted, "There were quite a few American flyers who were prisoners of war here in town. We fed them and furnished transportation to get them to an American camp."

Some men of B Company had a disconcerting experience while patrolling the town. The diary entry for May 5 reported, "An Austrian civilian who was a strong supporter of the Nazi Party hung himself in a shed this morning. TEC 5 John A. Minarchin cut him down. Lieutenant Gilbert A. Smith who is (Acting) G.R. [graves registration officer] employed some of the townsfolk to bury him." Suicides among party members and local officials became all too commonplace as the GIs moved across the territory of the former Reich.

After Braunau, the infantry continued to advance into Austria. The 319th advanced 95 miles and the 317th moved 52 miles, taking Vocklabruck before advancing to the Enns River.[2]

With the horrors of Ohrdruf and Buchenwald fresh in their minds, men of the 80th Division were confronted with further Nazi atrocities in Austria. While doing an advance scout, the 80th's 3rd Cavalry Reconnaissance Squadron discovered a large concentration camp about 60 miles from Braunau. The camp was hidden in a forest along a winding Alpine road leading up from scenic Traun Lake. When the squadron stumbled upon the camp, which was known as Ebensee, "the chimneys were still smoking from the burning of bodies. It was filled with piles of the dead and emaciated, dazed prisoners."[3] Units from the 80th followed close behind the 3rd Cavalry and are credited with liberating the camp.

One of the first 80th Division soldiers to enter Ebensee said, "It was hard to put up with—very hard . . . walking amongst the dead bodies and seeing them piled around the crematorium and then into the crematorium. . . . If you were not sick and crying by now, you would be before you exited."[4]

Ebensee had once held about 16,000 prisoners, who had been originally brought to the camp as labor for the construction of elaborate tunnels in the nearby mountains, which were designed to house underground factories for rocket production. Ebensee, however, had become the final destination for thousands of additional prisoners transported from camps farther east. As the Allied armies closed in, the Nazis shifted many prisoners to camps in Austria in a futile effort to hide their atrocities. About 8,500 had already died by the time the 80th arrived, and the American soldiers watched as many others were taken by starvation and disease. Most of the camp's SS guards had vanished, and the brutalized captives took their revenge by murdering the few Nazis who remained behind.[5]

Over the next few days, the men of the 80th began to establish water points, feed Ebensee's prisoners, and give them medical care. As soon as they gathered

---

2 After-Action Report, 80th Infantry Division, May 1945.

3 Jan Elvin, "Honoring the Liberators," April 16, 2010, accessed July 2, 2017, http://janelvin.blogspot.com/2010/04/honoring-liberators.html. (Accessed May 5, 2017.)

4 Hirsh, *The Liberators*, 247.

5 Elvin, *Box from Braunau*, 149-54; Hirsh, *The Liberators*, 249.

their strength, the refugees were moved to a U.S. Army displaced persons camp or, when possible, their country of origin. Transporting refugees became a regular occupation for B Company.

Groups of officers from the 80th were taken to observe the Ebensee camp and its inmates after its liberation.[6] One of them recalled, "Recalled the overpowering smell . . . . I didn't know why I'd come. I was sorry I had. It was so devastating, so depressing."[7]

The Enns River had been designated as a border between U.S. forces advancing from the west and the Red Army coming from the east. The 80th patrolled 15 miles beyond the Enns on May 4, but they encountered no Soviet troops.[8] On May 6, B Company headed 50 miles south from Ranshofen to Vocklabruck, arriving at 4:00 a.m. The company's vehicles quickly refueled and motored another 50 miles to Kirchdorf. The company remained there from May 6 to May 9 before moving on to Garsten, where they stayed until May 14, well past the end of the war.

B Company engaged in its last major combat operation at this time, just days before the German capitulation. While the company was billeted in Kirchdorf, each of its three platoons joined up with a special division-level task force whose mission was to destroy all enemy resistance north of the Inn River. The secondary mission of the three task forces was to contact "our ally, the Russians." The 1st Platoon joined Task Force James, the 2nd Platoon joined Task Force Simon, and Lembo's 3rd Platoon participated in Task Force Smythe, and code-named for its leader, assistant division commander Col. George W. Smythe.[9] The 3rd Battalion of the 317th was assigned as lead infantry. Other participants in Combat Team 317 were the 702nd Tank Battalion, the 80th Reconnaissance Troop, the 313th Field Artillery Battalion, and the 811th Tank Destroyers.[10] Second Lieutenant Lembo's

6 The daughter of Sgt. Erwin Knaubel, Rita Knauper Thomas, commented on the effect these camps had on American soldiers: "I remember being in high school or college when the world tried to say the Holocaust never happened. I asked my dad if he knew about the concentration camps during the war. I remember he didn't answer. Fast forward decades later and I see his writing on the back of [his photos of Ebensee]. Of course he was there!"

7 Elvin, *Box from Braunau*, 168.

8 After-Action Report, 80th Infantry Division, May 1945.

9 Dominique and Hayes, *One Hell of a War*, 221.

10 Surrender of the 6th German Army at Garsten, Austria, Interview with Maj. E. C. Kerr, assistant G-3, 80th Division, June 19, 1945, 1.

3rd Platoon of engineers operated with Task Force Smythe for at least three days, until the end of the war.

On May 6, Task Force Smythe took off from Kirchdorf and went down the Enns Valley in pursuit of about 10,000 SS troops, who had been reported to be in a well-fortified pass near Klause. As the small task force approached the German position, it sent officers to the German headquarters at Garsten to request their surrender. The Germans countered with unacceptable terms, far from the unconditional surrender that was demanded. The Americans believed the Germans were stalling to cover an escape to the south or perhaps positioning to fight the Soviets.[11]

After the German terms were refused, Task Force Smythe had no choice but to attack the much-larger German force. Despite the overwhelming odds, early the next morning, the task force's infantry element, the 3rd Battalion of the 317th, attacked the Germans retreating south in the vicinity of Garsten. Engineers had to clear enemy demolitions and fill craters and help the task force surmount a blown-out railroad bridge. An officer from the 317th recalled that the 317th was expected to attack a force of almost 200,000. The terrain was tortuous, easy to defend, and required the special skills of mountain divisions. All of these factors would have resulted in a disaster for the 317th."[12]

Fortunately for the GIs, shortly after the American attack began, the Wehrmacht commander contacted the task force and surrendered 20,000 troops who had been operating in the immediate vicinity. Soon after that Gen. Hermann Balck, commander of German Sixth Army, surrendered his entire command, 120,000 men, which had been fleeing the Red Army, even though, according to Allied policy, the army should have surrendered to its last battlefield opponents, the Soviets.

Before the capitulation, Balck requested a meeting with 80th Division commander Horace McBride, who was initially "rather cool" to him. The English-speaking Balck and McBride talked privately, and soon, according to Balck, "settled everything in short order. We selected assembly areas and the Americans established a security screen against the Russians that were pursuing us .... McBride warmed up and I accepted a cup of coffee from him. He bade me a hearty farewell as I returned to the Enns. . . . Years later an American told me how

11 Ibid., 1-3; Regimental history, 317th Infantry Regiment, May 1945, 3.

12 Dominique and Hayes, *One Hell of a War*, 221.

lucky I had been to encounter McBride. No other American general would have acted contrary to his orders to such an extent."[13]

On the morning of May 7, near Klaus, Combat Team 317th's Reconnaissance Troop was strafed and shot down the German fighter. An after-action report from the 80th Division concluded these were the "last shots in anger among American forces in the ETO."[14] Also on May 7, the entire gold reserve of the National Bank of Hungary was surrendered to the 80th Division.[15]

According to the surrender terms negotiated that day, any German troops that were not across the Enns by midnight on May 8 would be turned over to the Russians. An estimated 102,000 German soldiers poured across the Enns River Bridge and gave themselves up to the Americans.[16] Reportedly, many German soldiers drowned while attempting to swim the Enns River.[17]

The war in Europe was over. By May 9 the entire 80th Division was involved in maintaining law and order and handling prisoners and displaced persons.[18] On May 9, the company diary summarized: "The peace that had been in the offing so long will be official on 0100 on May 10." A ceasefire went into effect immediately.

It had been a very long, hard war. The men of the 80th Infantry Division had covered 3,015 miles across Europe since arriving at Utah Beach the previous August. Within the year some lucky troops expected to be headed home while others would be sent to the Pacific.

The 80th played an important role in the victory in Europe, but it paid a high price: 3,038 men died in combat and another 442 died of wounds. More than 12,000 others had been wounded.[19]

13 Hermann Balck, *Order in Chaos: The Memoirs of General of Panzer Troops Hermann Balck*, trans. David T. Zabecki and Dieter J. Biedekarten (Lexington: University of Kentucky Press, 2015), 439.

14 Drive from Regensburg to Vocklabruck, 3; see also Craig, *The 80th Infantry Division*, 57; Surrender of the 6th German Army at Garstan, Austria, 2.

15 After-Action Report, 80th Infantry Division, May 1945.

16 Surrender of the 6th German Army at Garstan, Austria, 3.

17 Walter Carr, quoted in Elvin, *Box from Branau*, 123.

18 After-Action Report, 80th Infantry Division, May 1945.

19 Craig, *The 80th Infantry Division*, 57.

CHAPTER 18

PEACE SETTLES IN: MAY 9-JUNE 10, 1945

B Company left Kirchdorf on May 9 and motored 45 miles to Garsten, Austria, where the terms of the German surrender had been negotiated a few days earlier. The company remained at Garsten for almost a week, helping with the immediate postwar cleanup. The men assigned to Task Force Smythe, including Lembo's 3rd Platoon, rejoined the company in Garsten, but for the time being continued to operate with the task force.

The timing of the surrender was fortuitous for those German troops who made it over to the American side of the Enns River. Soviet troops were closing in quickly from the east, and the Americans were moving in from the west, ready to join up. The American and Soviet forces subsequently met at the center of the bridge over the Enns and conducted a ceremony to mark the linkup in the nearby city of Liezen.

There was no doubt the Americans were ready for the war to end. By May 12, the men were filling out their rating cards and questionnaires for the Information and Education (I&E) On the Job Training program, which was slated to go into effect shortly, and B Company's Capt. Robert C. Marshall read out the Articles of War.[1] Nevertheless, the 305th Engineer Combat Battalion still had a heavy load of work to do in Garsten. The engineers went out to clear the Austrian roads of

---

1 Presumably, Marshall was reminding the troops of the strict rules against fraternization with German civilians, which was a major offense under the Articles of War. The soldiers would have been familiar with the other requirements.

abandoned and wrecked vehicles and roadblocks, fill craters, and reopen the road network in the 80th Division's sector.

The engineers' time was also filled with the ever-increasing number of German POWs. Surrendering troops brought with them enormous amounts of arms, ammunition, and demolitions, and naturally the job of collecting and destroying this materiel fell to the engineers, who were already fully engaged in other work. They took the prisoners to the army's overcrowded enclosures and camps and occasionally did guard duty. Most of the prisoners seemed happy to be in American rather than Soviet hands. Some of the camps set up by the 80th didn't even use barbed wire.

To resupply the division from the rear, Frank Lembo's 3rd Platoon put together a railroad using German facilities and equipment. The railroad brought supplies from the vicinity of Braunau to points as far forward as Kirchdorf. The railroad was also used to evacuate POWs to camps and enclosures as well as sick and repatriated persons from the forward areas to rear dispersal points. The scale of the rail operation grew so large that an officer was subsequently appointed as full-time railroad manager to coordinate and oversee operations.

The railroad moved 1,000 prisoners on May 11 and continued to operate under B Company control through May 13, when the company diary reported, "Company continued to operate a 30-mile run of railroad evacuating German PWs and stragglers from other armies." B Company's 2nd Platoon relieved the 3rd Platoon of its railroad duties on May 14, and the 179th Engineer Combat Battalion took responsibility for the railroad on May 15, when B Company moved 60 miles by motor convoy to Unterberg.

B Company engineers also constructed POW enclosures during the remainder of May and early June, a job that sometimes required ingenuity. Lembo's platoon scoured the area around Unterberg to salvage barbed wire and lumber, and Lembo scouted potential enclosure sites in Kirchdorf, Steinbach, and Muhldt. There seemed to be a perpetual call for secure places in which to house the tens of thousands of prisoners in the vicinity, many from the German Sixth Panzer Army, which had surrendered a little more than a week before.

A detail from Lembo's platoon also constructed latrines and other facilities for a "women's PW enclosure" in the vicinity of Scherfling, a task that continued through the first week of June. Scherfling housed two subcamps of the infamous Mauthausen-Gusen concentration camp, one for male inmates and one for females.

Peace brought a mixed attitude toward discipline. The company diary for May 16 reported the company had "the first reveille formation at 0630" since their arrival in France, followed by "twenty minutes of close order drill." But the diary also noted the acquisition of "26 cases of beer for a party."

Even though the war was over, the soldiers still took a dim view of deserters. On May 17, a general court-martial was held at the division forward command post for a B Company private who had "returned after an absence of a few weeks [beginning on March 1]." Captain Marshall and several enlisted men were called as witnesses, and the deserter was sentenced to 30 years in prison.

At the end of May and into June seven of the company's trucks transported refugees to Luxembourg and various Allied camps in the region. The transport of the DPs continued day after day. On May 24, the diary took particular note that "two trucks reported to Headquarters 305th Engr. with eight days rations to haul displaced persons."

On May 21, a squad checked the Leitzen airport for booby traps and mines, Lt. Gilbert Smith supervised the construction of a railroad bridge at Klause (a job that continued through June 4), a squad repaired a bridge on the main supply route in the vicinity of Wimbach, 2nd Lieutenant Lembo made a road reconnaissance of the main supply route, squads reconnoitered bridges, men constructed roadblocks in the vicinity of Eidig, and the company continued to haul a massive amount of arms and ammunition to the dump.

Mines were still a problem, and the company marked mines and booby traps in the vicinity of Wimbach. There was now a new wrinkle in mine clearing. On June 4, the diary reported the men "picked up 12 PWs to remove German mines in the vicinity of Lambach. Mines had already been picked up by another organization with PWs." Prisoners of war were forced to clear mines in Europe after the war, and some of them died doing so.

Squads went out on reconnaissance missions to find potentially useful materials that had been abandoned by the Nazis. Fuel was a particularly important commodity. Lembo and a detail of his men went to a railroad yard on May 21 and found six railroad cars filled with oil and gasoline. Lieutenant Smith led another mission to search for stores of enemy gasoline and oil and came up with 55,000 gallons for the division's use.

There were occasional tensions within the division when it came to allocating fuel supplies from enemy stores. An after-action report by the S-4 (the supply section) of the 305th Engineer Combat Battalion reported that one 305th unit "discovered [the] whereabouts of German gasoline in flat cars. Was able to obtain 1,000 gallons before G-4 stopped us and said further issues would be allocated. B Company had been selected as Task Force Engineers. We then had to give them the entire 1,000 gallons of German gasoline we drew the day before."[2] Unfortunately, when it was finally time for the unit to receive the allocation, it discovered the G-4 had sent a railroad car with diesel fuel instead of gas.

As peace set in, B Company engineers had time for recreation, which was important to keep the GIs occupied in the absence of wartime pressures. One night the company watched the movie See Here, Private Hargrove, which was based on a writer's humorous memoir of his experiences in the army. Men also built a softball diamond and a corral for six horses, which B Company had obtained on May 19 from the battalion. The area was flush with horses originally brought in by the Germans to move men and equipment (some horses had been used by the cavalry). Horseback riding became so popular that, on May 21, the company commander, Captain Marshall, went to Garsten to find more horses. He returned with 14 animals, and men found 20 additional saddles.

The men thought it was hilarious when "our horses broke out of their corral and had to be rounded up by Lt. Gilbert Smith and a detail of enlisted men." According to an article in the division newspaper, *80th Forward*, PFC Quinton Howell, who had handled horses all his life, helped collect the stampeding horses by chasing them in a jeep. The 3rd Battalion of the 317th Infantry subsequently had its own stock of horses, which the *80th Forward* dubbed the "Blue Ridge Riding Academy."[3]

On May 28, 2nd Lieutenant Lembo went out on reconnaissance to find equipment for a rifle range, and the men took turns with German .31-caliber rifles and Lugers, using ammunition provided by headquarters. There were volleyball and softball games every day, and the men built a backstop for their baseball diamond. The company also assumed responsibility for maintaining the battalion's swimming pool in Vocklabruck. Even the battalion's road marches were an opportunity to engage in athletic competition.

Not surprisingly, the GIs were happy to indulge their long-delayed thirst for beer. The company received 26 cases, and 2nd Lieutenant Lembo bought 7 kegs and 3 more cases for his platoon. They had beer in the evening and with every meal. They watched movies and had parties. Their "long sought Coca Cola rations" came through.

Men went on passes to Paris, the recreation area in Gmunden, and the rest camp in Thionville, France, on the Luxembourg border. In a case of Allied

---

2 Historical Journal of Supply, After-Action Report, 305th Engineer, May 1945.

3 *80th Forward*, July 30, 1945.

cooperation, one of the company's enlisted men traveled 90 miles to Liezen to receive a decoration from the Russians.

With the exception of the latrine detail, the men of B Company had a well-earned holiday on June 6, the anniversary of D day. June 9 saw the departure of longtime company commander Robert Marshall, who was again assigned as battalion S-3.

Also on June 9, Lembo led a detail on a long-distance quartering party to the Bavarian village of Aitrang. The company's motor convoy followed close behind Lembo's advance party and on June 11, after traveling a long 211 miles, arrived at the town. Two of the trucks immediately went back to Unterrogau for "eats and mattresses." The company waited to take over the buildings and areas in the village that were being vacated by the 111th Engineer Combat Battalion. The company diary indicated a misunderstanding about quarters involving the Russians, who were also lodged in Aitrang, temporarily brought all of the company's work to a standstill.

B Company stayed in Aitrang through the end of July—longer than anywhere since it arrived at Utah Beach—and, according to Frank Lembo, it represented some of his best memories of the war. Aitrang was a beautiful Bavarian village, and the men of B Company appreciated their comfortable quarters. Reportedly, the 305th's three-room mess hall was in a building that held an enormous mural of great German victories as well as deeply carved window moldings, mantelpieces, and entryways.

The 80th Infantry Division centered on the town of Kaufbeuren, which boasted a former Luftwaffe base. Battalion headquarters moved to Marktoberdorf, close to both Aitrang and Kaufbeuren. The 318th and other 80th elements settled in at nearby Kempten. The area around Kaufbeuren became an 80th Division "company town," and the men of B Company replaced all signposts in the town that did not pertain to the 80th.

With the move to Aitrang, leisure activities became B Company's norm and the engineers were free to enjoy them. The company's horses were unloaded at the rail depot in Marktoberdorf, and GIs from B Company rode them to a corral in Aitrang. According to the diary, the "Company acquired a Hungarian stable boy in the deal." The men built a shed to keep the saddles out of the rain.

Apparently a separate group of horses owned by the 3rd Battalion of the 317th—the so-called Blue Ridge Riding Academy—couldn't get on the train, so four enlisted men rounded up the horses and rode them 135 miles to Aitrang, a trip that took four days. The division newspaper reported the 317th's "bronco-busters"

B Company engineers construct POW camp. *US Army*

were being assisted by three former Russian cavalrymen who taught the new horsemen from the 317th "some Cossack tricks."[4]

Relationships with the Soviets billeted in the vicinity of Aitrang had some antagonistic moments. In an incident on June 13, the company diary reported that three men went out with the MG policeman[5] to pick up "a Pole" for stealing. The man, in fact, was a Russian and had not stolen anything. After he was released, the "Russians came to Aitrang and threatened the MG Policeman and chased him through buildings." The diary explained, "We took the Russians, the Policeman and the Burgermeister to the MG in Marktoberdorf to get the problem straightened out."

There was another problem with the Russians on June 17, when a Russian was locked up after stealing a motorbike. The incident again required headquarters intervention.

Still, there was some engineering work to do, although not enough to wholly interfere with the GIs' recreation. A new routine developed. Trucks daily hauled gravel to the battalion motor pool from as far away as Munich, and the company trucks oiled the streets. The engineers maintained their equipment and erected showers in the company area, using plumbing scavenged from the Kempten SS barracks. The company prepared for ordnance inspection, and the battalion commander found it to be "excellent." In the words of the diary, "The Company received a flag, so old glory will fly over Aitrang."

The boys in B Company apparently adopted a puppy as a company mascot. Several photos in Frank's collection show the dog posing in the company offices and with the company flag.

A good part of June was taken up building an enlisted men's resort for the battalion at a lake called the Elbsee, only a mile from Aitrang. At the same time B

---

4 "317th Third 'Cavalry' Bn.," *80th Forward*, July 30, 1945.

5 Police of the provost marshal general.

Company built quarters for up to 50 men, a dance hall, a dining hall, an obstacle course, stables, a baseball diamond, and a volleyball court. The company's men subsequently spent their free time at Elbsee, taking turns swimming, fishing, and riding horses.

The enlisted men's resort at Elbsee Lake was christened The Castle (a reference to the engineers' logo). The kickoff was an outing attended by hundreds of soldiers from the battalion in honor of Activation Day, July 15, 1942. Participants spent the day engaged in sports of all kinds. The company then went all out to finish their building projects.

As reported in the 305th Engineers' supply bulletin: "Large recreational program being planned for the battalion now that the war is over with in Europe. Secured three outboard motors from a neighboring Engineer Unit. Gave . . . our assault boats to 'A' Company who was going to use them on the lake." A later bulletin observed, "Since the recreation program is in full swing, more equipment was needed, especially boats. Some German storm boats and motors were spotted in Ried, Austria, and these were obtained. The motors were tuned up by the Motor Pool mechanics and taken to the lake." The battalion S-3 obtained forage for the horses.

B Company also helped construct facilities at the division's resort at Gmunden See and at the divisional headquarters in Kaufbeuren. The division's facilities offered ball fields, an obstacle course, a flytrap, a camouflage area, and a boxing ring. Considerable effort was expended to finish the divisional parade ground at the Kaufbeuren headquarters, putting up signs and moving bleachers into place before it was used for inspection.

There was real work to do as well. On June 28, Lt. Keith Eilers, a good friend of Frank Lembo's and the namesake for Frank and Betty's son, made a road reconnaissance on the main supply route, and others scouted far afield. Five trucks hauled displaced persons in Marktoberdorf.

On June 29, the company viewed movies on venereal disease, sex hygiene, and malaria. Nonfraternization policies had recently been relaxed.

It must have been quite a day when the motor pool brought the entire company to the new parade ground at Kaufbeuren. It was Independence Day and time to celebrate America's victory against Hitler in Europe. On the receiving stand in Kaufbeuren were Maj. Gen. Louis A. Craig, commander of XX Corps and acting commander of the Third Army (Patton was on leave in the United States). Craig reviewed the troops and presented the Presidential Unit Citation to the 2nd Battalion of the 318th Infantry Regiment for its outstanding performance in the relief of Bastogne between December 24 and 28. As an attached unit, B Company's 1st Platoon shared in the award.[6]

Second Lieutenant Lembo and his platoon were responsible for collecting and setting off demolitions for the July 4th fireworks at the celebration. As the newspaper of the 313th Field Artillery, the *Hamboner*, described it, "At the conclusion of Gen. Craig's address, forty-eight rounds of something that sounded like either heavy ammo, or dynamite, was fired off in rapid succession. With a loud roar for each of the forty-eight states it made it seem like the 4th of July celebration at home and was a fitting climax for this impressive ceremony."

The 305th Engineer Combat Battalion newspaper, *Fire in the Hole*, also reported on the event: "Lt. Lembo and a squad from his platoon under the direction of Sgt. Rutkowski had charge of producing the explosions. . . . With a novel setup, consisting of an electric battery, a copper plate, and four rows of nails, each of which was connected to a 5 lb. charge of explosives, 'Rut' calmly and efficiently counted to five between contacts and the engineer participation in the salute to Independence Day was completed. Thanks to these men for a good job of engineer ingenuity."[7]

Years later, Frank recalled the event and laughed that they had "broken every window in town."

On July 17, 17 men from the battalion, including 2nd Lieutenant Lembo, spent five hours on a train to see a Billy Rose show in Garmisch-Partenkirchen, Germany. The variety show was in a stadium where part of Hitler's 1936 Winter Olympics had been held.[8] Earlier they'd seen Marlene Dietrich, a Jack Benny show in Augsburg, and a Russian show in Marktoberdorf. The divisional newspaper *80th*

6 The August 13, 1945, edition of the division newspaper, *80th Forward*, reported that Lembo's platoon and other support units would receive the Presidential Unit Citation, "In keeping with the established policy of awarding the Presidential Unit Citation to all units which accompanied the famed 2nd Battalion of the 318th Infantry in their epic relief of the besieged Bastogne." An article in the battalion newspaper reported, "Forty-four officers and men of Company B, 305th Engineer Battalion, recently received the coveted gold-framed blue ribbon." The article also noted, "At the time it earned the citation, the platoon was commanded by Lt. Arthur G. Henke, now Pacific-bound."

7 PFC N. Stephenson, "B Company Furnishes 'Bang' for Division Celebration," *Fire in the Hole*, July 14, 1945.

8 PFC H. Brickman, "A Visit to Billy Rose's 'Diamond Horseshoe' Show," *Fire in the Hole*, July 21, 1945.

Forward reported that other entertainments for the 80th Division included performances by Bob Hope and the Radio City Music Hall Rockettes.

The 305th Engineers were thrilled to get word that General Patton would visit the 80th Division in Kaufbeuren and Kempten on July 19 for a day of demonstrations. The 305th's B Company was asked to close out the day's activities by constructing an infantry footbridge over the Iller River in Kempten. Despite the fact that Lembo was a junior platoon commander, his platoon had the honor of demonstrating the bridge construction.

As luck had it, shortly before Patton's visit, Lembo fell off the back of a jeep and broke his arm. He was getting his arm set while the demonstration went on without him. Later, Frank commented ruefully that, after ten months of war, he'd missed his final moment of glory.

The battalion newspaper *Fire in the Hole* reported: "General Patton, accompanied by Major Generals Craig and McBride and Brigadier General Smythe, arrived at the bridge site at 4:30 pm. At the starting signal, Gen. Patton, unknown to the majority, set a stopwatch. When the bridge reached the far shore, Maj. Gen. McBride stated that it had been assembled in a little less than six minutes. Gen. Patton then corrected him and said that the time had been five minutes and thirty four seconds."

Patton walked across the footbridge, asked some technical questions, and "mentioned that the last time he had crossed a river on this type of bridge was over the Sauer River, and that it had no handrails, was covered with bodies and under fire from Jerry artillery." Patton told the photographer to "take pictures of the bridge, you can get one of me anytime."[9]

In July, the division deployed to Garmisch,[10] which Frank much enjoyed. Later, he frequently remarked that the Bavarian Alps and Garmisch were the most beautiful places he had ever seen.

The last entry in the company's diary was dated July 31, 1945. The final morning report and after-action report had been long since been published. The war was over and there was no longer any need to chronicle B Company's fishing, swimming, and softball game scores. The diary closed with an annotation that "one squad worked on the lake. 'B' Company dropped another to 'C' Company. This time the score was 4 to 2."

9 "Gen. Patton Visits 305th Eng. Bn.," *Fire in the Hole*, July 21, 1945.

10 "Blue Ridge C.P. Shifts to Garmisch-Partenkirchen," *80th Forward*, September 10, 1945.

Portrait of Lt. Frank Lembo. *Betty Craig (Lembo)*

Co. B mascot, at Aitrang, Bavaria. *Lt Frank Lembo*

In late July, the 45th Infantry Division and 4th Armored Division joined the 80th Division. When it finally came time for the brass to decide, the GIs from the 80th—and their wives and sweethearts at home—breathed a deep sigh of relief when they learned they'd be headed home in December rather than to the Pacific. The men prepared to return to the States.

The 80th Division headquarters moved to Garmisch on September 10, 1945, but the division soon moved out of Bavaria to take up duty in Marienbad, Czechoslovakia, and B Company followed. The soldiers' time in Europe entered its final phase.

Frank T. Lembo was promoted to 1st lieutenant on September 5, 1945, as he waited in Czechoslovakia for his chance to go home with the rest of the division. His promotion was the culmination of a long dream. As reported in the 305th Engineer Combat Battalion newspaper, "Eloquent testimony to the platoon's efficiency was the battlefield commissioning of their . . . former squad leader, now 2nd Lt Frank T. Lembo."[11]

11 Ibid.

EPILOGUE

LIEUTENANT Frank T. Lembo faced a difficult decision in the fall of 1945, with the war over, and home and his sweetheart waiting to be rejoined. Frank had flourished in the army and enjoyed its challenges and camaraderie. In the army he had discovered strengths he hadn't imagined when he was in school and then working in his blue-collar job at Wright's before the war. It must have seemed like a very long time ago, and he wasn't the same young man anymore. The war had proven him to be capable, intelligent, and resourceful, as well as a natural leader.

His commanding officer encouraged Frank to re-up and promised him a positive career path if he decided to make the army his career. He had garnered enough points to go home, but the army had made his situation clear: "Officers who desire to remain in service, may so signify by signing a certificate stating that they elect irrevocably to stay on active duty for the duration of the emergency plus six months."

On the other hand, there was the irresistible pull of the girl back home, who he had loved for years and yearned for at night when he was sitting and writing letters. She had accepted an engagement ring in November 1943, but she didn't always seem certain about the wisdom of getting married right away, even if the romance had been dragging on long enough, and her daily letters to Frank had been loving ones. Frank couldn't have both the army and the girl. Betty Craig wasn't cut out to be an army bride. He would say later in life that the army offer was tempting and he would have seriously considered signing up if Betty had put him off again.

Lieutenant Frank T. Lembo went home on leave, proposed again, and offered Betty Craig an ultimatum: they would get married without delay, or he would sign back up and make a career of the army. Betty accepted his proposal at long last. After so many difficult months of waiting, she certainly didn't want to lose Frank again.

Frank returned to the States with other soldiers from the 80th aboard the Mt. Vernon Victory when it sailed for New York on January 3, 1946. Upon disembarkation, he went to Fort Monmouth, NJ, where he was formally discharged.

Frank and Betty receive congratulations from family and friends. *Mary Lembo (Randall)*

Keith, Lois, and Nancy at Daytona Beach, late 1950s. *Frank Lembo*

Frank and Betty were married only a few weeks later, on January 26, 1946. Betty wore a white silk suit and matching pillbox hat with hand embroidery that her father had had made for her in New York City on short notice. Friends, family members, and a smattering of army buddies were in attendance. Frank T. Lembo's days in the U.S. Army had drawn to a close. A new career, a new house, and a new family beckoned.

Considering how close he had been to Scotty, Eddie, and Whitey, and how indestructible the bonds of friendship forged during the months of struggle together had once seemed, "the boys" quickly lost touch as each went off to a new life in peacetime.

Frank and Betty moved into a spare room in the Craig household while Frank built a house at 76 Ruth Avenue in their hometown of Hawthorne, NJ. Frank's father, brothers-in-law, and friends pitched in to help build the house, and it was finished and ready for the family to move in by the beginning of 1948. Frank lived in the house on Ruth Avenue for the rest of his life, despite Betty's frustrated urgings to move to someplace larger or, as they got older, somewhere warmer. But by the time Frank settled down, he was settled for life. After Frank's passing, Betty sold the house to their beloved granddaughter Vanessa Jacobson, who found Frank's letters hidden in the rafters during renovations.

Betty had become pregnant with their first child, Keith, born in February 1947 while Frank rushed to complete the house. Their daughter Lois followed three years later and, after six years, Nancy was born to fill out the family. Frank's life had matched that of countless other American GIs who returned home to accept the responsibilities of families, homes, and jobs. After so many months of pain, deprivation, and uncertainty, life was good. And it didn't take long before Frank put the war behind him. The 1950s heralded a new era and, for the nation, the dark days of the war were overtaken by a new prosperity.

Frank was a man of his times. He put Betty on a pedestal and believed that the man of the family was the breadwinner and primary decision-maker—a role he had no intention of abandoning once he got home. Betty became the homemaker, responsible for the household and the family. The division of labor worked well for them, and the family flourished. Keith and Lois went on to college, and then on to successful careers after law school for Keith and an MBA for Lois. Nancy stayed close to home and got a position as chief bookkeeper for a Hawthorne manufacturing company, and later as manager of the Paterson Farmers Market. Frank reacted with absolute delight when Nancy gave him his granddaughters, Vanessa, Sarah, Maxine, and Liza. Nancy also took loving care of her parents as they grew older.

Frank and Betty enjoying a round of golf. *Keith Lembo*

Frank had worked in his father's construction business, Joseph Lembo General Contractor, before the war, and he joined his father when he returned home, seeing the firm renamed Joseph Lembo & Son in his honor. The business grew and Frank took over ownership when his father passed away. After retiring from the construction business, Frank began a new career in the 1980s as the Public Works Director in the Borough of Hawthorne. He brought to the endeavor all that he had learned during the war, and turned the Public Works Department into an efficient organization that kept Hawthorne's roads open, streets plowed, and water flowing.

While he was away in Europe, Frank speculated about going into radio and taking on photography as a serious hobby, but he discovered his true passion in golf, beginning with Sunday outings on the county course with three of his neighborhood friends, and later achieving his dream of joining the North Jersey Country Club, where he and Betty met a new group of golf partners and lifelong friends. Frank again showed off his penchant for hard work and flair for management, serving on North Jersey's Board of Governors in positions ranging from Greens Chairman to Treasurer. He was a pillar of the club for 38 years and was named emeritus when his golfing days ended.

Frank's letters home expressed his wish to travel with Betty to some of the places he had passed through as a soldier: Paris, the French countryside,

Luxembourg, and the Bavarian Alps. As he said in a letter home from Paris, "I'll always remember my trip there, and I hope someday we can both go to the city once more." He never seemed disappointed that he didn't get back to see these places whole again; Betty's fear of flying may have been just a good excuse for staying home. Golf came to dominate the family vacations, although summer vacations were few and far between because of the Lembo's seasonal construction business. Every three years, the kids packed up their schoolwork and the Lembo's took off south for three weeks in Florida. Later, Frank and Betty went on golfing vacations in warmer climes, playing at some of the best courses on the east coast.

During his big battles, Frank would write to Betty that he would "tell you all about it when I get home," but he never seemed to talk about the war much when the time came, either with the family or with outsiders. Although Frank never made a secret of the outline of his experiences in France, Luxembourg, Belgium, and Germany, they were seldom the main topic of conversation. For men like Frank, the war stories told to wives and then children focused on anecdotes about adventures and misadventures with "the boys" in the unit, and the surprising number of good memories that came out of the war. Still deeply felt but not articulated were the grim and frightening ones. The family heard affectionate stories about setting off a German howitzer, 4th of July fireworks, and missing the chance to build a bridge for Patton. But the answers about, for example, the Silver Star mission tended to be "It was nothing," or 'I don't want to talk about it."

Frank kept only a few keepsakes from his months in training and in Europe. In addition to the letters stored in the rafters above the basement ceiling tiles, Frank kept a large envelope with his battalion flag, a few Nazi souvenirs, his company diary, the Service Record kept by Betty, and a stash of news clippings and other ephemera. For the kids, looking through these materials made their Dad's days as a soldier real. Those materials form the basis for this book.

Later in life, Frank's culinary experiments in the army were put to good use as he became the family's chief cook. He took great pride in his ability to find the best bargains at the grocery store and to prepare prime rib, shrimp, and authentic Italian dishes.

Frank and Betty's love story continued for almost 60 years after their wedding. Frank passed away on January 4, 2006, after a long battle with congestive heart failure. Betty lived seven more years, establishing a new home at Van Dyke's Park Place in Hawthorne. They are buried together, near her parents at George Washington Memorial Park in Paramus, NJ.

FRANK T. LEMBO
SERVICE RECORD

DATE	RANK
Nov. 12, 1942	Private
April, 1943	Private First Class (PFC)
Dec. 26, 1943	Corporal
Jan. 10, 1944	Sergeant
Feb. 11, 1945	Staff Sergeant (S/Sgt)
March 8, 1945	Second Lieutenant (2nd Lt.)
Sept. 5, 1945	First Lieutenant (Lt.)

DATE	POSTING
Dec 4, 1942	Camp Forrest, TN
June 23, 1943	Camp Philips, KS
Nov 11, 1943	Yuma, AZ
April 5, 1944	Ft. Dix, NJ
June 30, 1944	Overseas

Appendix 2

Company B, 305th Engineers Locations

DATE	LOCATION
6 AUG 44	Utah Beach
6-7 AUG 44	St. Jores, France
8 AUG 44	Montsurs, France
9-10 AUG 44	La Bazouge, France
11 AUG 44	Conlie, France
13 AUG 44	St. Aubin-Du-Desert, France
14 AUG 44	St. Pierre-Des-Hids, France
15-16 AUG 44	Evron, France
17 AUG 44	Montree, France
18-21 AUG 44	Argentan, France
22-26 AUG 44	Medvey, France
26 AUG 44	Origny-Le-Sec, France
28 AUG 44	Cheniers, France
29 AUG 44	Vraux, France
30 AUG 44	Vraux, France
31 AUG 44	Revigny-Sur-Ormalm, France
1-3 SEP 44	Euville, France
4 SEP 44	Manon-Eu-Court, France
5 SEP 44	Preny, France
6-11 SEP 44	Fey-En-Haye, France
11-12 SEP 44	Blenod-Les-Pont-A-Mousson, France
13-17 SEP 44	Jezainville, France
19-20 SEP 44	Etton, France
21-22 SEP 44	Autreville-Sur-Moselle, France
23-24 SEP 44	Millery, France
25-26 SEP 44	Villers-Les-Prud-Hommes, France
27-30 SEP 44	Pont-à-Mousson, France

COMPANY B, 305TH ENGINEERS LOCATIONS, CON'T.

DATE	LOCATION
1-6 OCT 44	Pont-à -Mousson, France (con't)
7-11 OCT 44	Ville-au-Val, France
12-13 OCT 44	Serrieres, France
14-31 OCT 44	Ste. Genevieve, France
1-7 NOV 44	Ste. Genevieve, France (con't)
8-9 NOV 44	Benicourt, France
10 NOV 44	Thezey-Ste.-Martin, France
11 NOV 44	Mancheux, France
12-13 NOV 44	Meville-Sur-Nied, France
14-17 NOV 44	Baudrecourt, France
18-20 NOV 44	Brulange, France
21-23 NOV 44	Faulquemont, France
24-25 NOV 44	Cites Des Charbonnages, France
26 NOV 44	Bambiderstroff, France
NOV 44	Longeville, France
28 NOV 44	St. Avold, France
29 NOV 44	Guenviller, France
30 NOV 44	St. Avold, France
1-6 DEC 44	St. Avold, France (con't)
7-17 DEC 44	Helleringer, France
18-19 DEC 44	Rahling, France
20-21 DEC 44	Lintgen, Luxembourg
22-31 DEC 44	Chau de Birtrange, Luxembourg
1-20 JAN 45	Chau de Birtrange, Luxembourg (con't)
21-24 JAN 45	Niederfeulen, Luxembourg
25-26 JAN 45	Wiltz, Luxembourg
27 JAN 45	Christnach, Luxembourg
28-31 JAN 45	Waldbillig, Luxembourg
1-14 FEB 45	Waldbillig, Luxembourg (con't)
15-19 FEB 45	Biesdorf, Germany
20-25 FEB 45	Cruchten, Germany
26-28 FEB 45	Mettendorf, Germany

COMPANY B, 305TH ENGINEERS LOCATIONS, CON'T.

DATE	LOCATION
1-2 MAR 45	Idesheim, Germany
3-10 MAR 45	Seffern, Germany
11 MAR 45	Erpeldanger, Luxembourg
12-13 MARCH 45	Kaiferhaum, Germany
14-16 MAR 45	Zerf, Germany
17-18 MAR 45	Weiskirchen, Germany
19 MAR 45	St. Wendel, Germany
20 MAR 45	Niedernaer, Germany
21 MAR 45	Bad Durkheim, Germany
22-23 MARCH 45	Grundheim, Germany
24-27 MAR 45	Gundersweiler, Germany
28-30 MAR 45	Mainz, Germany
31 MAR 45	Lendorf, Germany
1-2 APR 45	Zinner, (Gudersberg), Germany
3-6 APR 45	Brasselburg, Germany
7 APR 45	Hania, Germany
8-9 APR 45	Seebergen, Germany
10 APR 45	Kleinrettbach, Germany
11-12 APR 45	Newerhauser, Germany
13 APR 45	Lebensten, Germany
14-15 APR 45	Oberwein, Germany
19-20 APR 45	Kettensdorf, Germany
21-27 APR 45	Nurnberg (Nuremberg), Germany
28 APR 45	Ober-Isling, Germany
29 APR 45	Wechshewn, Germany
30 APR 45	Sessau, Germany
1 MAY 45	Mamming, Germany
2 MAY 45	Rimbach, Germany
3 MAY 44	Senbach, Germany
4-5 MAY 45	Ranshefen, Austria
6-8 MAY 45	Kirchdorf, Austria
9-14 MAY 45	Garsten, Austria
15-31 MAY 45	Unterregau, Austria

COMPANY B, 305TH ENGINEERS LOCATIONS, CON'T.

DATE	LOCATION
1-10 JUN 45	Unterregau, Austria (con't)
11-30 JUN 45	Aitrang, Austria
1-31 JUL 45	Aitrang, Austria

American tank destroyer crews pause and confer about directions. *Army Signal Corps*

APPENDIX 3

DIVISIONAL CASUALTIES

THE infantry division in World War II was in a triangular form, meaning its basic fighting force consisted of three infantry regiments, each containing three battalions, each of which contained three companies.

The infantry division was designed to be self-sufficient, and its 14,000-plus soldiers also included a headquarters staff, cavalry reconnaissance, quartermaster, signal, military police, and field artillery, medical, and engineer battalions.

80TH INFANTRY DIVISION CASUALTIES BY MONTH			
(KILLED, DIED OF WOUNDS, SEVERELY WOUNDED IN ACTION)[1]			
	317th I. R.	318th I. R.	319th I. R.	Rest of Division
August 1944	35	310	21	24
September 1944	432	566	215	76
October 1944	282	288	148	46
November 1944	342	385	250	27
December 1944	251	183	166	20
January 1945	175	233	239	28
February 1945	149	311	208	27

1 Casualty numbers are derived from Robert T. Murrell, 80th Division Losses in Action. The official casualties are higher because the numbers discussed here include only the dead and severely wounded. See http://www.80thdivision.com/AfterActionReports/80th_Losses InAction_Murrell.pdf.

80TH INFANTRY DIVISION CASUALTIES BY MONTH, CON'T			
(KILLED, DIED OF WOUNDS, SEVERELY WOUNDED IN ACTION)			
	317th I. R.	318th I. R.	319th I. R.	Rest of Division
March 1945	130	142	79	7
April 1945	91	136	86	6
May 1945	21	11	10	1
Total	1908	2565	1402	173

The total rifle strength of an infantry division was 2,916 men in 243 rifle squads.[2] An infantry squad consisted of a squad leader, an assistant leader, seven riflemen, and a three-man Browning Automatic Rifle (BAR) crew. Casualties were often extraordinarily high in rifle companies. Unsurprisingly, casualties in the 80th Division were heaviest in the infantry regiments. The 318th had by far the highest casualties, followed by the 317th. Oddly, the 319th had significantly lower casualties than the other two regiments, suffering half the casualties of the 318th.

The worst months for the three infantry regiments of the 80th Division (killed and severely wounded in action) were:

FIVE BLOODIEST MONTHS FOR INFANTRY REGIMENTS IN THE 80TH DIVISION		
(KILLED AND SEVERELY WOUNDED)		
Month	Killed/SeverelyWounded	Combat Activites
September 1944	1213	Moselle crossing and fight for the hills
November 1944	977	Seille crossing and advance to the Saar
October 1944	718	Nearly month-long period of inactivity; major midmonth attack on Mount St. Jean, Mount Toulon, etc.
February 1945	668	Sauer crossing and advance on Prüm River
January 1945	647	Closing the bulge (Battle of the Bulge); lengthy period in reserve

2 Hugh F. Foster III, "History, Infantry Structure," 70th Infantry Division Association, accessed May 22, 2017, http://www.trailblazersww2.org/history_infantrystructure.htm.

Even though December 1944 included the bloody Battle of the Bulge attacks on Ettelbruck and Bastogne, casualties were low this month because the division spent more than half the month in reserve.

The army replacement system trained replacement troops to compensate for casualties, and as the war proceeded and casualties mounted, the original units increasingly became "replacement units."[3]

There were many sources of replacements. Initially, much of the supply came from replacement training centers, which produced newly trained soldiers who had been trained with the idea that they would become fillers in existing units. But the demand for replacements in the ETO was nearly insatiable, and as casualties mounted, it was necessary to use more extreme measures. These included:

- Stripping lower-priority divisions of officers and enlisted men. (This method was used both to "plus-up" deploying divisions to their full strength and later to provide replacements.) Heavy taxes were placed on a group of divisions in the fall of 1943, again in February 1944, and, heaviest of all, in the spring and summer of 1944. Between April and September 1944, 17 divisions lost nearly 80,000 men, an average of nearly 4,000 each.[4]
- Virtually terminating the Army Specialized Training Program (ASTP), which assigned promising soldiers to colleges, where they were expected to receive technical training and graduate as officers with special skills. These soldiers were reassigned to deployed divisions.
- Placing taxes on rear-echelon units and even non-infantry frontline units (such as engineers) to provide troops to meet the demand for riflemen.
- Converting units that were not needed in originally anticipated quantities (such as antiaircraft batteries and tank destroyers), often as a full unit, to another purpose, and many soldiers were converted to infantry replacements.

The replacement system never operated with full effectiveness. There were constant complaints about the quality of these replacements by the infantry regiments that received them. Moreover, despite the replacements, the rifle strength of many regiments continued to slip significantly. For example, Patton wrote on December 3 that Third Army was 11,000 men short with little chance of

---

3 The process of training and providing replacement soldiers is discussed extensively in Robert R. Palmer, *The Procurement and Training of Ground Combat Troops, The U.S. Army in World War II: The Army Ground Forces* (Washington, DC: Historical Division, Department of the Army, 1991).

4 Divisions that were particularly hard hit included the 63th, 65th, 66th, 69th, 70th, 71st, 75th, 76th, 78th, 83rd, 84th, 86th, 87th, 89th, 97th, 100th, 103rd, and 106th.

GIs taking a break. *Army Signal Corps*

getting replacements. "People do not realize that 92% of all casualties occur in the infantry rifle companies, and that when the infantry division has lost 4000 men, it has practically no riflemen left. Therefore, with 11,000 odd short in an army consisting of three armored and six infantry divisions, we are closely approaching a 40% shortage in each rifle company."

Shortly after this letter, Patton "taxed" all the non-infantry units of the Third Army to supply a percentage of their troops for conversion to infantry. Nevertheless, rifle companies went into the Ardennes counteroffensive well short of their authorized strength.

Despite the obvious shortfalls, though, the replacement system served its purpose of supplying replacements. Without these replacements, infantry divisions like the 80th would have ceased to exist.

MAIL AND THE GI IN WORLD WAR II

THE IMPORTANCE OF MAIL

THE delivery of mail was a frequent concern of Frank Lembo. Almost every letter he wrote to Betty included a statement of his gratitude for the latest letters he had received, and he often wrote about his concerns about the delivery of mail. A few examples include:

- August 12, 1944: "I've been in France for some time now, and I hope you don't mind the mail delay, but it's just one of those things that happens. I haven't had any mail in a few weeks but I'm not worried about it. I guess it will catch up with us sometime, usually your mind is so occupied you don't think of mail until one of your off moments."
- August 13, 1944: "I finally received a deluge of mail and letters from almost everyone, about 16 from you, so I was highly pleased."
- September 30, 1944: "Since the question of either mail or supplies has come up, we are doing without mail, which we gladly agree with. All our mail is back at some coast port, and it really must be stacked up."
- December 8, 1944: "Received two letters from you yesterday so all in all I'm in a good mood."
- January 4, 1945: "Thanks for the Air Mail stamps. I believe that most of the mail is going by boat, and will so until summer comes, but we're satisfied with mail whether it's late or early. I guess it's because we have to be." He let her know a lot of the mail coming through was from early November, "so you can see it's a screwed up affair. Every once

in awhile we'll get a letter that took about nine days to get here, but they are really few and far between."

- January 12, 1945: "No mail tonight outside of a package from mom, and we are hungry for letters and we miss it when evening rolls around without any mail."

Frank's correspondence with Betty is the backbone of this chronicle and an important part of Frank's and Betty's lives. But we also know that Frank wrote to and received letters from his parents, his sisters, his cousins, and friends from back home. His frequent references to mail and packages from other people show how important all this mail was to him.

Frank was in no way unique. Mail was just as important to everyone else caught up in the war—soldiers, airmen, and sailors as well as their loved ones back home—and the policy makers recognized how important mail was to maintain morale on the front lines and the home front.

Writing in the Army and Navy Journal, Postmaster General Frank C. Walker commented: "It is almost impossible to over-stress the importance of this mail. It is so essential to morale that army and navy officers of the highest rank list mail almost on a level with munitions and food."[1] Major General James A. Ulio, adjutant general of the army, supervised the Army Postal Service and agreed it was "a necessity for the maintenance of morale" and described mail as "mental ammunition."[2]

Mail and the Home Front

A report prepared by the U.S. Postal Museum stated:

Civilians were encouraged to write their service men and women about even the most basic activities. Daily routines, family news, and local gossip kept the armed forces linked to their communities. . . . Letters kept America's troops informed about home life and detailed accounts allowed them to be in the war and have that critical link back to their families. Others wrote to kindle new relationships and fight off the loneliness and boredom of wartime separation.

---

1 Frank C. Walker, "The Postal Service at War," *Army and Navy Journal*, December 7, 1942-December 7, 1943, 16.

2 James A. Ulio, "Adjutants General in the Theaters of Operations," *Army and Navy Journal*, December 7, 1942-December 7, 1943, 102.

The emotional power of letters was heightened by the fear of loss and the need for communication during times of separation. . . . Military personnel felt the most connected to home through reading about it in letters. Wartime romances adjusted to long distances and sweethearts and spouses separated by oceans used mail to stay in touch.[3]

DELIVERING THE MAIL

To ensure the speedy delivery of mail to and from all the fronts of the war, the Post Office Department had 1,300 U.S. post offices serving army posts and camps in the United States. Four hundred army post offices operated in more than 50 foreign countries. There were 2,000 postal facilities serving the navy on ships and at shore stations.[4]

Postmaster General Walker described how a letter was delivered from the home front to a soldier in camp.

The letter would be addressed to the soldier, with his military unit and the address of the Postmaster in New York.

The local post office would cancel the letter, sort it, and send it to the massive New York post office building that handled overseas GI mail.

"Still under the Post Office Department's immediate control, it arrives at the New York Post Office's Postal Concentration center, a great building whose entire facilities and hundreds of workers are engaged exclusively in the final processing of the mail before it is handed over to the military authorities."

The letter is sorted and separated and is put in a package with all other mail addressed to soldiers in the same company or other small unit.

The package is then handed over to army control at the New York Port of Embarkation Army Post Office (APO). The postmaster general noted, "The Army knows where [the soldier] is located; we do not."

The package goes by ship or plane to the overseas APO and then on to the unit.

The package is delivered to the mail orderly of the addressee's unit, and the letter is distributed to the soldier. If he has been transferred or is in hospital, the package is redirected.[5]

---

3 U.S. Postal Museum, "Letter Writing in World War II," V-Mail Online Exhibition, May 22, 2017, https://postalmuseum.si.edu/VictoryMail/index.html.

4 Walker, "Postal Service at War," 16.

5 Ibid., 140.

Adjutant General Ulio gave a few more details on the challenge the army faced once mail arrived in theater: "The forwarding of mail within a theater of operations presents a postal and transportation problem of the first magnitude, particularly in these days of fast-moving, mechanized warfare. . . . [It requires] careful study and planning [and] utilizing of all available transportation including a courier service."[6]

With mail written by the soldier, the process was similar, with the additional step of review by censors to make sure the soldier hadn't mentioned any sensitive information, such as references to specific locations or movements. Censors could either black out the objectionable part or go back to the soldier, discuss the sensitive information, and invite him to rewrite the letter. In Frank's case, his platoon commander, Lt. Arthur Henke, censored most of his mail. Frank understood the censorship rules. There were no censor marks in any of the 86 letters he wrote to Betty from Europe. Later, he became a platoon commander and censored the mail himself.

The process of preparing mail for delivery to the States seemed to go fairly smoothly most of the time, but there were a few delays within the APS. For example, Frank's February 9, 1945, letter was postmarked by the APS on February 12, but it didn't reach Lieutenant Henke until February 21. An even earlier letter, written on January 12, was postmarked January 16, but it didn't reach Henke until February 21 either. Perhaps the confusion of the Sauer River crossing and the movement toward Bitburg accounted for some of the delay—although other letters Frank wrote seem to have proceeded smoothly.

CONSERVING DEMAND: V-MAIL

A survey concluded that each of the 11.5 million members of the uniformed services was writing an average of six letters a week. The postmaster general estimated that over 5 billion pieces of mail went to and from people serving in the military each year.

The War and Navy Departments understood the mail was crucial to morale, but the volume of mail competed for cargo space with food, fuel, munitions, and other essential supplies. V-mail was introduced in June 1942 to reduce the volume of mail. V-mail involved microfilming each letter and sending it home (or to the front) with hundreds of others on a gigantic microfilm roll, then printing a very small paper version and delivering it to the addressee. V-mail was so small that

---

6 Ulio, "Adjutants General," 102.

1,500 to 1,800 letters could fit on a 90-foot microfilm roll.[7] And V-mail letters were flown home on empty airplanes, arriving within a little more than a week, compared to the monthlong journey surface mail could take. In Europe, the microfilming of GI mail was done by the Army Signal Corps, but in the States, Kodak had a contract and established six centers to do the microfilming of civilian mail to the soldiers.[8]

Although V-mail was an important means of communication, Frank was not a regular user. Of his 86 surviving letters, only 2 (written July 21 and 22, 1944, in England) went via V-mail.

In his November 1, 1944, letter, Frank wondered whether he should make the switch: "I haven't received much mail in the last eight days. I'm wondering if I should switch to V-mail. They claim weather conditions are cancelling a lot of plane trips." But apparently he never made the switch. Instead, he spent six cents for airmail postage for each letter while he was in Europe to avoid the month-long delay a voyage at sea would entail. He also relied on Betty to send him stamps and stationery. (From several references in Frank's letters to the speed of Betty's replies, it appears she used airmail as well.)

At the start of the war, airmail letters had been much more expensive to send (as much as 70 cents to remote areas of the Pacific), but the War and Navy Departments recognized the importance of regular mail service for morale and negotiated the special flat rate with the Post Office Department.[9]

Clearly, for Frank and millions of other soldiers, airmen, and sailors (as well as their friends and families back home), the mail provided a vital way to keep in touch and was an important morale builder. Considering the volume of mail, the number of locations of the dispersed soldiers, their constant movements, and the number of people and transportation modes involved in the process, the delivery of personal mail was a World War II success story. Frank's letters provide an eloquent testament to how important this service was to the soldiers at the front.

7 U.S. Postal Museum, "How Did V-Mail Stack Up?" V-Mail Online Exhibition, https:// postalmuseum.si.edu/VictoryMail/index.html.

8 Frank W. Towers, "V-mail, the Wonder of World War II," www.30thinfantry.org/ history_docs/v-mail.doc.

9 "American Armed Forces Airmail During World War II: Part 1, 1941-43," *Linn's Stamp News*, April 7, 2014, http://www.linns.com/news/us-stamps-postal-history/2014/april/ american-armed-forces-airmailduring-world-war-ii-p.html#

ENGINEER ROLES AND MISSIONS

THE 305th Engineer Combat Battalion was assigned to the 80th Infantry Division and functioned as engineers in direct support of the division's infantry regiments. It was not an inviolate rule, but it appears A Company of the 305th often supported the 317th Infantry, B Company often supported the 318th, and C Company often supported the 319th.[1]

FUNCTIONS OF DIVISIONAL ENGINEERS

Army Field Manual 5-5 (Engineer Troops) detailed the most common functions performed by divisional engineers:

1. Removal and passage of enemy obstacles, including minefields,
2. Preparation of obstacles by demolitions and other means, including mine fields and booby traps,
3. River-crossing operations to include use of assault boats, preparation of fords, and other stream-crossing expedients; and construction of vehicle ferries, portable bridges, and, in emergencies, ponton bridges capable of sustaining combat-team loads,
4. Emergency repair and maintenance of roads, and reinforcement, repair, and maintenance of bridges,

---

1 While the B Company diary is an inexact measure of support assignments, because it often mentions only the company's movements with no reference to work performed, B Company's assignment to the 318th seems to be supported by the fact the diary mentions working in support of the 318th on 50 occasions, in addition to 15 references to specific 318th Infantry battalions. In contrast, assignments to the 317th are mentioned only 7 times, including support of the 2nd Battalion during the first Moselle crossings. Support of the 319th by B Company is mentioned only twice.

Engineers clear mines. *Army Signal Corps*

5. Engineer reconnaissance,

6. Providing local security for own working parties.

Less common functions included the layout of rear positions, erecting markers, guiding troops, construction of fixed bridges and roads or landing fields, defense of minefields or other obstacles, and combat as infantry.[2]

In reality, the most commonly mentioned task in the B Company diary was clearing mines, booby traps, roadblocks, and other obstacles. During the August breakout after the collapse of the Falaise Pocket and the last few months of the war, the rapidly retreating German armies didn't have a chance to lay mines and other obstacles. But in the static warfare of the fall, winter, and early spring, the Germans littered their retreat or their fixed positions with mines and other obstacles.

2 U.S. War Department, *Engineer Field Manual: Engineer Troops* (FM 5-5) (Washington, DC: Government Printing Office, 1943), 52-53.

305th bulldozer clears wreckage.
Frank Lembo

The next most frequent task was building or repairing roads (building corduroy roads, clearing snow, filling craters, spreading sand on icy roads, etc.). An integral part of this task was the removal of abandoned or destroyed equipment and also the burial of dead animals.

The third most common task was reconnoitering riverbanks, bridges, and roads. In these missions, engineers searched for crossing points, went behind enemy lines to identify enemy positions, and searched roads for craters and destroyed bridges.

The fourth most regular task was building and repairing bridges and otherwise supporting river crossings. The diary mentions building footbridges, trestle bridges, treadways, and Bailey bridges. Other methods the company used to cross infantry included assault boats, ferries, and fords.

The final task in B Company's top five duties involved fighting as infantry. The engineers sometimes were assigned to fight as infantry (particularly in defense of new bridgeheads), but they often stumbled into their fights by moving into occupied towns. Particularly in the last few months of the war, the company frequently captured surrendering German soldiers.

Less common tasks mentioned in the diary include demolitions and digging in command and observation posts and artillery emplacements, setting up and moving water points, destroying bridges, laying mines, creating defensive positions, and blowing up enemy munitions.

After the shooting stopped, the men of B Company continued to clear mines, but their other engineering chores were superseded by such assignments as building POW enclosures, hauling displaced persons to other places, operating a railroad, and constructing recreational facilities.

Functions of Corps-and Army-Level Engineers (Supporting Engineers)

Other engineer battalions were formed to work at the corps or army level. The field manual described the corps engineer's separate responsibilities:

General engineer work in the forward part of the corps area, and such engineer work in the division services areas as may be taken over by corps. They reinforce divisional engineers or relieve them of engineer tasks so they may work farther to the front. . . . They follow closely behind the infantry divisions and take over the maintenance of roads to relieve the division engineer troops; replace the temporary bridge expedients with more substantial structures capable of carrying the heaviest military loads.[3]

The list of common functions illustrates the different assignments of the corps engineers:

1. Improvement and maintenance of roads, bridges, and landing fields, mainly in the corps service area,
2. Construction of or extension of barrier zones,
3. Engineer assistance to corps troops and to troops attached to the corps,
4. Engineer reconnaissance,
5. Reinforcement of division engineer units either by taking over engineer work in division rear areas or by attachment of subordinate units to divisional engineer units,
6. River-crossing operations to include use of assault boats, preparation of fords and other stream-crossing expedients, and construction of vehicle ferries, portable bridges, and ponton bridges capable of sustaining combat-team loads,
7. Providing local security for own working parties,
8. Removal and passage of enemy obstacles, including mine fields.[4]

These units were also referred to as supporting engineers. In general, the 305th worked cooperatively with the supporting engineers, but there was occasionally some friction and difficulties in communication between the two.

3 Ibid., 53-54.

4 Ibid., 54-55.

BIBLIOGRAPHY

ORIGINAL MANUSCRIPTS, LETTERS, AND REPORTS

Many of the division, regiment, and battalion records are available online at the 80th Division digital archives project, http://www.80thdivision.com/WebArchives. We are profoundly grateful for the effort Andy Adkins put into creating this invaluable record.

Betty Craig Documents
"His Service Record," 1942-1945 (notes and photos maintained by Betty Craig).
Items mailed home by Frank T. Lembo (postcards, Patton weather prayer and Christmas greeting, newspaper articles and photos [mostly *Stars and Stripes*], photographs, safe conduct pass, and souvenirs from Paris trip)
Letters from Frank Lembo to Betty Craig
Order to Report for Induction, Frank T. Lembo, November 10, 1942.
Scrapbook maintained by Betty Craig, 1942-45 (primarily newspaper articles on the progress of the Third Army)
Silver Star citation for Frank Lembo

Interviews (September 14-16, 2017)
Staff Sergeant Bob Burrows (2nd Battalion, 317th Infantry Regiment)
PFC Charles Faulconer (1st Battalion, 319th Infantry Regiment)
PFC Burt Marsh (3rd Battalion, 319th Infantry Regiment)
Cpl. Charles Parker (2nd Battalion, 319th Infantry Regiment)
Simon Petitot (Local Bambiderstroff historian)
PFC Ben Rupp (3rd Battalion, 318th Infantry Regiment)

Letters, Photographs, and Documents
Letter from Dwight Eisenhower to chief of staff George Marshall, April 15, 1945.
Letter from George S. Patton to Troy Middleton, April 24, 1945, http://www.unithistories.com/units_index/default.asp?file=../units/3rd%20US%20Army%20letter.asp.
Log of the President's Inspection Tour, 13-29 April 1943, http://www.fdrlibrary.marist.edu/_resources/images/tully/7_08a.pdf.

Photo and document collections at Army Heritage and Education Center: Files on the Third Army, 317th, 318th, 319th Regiments, 305th Engineers, George S. Patton, Manton Eddy.

80th Division Documents
After-action reports (G-2, G-3, and G-4).
80th Forward (Division newspaper, 1945).
The 80th Only Moves Forward, 80th Division scrapbook.
Interviews:
    Drive from Regensburg to Vocklabruck.
    Surrender of 6th German Army at Garstan, Austria.
Miscellaneous Reports:
    Moselle River crossing analysis.
    Dieulouard river crossing.
    Lorraine campaign.
    St. Avold time bomb incident.
Operational History

305th Engineer Combat Battalion
After-action reports (intelligence reports [S-2], reports of operations [S-3], journal of supply [S-4])
Fire in the Hole, vol. 1, nos. 3, 4, 5, and 6 (July-August 1945) (305th Engineer Combat Battalion newspaper).
"History of Company B, 6 August 1944 to 31 July 1945" (Typescript Diary of Company B, 305th Engineer Combat Battalion).
Interviews
Moselle crossing
Journal
Morning Reports
Unit Histories

317th, 318th, and 319th Infantry Regiments
After-action reports
Interviews
    317th: Moselle Operation; Seille and Nied River crossings and attack on Maginot Line; Bulge operations; crossing Clerf River; crossing Sure River
    318th: Seille and Nied River Crossings, relief of Bastogne, northern Luxembourg and Sauer Crossing
    319th: Seille and Nied River crossings, reducing the Bulge, Our River crossings
Morning Reports
Unit Histories

Other 80th Division or Attached Units
After-action report, 808th Tank Destroyer Battalion, September 25-October 31, 1944 (http://www.tankdestroyer.net/).
After-action reports, 810th Tank Destroyer Battalion, August, September, October, December 1944. http://cgsc.contentdm.oclc.org/cdm/ref/collection/p4013coll8/id/3615
After-action report, 150th Engineer Combat Battalion, February 1945 http://www.150th.com/reports/feb45.htm
Interview, 1135th Engineer Group, Bridging Sauer and Our Rivers

Interview, 166th Engineer Combat Battalion, "Crossing of the Sauer River at Dillingen, Luxembourg"

Interview, 150th Engineer Combat Battalion, "Our and Sauer River Crossings"

80TH DIVISION HISTORIES AND MEMOIRS

Adkins, A. Z., Jr., and Andrew Z. Adkins III. *You Can't Get Much Closer than This: Combat with Company H, 317th Infantry Regiment, 80th Division.* Havertown, PA, 2005.

Barnes, Wyatt E. "A Rifleman's Story," *World War II.* March 2003.

Beard, John. *Tales from Henpeck: Folklore of the 314th FA Bn.* N.p., n.d.

———. *The 314th FA Battalion in the ETO: A Footnote to History.* Ann Arbor: n.p., 1988).

Cannon, Jimmy. "A Village Lies Still in Death After War Hurtles Through." *Stars and Stripes,* December 1944.

Carr, Walter. "Breakthrough to Bastogne." *World War II.* January 1996.

Craig, Berry. *80th "Blue Ridge" Infantry Division in the ETO.* Paducah, 1991.

Cromie, Robert. "Civilians Help Patton's Army Capture Town." *Chicago Tribune,* November 28, 1944.

Dominique, Dean. "The Attack Will Go On: The 317th Infantry Regiment in World War II." Thesis, Louisiana State University, 2003.

——— and James Hayes. *One Hell of a War: General Patton's 317th Infantry Regiment in WWII.* N.p.: Wounded Warrior Publications, 2014.

80th Division. *Ever Forward.* 1945.

Elvin, Jan. *The Box from Branau: In Search of My Father's War.* New York: AMACOM/American Management Association, 2009.

———. "Honoring the Liberators," April 16, 2010, http://janelvin.blogspot.com/2010/04/honoring-liberators.html.

Forward 80th. Paris, 1945.

Gooby, Garland. "Heiderscheid Turkey Shoot." (unpublished). http://www.thetroubleshooters.com/702nd/maddog002.html.

Harmon, George W. "Memories of Heiderscheid" (unpublished). http://www.thetroubleshooters.com/702nd/maddog002.html.

Hogue, Thaine Ray. "Recollection of World War II" (unpublished).

Irzyk, Albin. "8th Tank Battalion's Daring Moselle Crossing," *World War II.* September 1997.

Janes, Terry D. "The Battle for Heiderscheid" (unpublished). http://www.thetroubleshooters.com/702nd/maddog002.html.

———. "Farebersviller, France, an In-Depth Study" (unpublished). http://www.thetroubleshooters.com/80th/farebersviller0003.html.

Levin, Meyer. *In Search, an Autobiography.* New York: Horizon Press, 1950.

Murrell, Robert T. "80th Losses in Action."

———. *Operational History, 80th Infantry Division.* N.p., 2016.

———. *Stories of the Men of the 80th Infantry Division.* N.p., 2015.

———. *317th Infantry Regiment History WWII.* N.p., 2001.

———. *The Blue Ridge Division Answers the Call in World War II,* N.p., 2015.

Rondeau, Tristan. "Baptism by Fire in Argentan: The First Engagement of August 18-19, 1944." *Normandie 1944* no. 6 (English translation by Dennis Adams, 2013). http://www.80thdivision.com/PDFs/Argentan_1_TristanRondeau.pdf

Smothers, Jimmy. "World War II Veteran Recalls Scenes at Death Camp." *Gadsden Times,* May 4, 2009.

Staff Group D, Section 16. "The 80th Infantry Division Assault Across the Sauer, February 7, 1945," Fort Leavenworth, KS, n.p., 1984.

Stanchak, Peter J. et al. "History Second Battalion 318 Infantry Regiment 80th Division."

"Town of Jena Taken After 'Honor Battle,'" Associated Press, April 13, 1945.

Vannoy, Allyn. "American Drive to the Moselle." *Military Heritage*, August 2009.

Wignall, Jeff. *Farebersviller 1944*. Peabody, MA: n.p., 2009.

Witzgell, Fred, comp. "318th History, Month by Month." 80th Division Veterans Association.

ARMY CENTER FOR MILITARY HISTORY U.S. ARMY IN WWII SERIES (LISTED CHRONOLOGICALLY BY CAMPAIGN)

Blumenson, Martin. *Breakout and Pursuit*. The U.S. Army in World War II: The European Theater of Operations. 1961. Reprint, Washington, DC: Center of Military History, U.S. Army, 1993.

Cole, Hugh M. *The Lorraine Campaign*. The U.S. Army in World War II: The European Theater of Operations. Washington, DC: Historical Division, Department of the Army, 1950.

MacDonald, Charles B. *The Siegfried Line Campaign*. The U.S. Army in World War II: The European Theater of Operations. Washington, DC: Office of the Chief of Military History, Department of the Army, 1963.

Cole, Hugh M. *The Ardennes: The Battle of the Bulge*. The U.S. Army in World War II: The European Theater of Operations. Washington, DC: Government Printing Office, 1965.

MacDonald, Charles B. *Victory in Europe, 1945: The Last Offensive of World War II*. Dover Books on History, Political and Social Science. 1973. Reprint, Mineola, NY: Dover Publications, 2007.

Ziemke, Earl F. *The U.S. Army in the Occupation of Germany*. U.S. Army Historical Series. Washington, DC: Center of Military History, U.S. Army, 1975.

Palmer, Robert R. *The Procurement and Training of Ground Combat Troops*. The U.S. Army in World War II: The Army Ground Forces. Washington, DC: Historical Division, Department of the Army, 1948.

OTHER BOOKS, MANUALS, AND ARTICLES

Abzug, Robert H. *Inside the Vicious Heart: Americans and the Liberation of Nazi Concentration Camps*. New York: Oxford University Press, 1985.

Balck, Hermann. *Order in Chaos: The Memoirs of General of Panzer Troops Hermann Balck*. Trans. David T. Zabecki and Dieter J. Biedekarten. Lexington: University Press of Kentucky, 2015.

Barron, Leo. *Patton at the Battle of the Bulge: How the General's Tanks Turned the Tide at Bastogne*. New York: NAL Caliber, 2014.

Beck, Alfred M. et al. *The Corps of Engineers: The War Against Germany*. Washington, DC: Center of Military History, U.S. Army, 1985.

Bergstrom, Christer. *The Ardennes, 1944-1945: Hitler's Winter Offensive*. Havertown, PA: Casemate Publisher, 2014.

Bilder, Michael C., and James G. Bilder. *A Foot Soldier for Patton: The Story of a "Red Diamond" Infantryman with the U.S. Third Army*. Drexel Hill, PA: Casemate, 2008.

Blumenson, Martin, comp. *The Patton Papers*, Vol. 2, 1940-1945. Boston: Houghton Mifflin, 1974.

Bradley, James, and Ron Powers. *Flags of Our Fathers*. New York: Bantam Books, 2000.

Bradley, Omar. *A Soldier's Story*. New York: Holt, 1951.

———, and Clay Blair. *A General's Life: An Autobiography*. New York: Simon and Schuster, 1983.

Bradsher, Greg. "Nazi Gold: The Merkers Mine Treasure." *Prologue: Quarterly Magazine of the National Archives and Records Administration*, vol. 31, no. 1 (Spring 1999), https://www.archives.gov/publications/prologue/1999/spring/nazi-gold-merkers-mine-treasure.html.

Bruning, J. M. *The Battle of the Bulge: The Photographic History of an American Triumph.* Minneapolis: MBI Publishing Co. and Zenith Press, 2009.

Childers, Thomas. *Soldier from the War Returning: The Greatest Generation's Troubled Homecoming from World War II.* Boston: Houghton Mifflin Harcourt, 2009.

Codman, Charles R. *Drive.* Boston: Little, Brown, 1957.

Colley, David P. *The Road to Victory: The Untold Story of World War II's Red Ball Express.* Washington, DC: Brassey's, 2000.

Doubler, Michael D. *Closing with the Enemy: How GIs Fought the War in Europe, 1944-1945.* Lawrence: University of Kansas Press, 1994.

Eisenhower, Dwight D. *Crusade in Europe.* Garden City, NY: Garden City Books, 1948.

Essame, H. *Patton: A Study in Command.* New York: Scribner, 1974.

Felix, Charles W. *Crossing the Sauer: A Memoir of World War II.* Short Hills, NJ: Burford Books, 2002.

Fowle, Barry W., gen. ed. *Builders and Fighters: U.S. Army Engineers in World War II.* (Fort Belvoir, VA: Office of History, U.S. Army Corps of Engineers, 1992.

Fox, Don M. *Patton's Vanguard: The United States Army Fourth Armored Division.* Jefferson, NC: McFarland, 2003.

Fussell, Paul. *The Boys' Crusade: American G.I.s in Europe: Chaos and Fear in World War II.* London: Orion, 2004.

Gabel, Christopher. *The Lorraine Campaign: An Overview, September-December 1944.* Fort Leavenworth, KS: Combat Studies Institute, U.S. Army Command and General Staff College, 1985.

Green, Michael, and James D. Brown. *Patton's Third Army in WWII: An Illustrated Guide.* Minneapolis: MBI Publishing Co. and Zenith Press, 2010.

Greenfield, Kent Roberts, ed. *Command Decisions.* New York: Harcourt, Brace, 1959.

Hirsh, Leo. *The Liberators: America's Witnesses to the Holocaust.* New York: Bantam Books, 2010.

"How the Army's Amazing Bailey Bridge Is Built." *The War Illustrated* 8, no. 198, January 19, 1945, 564.

Irzyk, Albin F. "8th Tank Battalion's Daring Moselle Crossing," *World War II.* September 1997.

Jordan, Jonathan W. *Brothers, Rivals, Victors: Eisenhower, Patton, Bradley, and the Partnership That Drove the Allied Conquest in Europe.* New York: NAL Caliber, New American Library, 2011.

Keegan, John. *Six Armies in Normandy: From D-Day to the Liberation of Paris, June 6th-August 25th, 1944.* New York: Viking Press, 1982.

King, John. *The 166th Engineer Combat Battalion from Utah Beach, August 6, 1944, to Czechoslovakia, May 8, 1945.* N.p., 1995.

Levinson, Lelia. *Gated Grief: The Daughter of a GI Concentration Camp Liberator Discovers a Legacy of Trauma.* Brute, WI: Cable Publishing, 2011.

Levitt, Saul. "Ohrdruf Camp," *Yank Magazine,* May 18, 1945.

MacDonald, Charles B. *Company Commander.* 1947. Reprint, Short Hills, NJ: Burford Books, 1999.

———. *The Mighty Endeavor: American Armed Forces in the European Theater in World War II.* New York: Oxford University Press, 1969.

McManus, John C. *The Deadly Brotherhood: The American Combat Soldier in World War II.* New York: Presidio, 1998.

McNab, Chris, ed. *Hitler's Fortresses: German Fortifications and Defences, 1939-1945.* Oxford, UK: Osprey, 2014.

Miller, Edward G. *Nothing Less than Full Victory: Americans at War in Europe, 1944-1945.* Annapolis, MD: Naval Institute Press, 2007.

"Edward R. Murrow Reports from Buchenwald, April 15, 1945." http://www.lib.berkeley.edu/MRC/murrowbuchenwaldtranscript.html.

O'Brine, Jack. "How Tank-Carrying Bridges Are Built," *Popular Mechanics*, December 1943.

O'Neill, James H. "The True Story of the Patton Prayer." *Review of the News*, October 6, 1971, http://www.pattonhq.com/prayer.html.

Patton, George S., Jr. *War as I Knew It.* Boston: Houghton Mifflin, 1947.

Pergrin, David E., with Eric Hammel. *First Across the Rhine: The 291st Engineer Combat Battalion in France, Belgium, and Germany.* St. Paul, MN: Zenith Press, 2006.

Phillips, Henry G. *The Making of a Professional: Manton S. Eddy, USA.* Westport, CT: Greenwood Press, 2000.

Province, Charles M. *Patton's Third Army: A Daily Combat Diary.* New York: Hippocrene Books, 1992.

Radford, Albert E., and Laurie S. Radford. *Unbroken Line: The 51st Engineer Combat Battalion, From Normandy to Munich.* Woodside, CA: Cross Mountain Publishing, 2002.

Reagan, Bruce W., and Jack N. Duffy. *An Odyssey with Patton.* Bennington, VT: Merriam Press, 2015.

Rice, Douglas. *Through Our Eyes: Eyewitness Accounts of World War II.* New York: iUniverse, 2008.

Rickard, John N. *Patton at Bay: The Lorraine Campaign, September to December 1944.* Washington, DC: Praeger, 2004.

Rottman, Gordon L. *US Combat Engineer, 1941-1945.* Warrior, no. 147. Oxford, UK: Osprey, 2010.

Russell, Lia. "World War II Vets Recall Horrors of Buchenwald." *Virginian Pilot*, November 8, 2009, http://pilotonline.com/news/local/world-war-ii-vets-recall-horrors-of-buchenwald/article_2 5bbe7d6-3805-5cef-bd6f-4b8e7f0759b6.html.

Schrijvers, Peter. *Those Who Hold Bastogne: The True Story of the Soldiers and Civilians Who Fought in the Biggest Battle of the Bulge.* New Haven, CT: Yale University Press, 2014.

Southergill, Norman C. *A Combat Engineer Remembers.* Victoria, BC: Trafford, 2002.

Steinbeck, John. *Short Novels: Tortilla Flat, The Red Pony, Of Mice and Men, The Moon Is Down, Cannery Row, The Pearl.* New York: Viking Press, 1953.

"Ten Most Devastating Bombing Campaigns of World War II," http://www.onlinemilitaryeducation.org/posts/10-most-devastating-bombing-campaigns-of-wwii.

Towers, Frank W. "V-mail, the Wonder of World War II." www.30thinfantry.org/history_docs/v-mail.doc.

Ulio, James A. "Adjutants General in the Theaters of Operations." *Army and Navy Journal*, December 7, 1942-December 7, 1943.

U.S. Army. Third Army. *A Souvenir Booklet for the Officers, Enlisted Men, and Civilians Who Made History with the Third US Army in the European Theater of Operations, 1944-1945.* N.p., 1945.

U.S. Army Information and Education Branch, Army Service Forces. *Instructions for American Servicemen in France During World War II. 1944.* Reprint, Chicago: University of Chicago Press, 2008.

U.S. Holocaust Memorial Museum. "Freeing of the Prisoners." http://hitlersholocaust.wix.com/liberation#!about

U.S. Postal Museum. "Letter Writing in World War II" and "How Did V-Mail Stack Up?" V-Mail Online Exhibition, https://postalmuseum.si.edu/VictoryMail/index.html.

U.S. War Department. Basic Field Manual: Engineer Soldier's Handbook (FM 21-105). Washington, DC: Government Printing Office, 1943.

——. *Engineer Field Manual: Engineer Troops* (FM 5-5). Washington, DC: Government Printing Office, 1943.

Vento, Carol Schultz. *The Hidden Legacy of World War II: A Daughter's Journey of Discovery.* Mechanicsburg, PA: Sunbury Press, 2011,

Walker, Frank C. "The Postal Service at War." *Army and Navy Journal*, December 1942-December 1943.

"Wheeled Pontons Give Fast, Safe River Crossings." *Popular Mechanics*, December 1943.

Whitaker, W. Denis, and Shelagh Whitaker. *Rhineland: The Battle to End the War*. New York: St. Martin's Press, 1989.

Yeide, Harry. *Tank Killers: A History of America's World War II Tank Destroyer Force*. Havertown, PA: Casemate, 2010.

Zaloga, Steven J. *Battle of the Bulge*. Oxford, UK: Osprey, 2010.

——. *George S. Patton: Leadership, Strategy, Conflict*. Command, no. 3. Oxford, UK: Osprey, 2010.

——. *Lorraine 1944: Patton vs. Manteuffel*. Praeger Illustrated Military History. Westport, CT: Praeger, 2000.

——. *The Siegfried Line, 1944-1945: Battles on the German Frontier*. Campaign, no. 181. Oxford, UK: Osprey, 2007.

WEB SITES (SELECTED LIST)

In addition to the above references and 80th Division site mentioned earlier, we also found these web sites to be useful reference tools

150th Engineers: http://www.150th.com/. Daily reports, history, photographs, soldier recollections, etc.

300th Engineers: History, photos, documents of the unit plus an excellent discussion of several of the most basic engineer functions, building bridges and roads, laying and clearing minefields, etc. http://www.300thcombatengineersinwwii.com/bridges.html.

Carl Henry. Web site by the daughter of a soldier in the 80th Infantry Division. http://www.frontseattowar.com.

Hyperwar. Vast collection of hypertext histories of World War II, including the entire "US Army in World War II" series, Center for Military History, etc. http://www.ibiblio.org/hyperwar.

Ike Skelton Combined Arms Research Digital Reference Library. A large collection of Army research papers. http://cgsc.contentdm.oclc.org.

Lone Sentry. http://www.lonesentry.com. Vast collection of photos, manuals, unit histories, and other publications from World War II.

Luxembourg: WWII in the Sauer River Area http://www.pararesearchteam.com/Luxemburg/Luxemburg.html.

The Troubleshooters. Terry Jane's web site on the 80th Division and specifically the 702nd Tank Battalion. http://www.thetroubleshooters.com/ww2/pt0001.html.

ACKNOWLEDGMENTS

FIRST of all, we want to thank Frank and Betty Lembo for their service, their love story, and this extraordinary correspondence that propelled this book. We feel like we live with them every day and, besides being "mom and dad," they are also this fascinating couple, "Frank and Betty."

We also want to express our deepest gratitude to our niece, Vanessa Jacobson, who with her husband Josh discovered Lembo's WWII letters while they were remodeling the basement of the house they'd bought from my father.

We are also grateful for the support for this project and the memories shared by our aunts, Mary Randall, Genevieve Jerome, Jo Anderson; our siblings George and Nancy Czahlo and Keith and Barbara Lembo; and our nieces Vanessa Jacobson, Liza Czahlo, Sarah Koroski, and Maxine Dembicki.

We are also grateful for the online archive of the 80th Division that was painstakingly compiled by Andrew Z. Adkins and the 80th Infantry Association. This book would not exist without the letters and this core source of information.

We learned valuable information from other 80th Division memoirs and histories, and appreciate the efforts of authors, Andy Adkins, Jan Elvin, Dean Dominique, James Hayes, Jeff Wignall, Robert Murrell, and John Beard.

At Gettysburg, we benefited from good advice and suggestions about World War II, information sources, and the publishing business from Stuart Dempsey, Bernadette Loeffel-Atkins, and park ranger John Heiser.

The library staff at the Army Heritage and Education Center, Carlisle, PA, and the National Archives and Records Administration, College Park, MD, were extraordinarily helpful in finding sources and pointing out further directions to pursue.

Oral historian Rishi Sharma and local Bambiderstroff, France, historian Simon Petitot were very generous with their time and knowledge.

Our map-maker, George Skoch, came to the rescue in an hour of need and did a great job with our maps.

To our editorial and promotion staff at Savas Beatie, notably Theodore P. Savas, Steve Smith, Lee Merideth, Ed Curtis, Sarah Keeney, and Lisa Murphy, we are grateful for the faith you showed in this project and your incredibly professional work to turn it into a publishable manuscript.

Within the 80th Division family, we want to thank the daughter of another 305th Engineer Battalion veteran, Rita Knauper Thomas, for the photographs and memories she shared with us. We also wish to thank officers and members of the 80th Division Veterans Association for their warm welcome at the 2017 and 2019 conventions, including Bill Black, Paul Stutts, Lee Anthony, and Brian Faulconer.

Finally, extraordinary thanks to 80th Division veterans Staff Sgt. Bob Burrows (317th Regiment, headquarters company); Burt Marsh (319th Regiment, M Company); PFC Charles Faulconer (319th Regiment, A Company); PFC Ben Rupp (318th Regiment, 3rd Battalion); and Corporal Charles Parker (319th Regiment, G Company) for their courage, their service to the country, and the memories they generously shared with us.

—Lois Lembo and Leon Reed
January 2020, Gettysburg, PA

Index